S0-BCO-009

PRIVATE LIES

Also by Frank Pittman

TURNING POINTS: TREATING FAMILIES
IN TRANSITION AND CRISIS

PRIVATE LIES

Infidelity
and the Betrayal
of Intimacy

FRANK PITTMAN, M.D.

W. W. Norton & Company

NEW YORK   LONDON

Copyright © 1989 by Frank Pittman
All rights reserved.
Printed in the United States of America.

First published as a Norton paperback 1990

Acknowledgement is made to the following for permission
to reprint lyrics: to Stephen Sondheim for "Buddy's Blues"
(Stephen Sondheim) © 1971 — Range Road Music Inc., Quartet Music Inc.,
Rilting Music, Inc. and Burthen Music Co., Inc. All rights
administered by Herald Square Music Inc. Used by permission; and
to The Cole Porter Trust for "Just One of Those Things"
by Cole Porter.

The text of this book is composed in
CRT 11/13 Avanta and 9/11 Technica Medium,
with display type set in Spartan Black and Trump.
Composition and manufacturing by the Haddon Craftsmen, Inc.
Book design by Margaret M. Wagner

To Betsy,
with all my love

Contents

10   CONTENTS

Author's Note

I've spent my life in the middle of other people's affairs. At first it was exciting. When I was a young psychiatrist in my twenties, I was fascinated by the stories I heard of adulterous excitement and intrigue, even envious of the intense passion and narrow escapes. Then I began to notice that the enemy in all these adventure stories was the spouse, and I realized that adulterers live with their greatest enemy—they spend their lives behind enemy lines. In time, the stories began to run together, and I came to see the similarities and the inevitable outcome. My curiosity lessened and my rescue fantasies were aroused. Since then, I have tried to stop people from risking so much for so little.

Have you ever tried to stop anyone from having an affair? I recall a joke about a couple making love on the railroad tracks. The oncoming train was barreling down, blowing its whistle, but the couple proceeded energetically with their chosen activity. The train screeched to a halt inches from them. The wreckage of boxcars and passengers littered the landscape. The conductor looked down at the now spent couple and demanded, "Why the hell didn't you move?" The relaxed man grinned. "You was coming and I was coming, and you were the only one with brakes."

My family, like all families, I suppose, had its mythology about infidelity. According to family legend, a great-uncle by marriage had a scandalous relationship with his secretary in 1907, an affair that greatly affected his life, and ultimately mine. Great-Uncle Jos had married my great-aunt Ora and had become treasurer of the family cotton mills in Griffin, Georgia. He took a liking to his secretary, whom I'll call Cat Cole, and "wore the office wall thin with her." To cover some Christmas gifts to Cat Cole, he embezzled a little money, faked the books, and gambled in cotton futures to recover his losses. Good money was thrown after bad, there was a crisis of confidence with the stockholders, and Great-Uncle Jos went to trial for larceny after trust, and then to prison. Great-Aunt Ora waited for him, and took him back. We have no idea what became of Cat Cole, as she left Griffin to seek her fortune elsewhere. The cotton mills failed. My grandfather—a lawyer, judge, senator, writer—was not a businessman, yet he inherited the problems. He fell sick, took to drink, and died soon afterward.

My grandmother, who told me this story so many times, was left with two small daughters, all the debts, and the newspaper my grandfather had bought so he could have a place to publish his poetry. She moved in with relatives, edited the paper, and struggled to pay off all those debts. My grandmother had little tolerance for her brother-in-law Jos' behavior, and some doubts about Ora's wisdom in taking back the prodigal husband. Grandmother was sure she would not have taken him back.

I never met my great-uncle Jos—my grandmother wanted nothing to do with a person of such weak character. "If he would lie to his own wife, he'd lie to anybody," she said. "How could his stockholders be so naive as to believe he'd be honest to them?"

I don't believe my grandmother quite understood that Great-Uncle Jos and Cat Cole might not have been the only adulterous couple in Griffin, Georgia, at Christmastime of 1907. When she had her stroke—shortly after her eightieth birthday party and just before my wedding—it was 1960, and by then Kinsey had published his report on the sexual behavior of human males. My grandmother refused to acknowledge it. She made it a point to read only British mysteries written by Agatha Christie or other well-born women. Murder was an acceptable topic for polite examination; adultery was not. Her newspaper, like most respectable papers, chose to ignore news of sexual indiscretion. Her belief was actually the prevailing belief of the time, the prevailing belief until quite recently. "It is best not to know people's secrets. People must have a good reason for keeping their secrets secret. If you knew people's secrets, you might have to think about them, and that would be distracting. It is just best not to know."

Had Grandmother not already had her stroke, it would certainly have been brought on by my announcement that I had chosen psychiatry as my life's career. She had heard enough of Freud to know that she wanted nothing to do with a man who would devote himself to uncovering other people's secrets. And she would have approved my mother's (her daughter's) warning about my own psychoanalysis—"If you discover you have an Oedipus complex, I want you to know that it comes from your father's side of the family, not mine."

I certainly wouldn't want society to go in the direction my grandmother took, of declaring adulterous people beyond the pale and refusing to receive them socially. (They may be the majority anyway.) We won't go back to the times when adulterers were put in the stocks and publicly humiliated, or become one of those societies—and there are many—in which adultery is punishable by death. Society in any case is unable to enforce a rule that the majority of people break, and infidelity is so common it is no longer deviant. But that doesn't stop it from being problematic.

I wrestle with infidelity and its aftermath every day in my office. Now, though my grandmother would find it unseemly, I would like to bring it out into the open and take a look at the secrets around which so many people center their existence. Why, we must ask, would otherwise sane people—people who buy insurance, who stop for traffic lights, who brush after every meal—risk everything in their lives for a furtive moment of sex?

That is the crucial question this book attempts to answer. As I write this, I find myself saying to you what I keep saying on the subject to my patients, my friends, my kids, my professional colleagues. I try to define for you the nature of infidelity, particularly the fact that the infidelity is not so much in the sex but in the dishonesty and secrecy of the act. I ask you to look with me at the popular mythology of infidelity, and attempt to strip away the mistaken notions about it. I explore with you the helpfulness of two much unappreciated emotions—guilt and jealousy—both of which, in small enough doses, are necessary for honesty and intimacy. I examine the brittle institution of marriage, the reasons why some people find it difficult, and the turning points in the course of a lifetime when people find it most fragile. I reveal what I find in the affairs that come into my office.

I then describe four patterns of infidelity, and the crises that develop in the course of each pattern. I explain to you my thoughts about how affairs lead to divorce (and how to keep that from happening), and why affairs are a shaky basis for remarriage (and how, if you must go ahead with such a star-crossed marriage, to increase the chances of it working). I look with you at the damage done to the children in these marriages, with some thoughts about how to reduce the sacrifices they must make for their parents' infidelities. Finally, I offer you my best advice on what people should do if they find themselves in a relationship or in a marriage in which there is or has been an infidelity, and tell you what I've learned about making monogamy work.

I am very much aware of the AIDS epidemic, which has already devastated the homosexual community and is making inroads into the heterosexual. We shall see whether the fear of death causes people to put on the sexual brakes. With AIDS, we are all sexually connected to our past and future sex partners, and to theirs. Sex has ceased to be a private matter, if it ever was private. And while this book was conceived before AIDS became an issue, the existence of AIDS makes sexual secrets even more intolerable. Our infidelities, and our partners' infidelities, are no longer simply threats to the stability of our marriages, our children, our happiness, but are virtually life threatening.

I hope this book might save some marriages, some sanity, and perhaps even the lives of some people who are having affairs, have had affairs, might have affairs, might be married to people who might have affairs, or have some involvement with the problems created by affairs. I have the firm hope that these things can be gotten out into the open where they can't hurt us as much.

I want to thank all those patients, friends, and even relatives who did the fieldwork for me by having their own affairs and letting me see the consequences. Even though many have urged me to tell their stories straight and unshielded, I have disguised the identity of those people whom I have known personally, and I have often combined two or more similar stories to further protect privacy.

In writing this book, I am especially grateful to my wife, Betsy, who has made honesty, intimacy, and therefore fidelity easy, and has brought inestimable other pleasures into my life too. She has permitted me the time and isolation to write the book, while carrying more than her load in our life.

I want to thank my friend Rich Simon, editor of the *Family Therapy Networker* and publisher of my movie reviews over the last five years, for trying so hard to teach me how to write. I also want to thank Susan Barrows, the editor for my previous book, *Turning Points: Treating Families in Transition and Crisis*, who encouraged me to go ahead and write for the professional audience about this subject, the forbidden topic in the family therapy literature. And finally, I want to thank my wonderful editor for this book, Carol Houck Smith, who believed that what I have learned on this subject deserved a wider audience. She has firmly kept me within the limits of my expertise and tried diligently to keep me within the limits of good taste, while challenging me to clarify my thinking and my language. I've felt myself in strong, sure hands throughout the process of getting this book thought out and written out.

FRANK PITTMAN, M.D.
Atlanta, Georgia

PRIVATE LIES

1 / What Is Infidelity?

"Now, just what is infidelity and how can we get involved?"
DABNEY COLEMAN AS TV TALK SHOW HOST, "BUFFALO BILL"

What is infidelity? This question of just what is an infidelity, and what isn't, is a suprisingly touchy one, as I discover each time I talk to either professional or nonprofessional audiences. I try to define infidelity, and describe it as best I can, and somebody will invariably come up to me anxiously and sheepishly and tell me about some experience, and ask for reassurance that this act was not an infidelity. Sometimes a bright-eyed couple seem to be asking me for my forgiveness, with the question "Was what we did all right?" or "Does so and so count?"

Then others will take issue with me, pointing out that I had no business disapproving of whatever their activity, since it was quite natural for them, and they felt no guilt about it at all. Furthermore, I was being just like their former marriage partner in trying to impose my screwed-up values on an otherwise perfectly satisfactory life.·

After that I have a hard time explaining that I have not been granted whatever power it would take for me to go around approving or disapproving, forgiving or condemning other people's behavior. And I tell them that whatever I say is not said from a religious or a legal posture. In fact, I firmly believe that religion's involvement in people's sexual behavior is likely to make things more difficult for everybody. It is hard enough for people to keep the faith in a marriage, without having to concern themselves with all sorts of rules from above, below, and aside. So I keep telling people that if it is OK with both marriage partners, if it leaves no permanent scars, and if they don't do it in the streets and scare the horses, then I promise not to make a fuss over it.

The way I define it, infidelity is a breach of the trust, a betrayal of a relationship, a breaking of an agreement. There are many kinds of infidelity, but here we are talking about a sexual infidelity in monogamous marriage or a relationship that is tantamount to marriage. Most couples agree to strict sexual exclusivity within the marriage, permitting masturbation and whatever fantasies each would like to have, but insisting that the genitals stay out of the hands or whatever of outsiders. Different couples may have different codicils to their agreement, and most of those have to be negotiated as they go along. The desperate pregnant woman in one couple I worked with agreed not to interfere with the man's philandering if he would only marry her and give the child a name. He did marry her, but quite quickly she found she couldn't tolerate his infidelities after all. She was not expecting them to have such a profound effect on her. He in turn saw her objections to his affairs as the *real* infidelity, the betrayal of the agreement they had made when they married.

Some couples have worked out their own set of rules about what is and what is not an infidelity. I've seen prostitutes, male and female, who were granted sexual exception when it was done for business, but not for pleasure. Swingers have encouraged mate swapping and orgies as long as the sex was public, but have been outraged over private intimacies. Traveling people have been granted permission to be unfaithful when outside the city limits, or, in one case, "more than a four-hour drive from home." A few couples have decided that homosexual behavior outside the marriage would be considered acceptable, while heterosexual behavior would be disapproved. And there are some marriages in which men are permitted to have affairs while women are not. Couples have justified this arrangement by insisting that men can have affairs casually, while women are in danger of becoming romantically involved. Conversely, I have seen at least one couple who decided that the woman could have affairs, but the husband couldn't because he might be expected to spend money on other women, which would create problems with the family budget.

Whatever the agreement (if it really *is* an agreement), that is the accepted ideal for this couple in this marriage. The infidelity is in the breaking of the agreement.

While words in our casual language don't seem to retain specificity, we might make a distinction between infidelity and adultery. Adultery might be considered the religious and legal concern, in which certain acts are sinful or unlawful in themselves, independently of the relationship between the marriage partners. I'm not much concerned, in this book or elsewhere, with adultery if all partners consent to it. If it is lied about or kept secret, or done over the partner's objection, then it is an infidelity, a betrayal of the marital agreement that the couple would keep their sexual activities within the relationship, within whatever guidelines the two of them—having an equal voice in the matter—have agreed to.

A familiar example of a conflict over the definition of infidelity would be the situation that occurs when one partner has engaged in flirtation, clandestine meetings, or furtive sex play with a co-worker or social acquaintance, but insists that nothing that has taken place has been "wrong," since there was no intercourse. The partner, seeing the direction of things, feels a threat to the security of the marriage and would feel more comfortable distancing the flirtation partner. Even more common, couples might have to debate the wisdom of having lunch with a former affair partner, or a former spouse. The effort to avoid discussing the matter might well be a betrayal of the honesty of the relationship. If one partner bullies the other into agreeing to tolerate a friendship with so much sexual tension or sexual history, there has been a betrayal of respect for the current partner's feelings in the matter.

So when a man asks me whether something is or is not an

infidelity, I suggest that he ask his wife. When a woman asks me if she has done something wrong in a certain situation, I reply that if she kept it secret from her husband, she must think so.

Under unusual circumstances, a couple might agree to keep certain activities secret, and maintain certain barriers to their openness and intimacy. I recall a man who spent years in the jungle prospecting for gold, and had sexual liaisons with the locals, while his wife stayed home with the children and with some intimate male friends. This couple had long ago agreed that they didn't want to talk about what they did when they were apart. She was outraged when he asked her whether a certain man had been one of her sex partners. This couple had made an agreement about the way they would live their lives, and if they began to include each other in their lives apart, it might lead them to experience guilt and jealousy, or even to miss each other. That degree of intimacy would be incompatible with the lives they had set up. The wife, considering that, declared the husband's question to be out of order, and really an infidelity, as it broke their agreement. He, on the other hand, felt that he would have been commiting a greater infidelity by remaining silent when he was beginning to consider the feasibility of changing their arrangement to something more open and intimate.

We might define adultery as a sexual act outside the marriage, while we might define infidelity as a sexual dishonesty within the marriage. Adultery may be against the law or against God's will, but infidelity is against the marriage and is thus a more relevant and more personal danger.

Infidelity may not be the worst thing that one marriage partner can do to another, but it may be the most confusing and disorienting and therefore the most likely to destroy the marriage—not necessarily because of the sex, but because of the secrecy and the lies. A lie may be a more direct betrayal than keeping a relevant secret, but the two ultimately amount to much the same thing— the deliberate effort to disorient your partner in order to avoid the inevitable conflict over some breach of the marital agreement.

In writing about infidelity, I find myself at the mercy of English pronouns and the difficulty of saying anything about individuals without specifying their gender. Devices to get around this, like "s/he," unfortunately just call attention to the problem, and I have no idea how people read such contrived words. I don't want to use "he" to refer to the person who is being unfaithful, or "she" to mean either the person "he" is being unfaithful with or the person "he" is being unfaithful to, unless that is what I mean. And if I use either "she" or "he" for all three characters, the sad domestic drama being described would take on quite different implications. I've tried to make sure that when I say "he" or "she," that is just what I mean.

If pronouns are a problem, so are nouns. What should we call the players in this drama? The drama of infidelity always has at least three players—the betrayer, the one betrayed, and the affair partner. The betrayer, the person I sometimes call the *infidel,* is the one who is committing the infidelity by doing something sexual outside the marriage agreement. I realize that the word "infidel" implies a nonbeliever, one who does not keep the faith. Exactly.

I know it is customary for affair partners to be called "lovers." I have watched, with impotent protest, the decline of our language via euphemism, but I feel I must take a stand against calling affair partners lovers. Affairs are emotionally complex, and involve considerable anger, some toward the marriage partner, some toward the affair partner, some toward the institution of marriage, and much of it toward the gender seen as "opposite." Very often love is a minor ingredient in this emotional stew. The dictionary says an affair is a "romantic or passionate attachment typically of limited duration." I want the implication here of unreality, enchantment, illusion, and impermanence. I sometimes refer to the affair partner as the *affairee.*

The victim of the affair is the marriage partner who is being betrayed, escaped, and hidden from. The term *cuckold* comes to mind. "Cuckold" used to be a derisive term for a man whose wife was pregnant by someone else. The cuckoo is a large grayish brown bird with the peculiar habit of laying its eggs in the nests of other birds. The other bird, after hatching what she assumes to be one of her own offspring, is surprised when the egg breaks open and out comes a cuckoo bird. This is also the joke behind the cuckoo clock.

The word "cuckoo" has entered our slang not only as "someone who is in the wrong nest" but as "a silly and addle-brained person." Someone who is being unfaithful is rightly considered to be cuckoo, and the spouse of someone who has gone cuckoo is, most sympathetically, the cuckold.

INFIDELITY AND MENTAL HEALTH

It may seem extraordinary that the members of the mental health professions have devoted so much of their time to treating the effects of affairs on marriages and thus on life, and so little time noticing and discussing the extramarital affair itself. Why have professionals been so preoccupied with sexual fantasies and so little concerned with sexual secrets? Perhaps because psychoanalysis has been conducted in secrecy, preoccupied with confidentiality, it seemed only appropriate that sex be conducted the same way. When I first began raising the subject in family therapy circles a decade ago, I found very little in the literature, and few therapists who were comfortable with the topic.

There were several expectable reactions: "Infidelity is not a mental health issue, it's a moral issue." This reaction derives from a number of fascinating assumptions: "Mental health is attained when the restrictions of moral judgments are overcome. Whatever frees one from sexual restraint must be mentally healthy. The problems inherent in infidelity are (a) guilt and (b) jealousy. If guilt and jealousy can be overcome, infidelity will cease to be a problem. Unfortunately, guilt and jealousy are rarely overcome in a single lifetime, so infidelity must be kept secret, and therapists and reporters should work to protect the secret." Or so the thinking seems to go.

Another reaction: "Affairs are the healthy, normal expression of normal impulses. Marriages must learn to accommodate them." The problem as stated here is marriage itself, seen as an unhealthy, unnatural restriction on sexual freedom. This philosophy assumes that people resent marriage, find it restrictive and cramping, and spend their lives fighting against it or seeking escape from it. Of course, people who protect infidelity are protecting it against mar-riage.

Either attitude, blaming morality or blaming marriage for inter-fering with affairs, produces a dead end for therapists or anyone else dealing with affairs. More important, our confused attitude pro-duces an impasse for those who are trying to live with affairs—their own and those of their loved ones.

Making value judgments is no problem for most people. Most people make them all the time, and know they are doing it. They must do so in order to develop for themselves a workable system of values in a society that does not really offer one. But psychothera-pists are supposed to avoid making value judgments. Some psycho-therapists believe that we are supposed to free people from guilt. They believe we have so much power that we run the risk of instilling our personal values in our patients, so we must be neutral in order to protect our patients from the guilt that we therapists are inadvertently arousing. I think this is naive. It assumes that one can live without values, it assumes that problems come from values too strongly held, and it assumes that psychotherapists have a lot more power than I notice myself having.

I believe that if people understand the workings of their mind, they are better able to behave in a manner that works for them in the long run. But this does require an examination of values, the patient's, the therapist's, and the society's. (Just declaring it healthy for everybody to do whatever he or she feels like doing would make civilization impossible and tie up rush hour traffic.)

It really is mentally healthy to experience guilt over harmful actions. Bob Beavers, in his book *Successful Marriage*, said, "Guilt is good for you, if it lasts no longer than 5 minutes and brings a change in behavior." Guilt, if briefly sustained, can make people think more clearly about how to behave next time.

It seems both sick and pointless, however, to feel guilty over the workings of one's mind. Few experiences are quite so gratifying as the satisfaction of behaving properly against the inclination of one's emotions. We all have sexual fantasies, and we populate them with people other than our usual sexual partner. This is one of life's safest and healthiest pleasures, especially if we know we're not going to act on these fantasies. We not only get the pleasure of the turn-on, we also get pride from controlling our actions, and a victory over guilt, because we are going through this delightful inner struggle without risking anything or hurting anyone. Whatever turn-on we experience can then be taken home. I do hope people feel comfortable with their fantasies, and do not consider them to be a betrayal of marriage. Ordinarily, keeping fantasies private, while encouraging one's partner to do the same, enables one to enjoy them more freely.

People who declare certain emotions as forbidden, and then feel guilt over sexual thoughts or angry emotions, are severely restricted in the situations they can comfortably enter. I've known people who suffer extreme guilt over long-past indiscretions or idiosyncratic infractions. Other people set unrealistic standards, and give higher allegiance to those standards than to any consideration of how their actions are affecting other people. One woman felt guilty for the angry thoughts she had in sluggish traffic. To relieve her anger, she abandoned her car on the expressway. Though her guilt abated, the traffic was stalled completely. Considerate people, unlike this selfish woman, try to choose their values wisely and generously, and then live close to those values. That way, when they experience guilt, it is a warning that they are betraying their own values, hurting themselves and others, and they need to consider why. What problem, they need to ask themselves, are they trying to solve?

THE VALUE OF MONOGAMY

All people do not value monogamy, honesty, intimacy. Some people put a higher premium on a quite different set of values regarding fidelity and infidelity. I have heard some people, most often men, insist that there was nothing wrong with their affairs because they were purely for sex and never involved closeness or caring. These men value emotional detachment. To them, the form of extramarital sex that would be least threatening to their marriage would be with a nameless, faceless prostitute—a different one each time. Other men have maintained that there was nothing wrong with their infidelities because they never lied to the other women about their marital status or emotional nonchalance. The "valued" value here has been the honesty with women outside the marriage, and the thoughtful dishonesty with the woman at home.

On the other hand, some people, most often female, tell me that their infidelities are no problem as long as they are respectful and involve a state of being in love. As long as the affair partners don't exploit each other, the relationship is not "wrong." These same women want to be sure that they are being unfaithful without being hostile. As they see it, the fact that the affair is carefully kept secret demonstrates that it is not an act of hostility, and it is not an effort to hurt one's marriage or one's partner. The whole thing is without mean intent, and is therefore valued for its lack of exploitive motivation.

There are cultures, and subcultures in our own society, in which it is expected that married people will have affairs, and these affairs are viewed without much disapproval. The rule is that the affairs must be kept secret. The prevailing value is that the spouse must never be put in the position of having to deal with this unpleasant reality. Honesty, in such cultures, is not seen as a virtue at all, but rather as a brutal and unpleasant act. Marriages are formal, respectful arrangements, in which the most compelling value is polite respect for distance. One older widow, mourning her late husband whose virtues were by most standards minimal, said that the thing she appreciated most about Wilbur was that he was always careful to deny his philandering, so that she was never put into the position of having to go through any unpleasant confrontations about them. I had seen Wilbur for his alcoholism, and I believe he was being honest with me when he insisted that he had never been unfaithful to his wife. In fact the poor man had never had much love from anyone, since his wife believed all those years that he was, like her father and all the other men in her family, just naturally a philanderer, and therefore best handled by not getting too close or asking any questions.

These ways of looking at infidelity involve values and value judgments, but these are not the values we usually associate with traditional morality. Morality is a middle-class concern, i.e., behaving in a manner that seems appropriate to others and providing reassurance that you can be trusted to consider their feelings and not be utterly self-centered. I suppose "middle-class" morality has gotten a bad name for being more concerned with appearances than with realities, more concerned with what the neighbors think than with how something affects one's loved ones. Sexual behavior does affect one's loved ones a great deal more than it affects the neighbors, and the people who are affected need to be considered. Lawrence Durrell in *The Alexandria Quartet* quoted Freud: "I am accustoming myself to the idea of regarding every sexual act as a process in which four persons are involved." I don't know that Freud was talking about infidelity, but Durrell was.

As I see it, people's sexual choices do affect other people. Extramarital sex, when it occurs in a marriage that has agreed to monogamy, should be considered symptomatic, problematic behavior, and its specific meaning should be explored to determine what problem it is symptomatic of. Extramarital sex that follows the particular marital contract between the two marital partners may be no problem whatever, even though it may produce some discomfort for casual observers. Marital contracts that call for something other than monogamy may not be as benign as they appear to be, and may indicate some problem in the commitment, balance, or practicality of the marriage, but that is a different, far simpler, level of problem—even if it's kinky, it's honest.

I hope this value judgment of mine is not misunderstood to be antisexual. It may be just the opposite. Many people are so uncomfortable with sex in general that they can't make distinctions about when they are behaving appropriately and when they are not doing so. Such people are struggling so hard to convince themselves that sex *itself* is acceptable that they don't make the distinctions between the sex that is part of their marital agreement and the sex that is a betrayal of their marriage.

With the specter of AIDS, we are seeing an end to the sexual freedom of the sixties and seventies. Monogamy may even come back in style. Marriage has been endangered in recent decades. With casual sex potentially lethal, sexual honesty might become necessary. Whether people practice monogamy or not is their affair, but it cannot be a unilateral decision. Even if we value politeness more than we value honesty, or casualness more than intensity, we can no longer afford to keep sex secret. It is other people's business. If we did not appreciate that while the divorce rate was spiraling, we should certainly appreciate that in the era of AIDS, when a few false sexual moves might wipe out a community.

THE IDEAL

We humans commit a lot of infidelity. It may well be that most marriages are adulterous. Yet when we are polled on the matter, we confirm our belief in marital fidelity. Something like 85 percent of us believe that monogamy is the ideal. We yearn for it, we glorify it, and we read books and magazines on how to achieve it. Drugstores and airports are stacked with self-help books on how to keep one's marriage sexually exciting and monogamous. The romance novels give us dreams of a love so total that a betrayal of it would be unthinkable. Even as fidelity is our ideal, we may not quite believe that it is achievable; at times we treat it less as an ideal than as a fantasy, something that would be wonderful if it were humanly possible.

Even as we fail to practice fidelity, we seem to believe that infidelity should not be tolerated. Throughout all cultures, in all great literature, infidelity is rarely rewarded. The punishment may actually be quite intense. Faithless lovers seem doomed to die dramatically in the last act. There are few heroic infidels in our literature and mythology. We have to go all the way back to the ancient Greeks, who found women a threat and, at best, a nuisance, to find an adulterer who is not punished for his misdeeds. Ulysses, of course, comes to mind. He did indulge in various dalliances during his years of travel, and he stayed for quite a while with both Circe and Calypso, but he was unhappy throughout for not being at home with his wife, Penelope, who was weaving by day and unraveling by night to keep the suitors away. Ulysses, however wily and resourceful, was not a totally admirable character, and he was far from gracious about matters of infidelity. Upon his return, he slaughtered both Penelope's suitors and the unfaithful servants.

One of the great classic love stories is *Brief Encounter*, written by Noël Coward and directed by David Lean. In the 1946 film, doctor Trevor Howard and housewife Celia Johnson lust after each other interminably in a train station, never quite get together, suffer horribly for their attraction, and finally go on about their business—all to Rachmaninoff's Second Piano Concerto. Everybody on and off the screen chokes back tears, and it is terribly noble. But the lovers are made to suffer for their clandestine (but never quite consummated) love.

Forty years later, we would seem to have reached a higher level of tolerance for infidelity, and we theoretically should be able to tolerate adulterous love stories. Accordingly, a 1984 film called *Falling in Love* starred Meryl Streep and Robert De Niro as two happily married but not very articulate people who bump into each other and fall in love. The audience watches in horror as they become tortured by their guilty love, proceed to wreck their marriages, get divorced, and get together. The script is careful to make sure they never actually have sex before they get together. Still, the film alienates the audience. We like Streep's husband and De Niro's wife too much. We are torn between the romance and the marriages. Audiences rebelled against the situation, and the film bombed. We can accept infidelity if the cuckold is presented as a monster, but adultery can't be rewarded if both the infidel and the cuckold are good guys. (It might be acceptable for Mr. Rochester to pursue Jane Eyre, though he is married, because his mate is the crazed pyromaniac imprisoned in the west wing. Still, he has to lose an arm and go blind and the loony lady has to die before he and Jane can have a final clinch.)

Perhaps the classic test of societal sentiments about infidelity is the story of Camelot. King Arthur brings together the last remnants of civilization in post-Roman Britain. These knights of the Round Table are, above all, defenders of the right. But Arthur's wife Guinevere and Arthur's best friend, Sir Lancelot, get into an affair. Their affair breaks up the Round Table and hurls Britain into the Dark Ages. How do we, the audience, react? How does the story end? There are several versions, and none is really emotionally satisfying. Recent versions show both Guinevere and Lancelot as contrite and Arthur as forgiving, but what then? Some versions get Guinevere and Arthur back together, and let them live happily (for a time). In others, Arthur quickly and dramatically dies. In still other versions, Guinevere gets herself to a nunnery. But there don't seem to be any versions in which Guinevere and Lancelot live happily ever after, with Arthur's blessing, in the ruins of civilization.

Something further to consider. Infidelity has been blamed not just for the end of civilization, but for the end of the world. Richard Wagner's *Ring* cycle sets the Teutonic legends to music, and explains how a series of infidelities and deceits led directly to the twilight of the gods.

In Wagner's *Ring of the Nibelung*, Wotan, the wily King of the Gods, gives up an eye in his struggle to marry Fricka. Lacking binocular vision, he promptly begins heroic philandering and produces a bumper crop of illegitimate children, including nine Valkyries, chief of whom is Brunnhilde. Fricka, who loves Wotan and wants his love in return, is not amused. Wotan's power comes from his reliability—he in effect rules by contract, and he must maintain his agreements. He must also have his wife's approval of his actions. He tries to impress Fricka by building her a grand castle, but in his guilt for his misdeeds, he becomes too extravagant. He has even agreed to trade his sister-in-law, and with her the immortality of the gods, for this home of Valhalla. Fricka's displeasure increases, and Wotan's power fades.

Wotan tries to produce a hero to save the gods, so he mates with a human woman and produces even more illegitimate children, this time the twins Siegmund and Sieglinde. They are separated from their mother while young. When they meet again, they are both beleaguered and travailed, so they fall in love and run off together. The fact that they are brother and sister doesn't seem to bother anyone very much, but the fact that Sieglinde is married (to the brutal Hunding) strikes Fricka, ever the defender of marriage, as a shocking departure from propriety. Fricka demands that Wotan prevent Brunnhilde from rescuing the incestuous, and now pregnant, lovers. She requires Wotan to sacrifice his beloved illegitimate son, his hope for the future. But his unborn grandson, Siegfried, is saved.

A couple of operas later, Wotan's grandson Siegfried has grown up, has married his aunt Brunnhilde, and is all set to save the world. But the family enemies confuse Siegfried into forgetting that he is married and trick him into getting involved with another woman. This results in Siegfried's death. Brunnhilde responds by bringing about the flooding of the Rhine, the burning of Valhalla, the destruction of the gods, and the end of the world. Brunnhilde is a powerful woman and she is not happy that her husband forgot that he was married to her, and hell hath no fury like a Valkyrie forgotten.

It should be apparent that infidelity can cause all manner of problems, some immediate, some generations later. One would think people would know that by now. Nonetheless, every time people commit an infidelity and all hell breaks loose, they look so surprised. Even after twenty-seven years as a psychiatrist and family therapist, devoting much of my time to cleaning up the emotional mess after other people's affairs, I never cease to wonder at the naïveté of people going through it.

2 / Some Myths about Infidelity

"Humankind cannot bear very much reality. "
T.S. ELIOT, *MURDER IN THE CATHEDRAL*

"The most costly of all follies is to believe passionately in
the palpably not true."
H. L. MENCKEN

---

nfidelity is the primary disrupter of families, the most dreaded and
devastating experience in a marriage. It is the most universally
accepted justification for divorce. It is even a legally accepted
justification for murder in some states and many societies. The
crises that follow infidelities fill the offices of family therapists,
lawyers, and plastic surgeons. I doubt if there is any problem on
which we all devote more energy. At the beauty parlor or the health
club, it is a major topic of conversation. Yet the subject is fraught
with misinformation and mythology.

There is a lot of nonsense in the popular mythology about
extramarital affairs. There are some ideas that are fallacious, but
rather universally accepted as true. From all the socially accepted
fallacies about infidelity, what causes it, and how to handle it, seven
myths stand out as especially misleading. These myths show up in
adulterous families, in "Dear Abby," in popular magazines, and
even in the literature on family and marriage (where thick books
on marriage therapy often bypass the problem entirely).

They are:

1. Everybody is unfaithful; it is normal, expectable behavior.
2. Affairs are good for you; an affair may even revive a dull marriage.
3. The infidel must not "love" the cuckold; the affair proves it.
4. The affairee must be "sexier" than the spouse.
5. The affair is the fault of the cuckold, proof that the cuckold has failed the infidel in some way that made the affair necessary.
6. The best approach to the discovery of a spouse's affair is to pretend not to know and thereby avoid a crisis.
7. If an affair occurs, the marriage must end in a divorce.

All of these ideas, like the proverbial stopped clock, are right some of the time. Many people are unfaithful, sometimes a marriage is better after an affair or some other crisis, people who don't define themselves as being "in love" with a spouse are at greater risk for infidelity, many people do choose affair partners for purely sexual qualities, a few people do encourage their mates to have affairs, many marriages have not developed tolerance for openness, and the divorce rate in adulterous marriage is high. But these observations, even at times when they are true, are misleading.

Myth #1: *Everybody has affairs.* The data on the frequency of infidelity is fairly consistent. About half do and half don't. Traditionally, more men than women have been adulterous, but the women seem to be catching up. Surveys in the last few years tell us that about 50 percent of husbands have been unfaithful, while 30–40 percent of wives have been. The younger generation of women is more likely to be unfaithful than the older generation was at that age or is now. In the very youngest groups, the husbands and wives are equally unfaithful, while among the oldsters, infidelity is largely a male activity. As the percentage of adulterous wives goes up, the percentage of adulterous husbands may actually have been going down.

If infidelity of some sort takes place in over half of all marriages, that's a lot of infidelity. The figures are misleading, though. Many adulterers have had only one affair, most only a few. Much of the infidelity takes place (as cause or effect) in the last year of a dying marriage. Intact, continuing marriages are far less adulterous. Marital fidelity remains the norm, in that most marital partners are faithful most of the time. The same surveys that show most marriages as adulterous also show that the vast majority of people believe strongly in marital fidelity, certainly for their spouse and generally for themselves. It remains the ideal, even if it is not always achieved.

It seems to me that people who screw around assume that everyone else does too, while those who don't screw around assume extramarital sex is unusual behavior. Quite obviously, people who grew up in families in which the adults had affairs are more likely to see this as normal behavior and to do it themselves.

There are several different kinds of infidelity. Some of it is infrequent, occurs under unusual circumstances, is perhaps even unique and accidental ("Accidental Infidelity"). Some of it is a rare but intense passion that threatens the marriage and feels like love ("Romantic Affairs—Falling In-Love"). Some of the infidelity is open and part of the marital arrangement, either cooperative or defiant ("Marital Arrangements"). Continuous, recurrent infidelity ("Philandering") may occur in no more than 20 percent of intact marriages. Much of the philandering is not even secret, and some is with the active cooperation of the spouse.

Fidelity is relative. One unforgettable case illuminates that matter, while it points up the problems that occur when people assume that "everybody does it." Larry had many businesses, some legitimate and some not. The source of his fortune was his liquor stores, but the source of his pleasure was his strip joint. He liked sex; since puberty, he had known that he liked it several times a day, and had arranged his life around this hobby. His hero was Hugh Hefner, who helped him escape from the sexual guilt of his divorced mother's fundamentalist religion. In his youth, he had preferred to have many different women. As he grew older, he preferred the same few familiar women each day.

He even decided to try marriage again, for the first time since a youthful disaster. He assumed that all men had affairs, so he arranged his marriage to accommodate active infidelity. He married a young, compliant, naive girl who also assumed that men would be unfaithful. He did not want his hobby to damage this marriage, so he moved his wife and children to another town, where they wouldn't get in his way. During the week, he lived with the women who worked for him, and then on the weekends, when he wasn't too busy, he'd visit his wife and children. He traveled with one or more of his women, and would sometimes bring them with him to visit his family. His wife quickly learned not to object. As Larry saw it, he had the life all men envy. It might even have been the life his father had had before his untimely death. He assumed that all men were devoting their full attention to having as much sex with as many different women as possible. He felt good, though his trips home weren't much fun because of his wife's depression.

The crisis in Larry's life occurred when the scandal hit and everyone learned the details of his life style. To Larry's surprise, people disapproved of him rather than admired him. People even convinced his wife that this is not the way marriages are ordinarily conducted. She tried to talk to him about it. He ran away. She fussed. He said, "If I wasn't married, what I'm doing wouldn't be wrong, so it is your fault for being married to me." She brought him to me, and I suggested that Larry give monogamy a try, but he acted as if I were trying to recruit him into some weird religious sect.

He did tell the story to the next woman on his sexual rotation that day. She assured him that he was right. Larry liked that and began talking to her more. That was fine for a while, but soon the mistress did something no woman had ever done to Larry before: she demanded that he give up all other women and be faithful to her, or else she would leave him for another man. Larry panicked. No woman had ever spurned him before. He pursued her, leaving his wife for her. She accepted him, but she demanded fidelity. He'd tried many new things with this young woman—new drugs, new positions, new combinations—but this concept of fidelity was certainly the kinkiest. He tried it, though. He even called to tell me how happy he was. As he put it, "I never thought I could do it, but I've been almost completely faithful to her for nearly three weeks now."

Larry's narcissistic naïveté is extreme. Most people really do know that infidelity is not usual behavior, even as they try to convince themselves that everybody is doing it. Most people in intact marriages are not being secretly adulterous. When someone is being secretly adulterous, it should be considered a problem that is specific to those involved rather than behavior that is typical of a gender or an era or a society. If adultery were dismissed as normal, expectable behavior, and were even anticipated, that would interfere greatly with trust and intimacy in the marriage. Its specific meaning would then not be explored. Therefore, it is not only more accurate, but also more helpful to consider infidelity as out of order and symptomatic. Then we need to determine what it is symptomatic of.

Myth # 2: *Affairs are good for marriage.* Somehow the idea has been foisted upon us that affairs can revive dull marriages. I've found that idea expressed in *Playboy* and in *Cosmopolitan*, which is not surprising since those magazines are selling sexy fantasies, but I've also heard it from marriage and family therapists, which is frightening. People must want desperately to believe this, as many do believe it while all the evidence points to the contrary.

It may be that the idea comes from a belief (on the part of certain magazine editors and certain psychotherapists) that marriage itself is dull. Believing that their own experience with marriage is the universal experience, they assume that fidelity would produce resentment in people who wanted to be unfaithful, and the deprivation would produce rancor in marriage. Therefore, if people felt free to be unfaithful, they would not be so angry about marriage. Such a belief assumes people are basically passive-aggressive and marriage is unnatural and fragile. Some people indeed are too angry and passive-aggressive for fidelity, and must either negotiate some other arrangement or live a life of secrecy and basic enmity with their partner.

For most people and most marriages, infidelity is dangerous. The exceptions are unusual and should be approached cautiously. I have seen marriages in which an affair did trigger a crisis that led to a fight in which some long-standing problem got solved. I've also seen marriages in which an automobile accident or a child's illness produced such a beneficial crisis. To have an affair in order to trigger a crisis from which the marriage might eventually benefit is truly a screwball, convoluted approach to problem solving.

Affairs do great damage. Marriages can recover from affairs, but it takes a hell of a lot of work and pain. A battle-scarred marriage might be wearier, and the partners might expect less from it, but it is nobody's ideal. Even a little bit of infidelity can set forces in motion that eventually wreck a marriage.

Carly was a lady of the utmost dignity. She confessed her infidelity with less shame than I might have expected, and far more sadness. Her affair partner was her husband's business partner and best friend, the husband of her own best friend. This very sad affair was now in its twentieth year. The two couples played bridge together, as they always had, every Monday, had dinner together every Wednesday, went dancing together every Friday, and went to church together every Sunday. The husbands worked together every day, the wives carpooled and baby-sat, first their children and now their grandchildren, anytime they weren't golfing or shopping. But every Thursday, for twenty years, Carly and her affairee sneaked off secretly for lunch to discuss their affair. They had tried sex once, it went badly and far too quickly. Now they had to meet to talk about how to keep it secret, and ponder whether their spouses suspected, and even consider whether they might try it again.

Carly's preaffair life had been pleasant and comfortable, but she had thought that her lack of premarital sexual experience might be making her marriage less exciting than she thought it should be. She read an article, back in the sixties, about variety being the spice of life, and she decided to add some spice to her life. But not being very adventurous, she didn't want to stray too far from home. She chose Clovis, and that was that. She found herself stuck now with even less of a marriage, and with an affair that added nothing except tension to her life. Carly was sad about the lack of romance and the lack of adventure and, indeed, the lack of sex, but she had devoted every day of her life for twenty years to thinking about this relationship, and it was too late to get all the way back into the marriage, or to bring about any change in the affair. After all, as Carly said, "I can't get along without him. He's the only one I can talk with about this central secret of my life. Now that I've betrayed my husband and my best friend, he's the only person I can relax with. I just wish I liked him better. The saddest part of all is that I like my husband better than I like my lover, but I can't tell him."

Myth #3: *Affairs prove that love has gone from the marriage.*
The reasons for affairs are rich and varied. Most of the reasons have to do with the ego state of the person having the affair rather than the person against whom the infidelity is being committed. The reasons can range all the way from "hobby" (the infidel belongs to a club in which they do this weekly) to "politeness" (the infidel stumbled into an awkward situation in which it would have been rude not to commit an infidelity). Even if someone did not love the spouse, an infidelity would be a rather complicated and indirect way to say so, and an inefficient way to approach the problems in the marriage. The feelings one spouse has for another are complicated from the beginning. The degree of complexity of the emotions in long-standing marriages is staggering. To reduce this complexity to a question as adolescent as the presence or absence of "love" is idiocy of the highest order. That question is best left to the petals of daisies.

Everyone involved (the infidel, the cuckold, the affairee, the children, the in-laws, the neighbors, etc.) must recognize that marriage abounds in love, hate, lust, disgust, envy, guilt, pity, admiration, dependency, fear, and all other emotions known and unknown.

The issue is not one of emotion, but one of choice—whether the commitment of marriage has or has not been abandoned. This commitment seems somewhat independent of the emotions of the moment and may have much more to do with the choosing spouse's sense of his or her own identity and system of values—

whether he or she "feels married" or not and what implications that has for behavior. Fidelity has to do with what one *intends* to do, not what one is inclined to do. Some people make rather fragile commitments and abandon them as soon as they notice an un-desired feeling toward the spouse or an attraction for someone else. Such people may talk of love as an engulfing totality and mislead everyone around them about the actual intricacy of the situation. Such people want the security and the high of an in-love state so intense that any outside attraction or unpleasant reaction would be intolerable. Such people, of course, have little concept of ego con-trol, of choice, of decision. They want the simplicity of living on pure and determinant instinct.

The instinctual nature of the human animal may be such that we bond, as other monogamous species do, to our sexual partner, our mate. Humans have the capacity to survive our mate—if he or she should die, we, unlike some monogamous birds, can recover and find another mate. However, if we mate with others while our partner is still around, we may break the bond that holds the pairing together. We may, by having affairs, loosen the attachment and "fall out of love" with our partner. It is therefore not that we fall out of love and thus have affairs, but that we have affairs and thus fall out of love by breaking an instinctual bond. The flexibility of the human animal, the relative weakness of our instincts, pro-vides us with possibilities of escape from instinctual control, but it opens us to the possibilities of unpredictable flirtations with dan-ger.

It is routine for a frantic cuckold to ask the question "Do you love him/her?" There is something so romantic and innocent in reducing these complex matters to such a simple yes or no question. Affairs may be driven by hate as often as by love. Certainly, I've seen more affairs in which friendship is the primary emotion than those based on being in love. Many affairs begin as friendships, and continue as friendships until the sex occurs. Once the sex occurs, the friendship then goes through a period of growing more intense and complicated, until it finally makes the friendship too uncom-fortable to continue. What is so sad, and seems so foolish about affairs, is that many of them might have been wonderful, utterly unthreatening friendships had they not been so naively sexualized by people who are overly preoccupied with gender differences, and just don't know how to have a friendship with someone of a different gender.

Lou was happily married, and had been for fifteen years. She was proud of Lefty, she enjoyed his company, and she loved to look at him. He was a great-looking jock; just looking at him was a turn-on. He was a good man and he made her proud. She didn't know whether he was any good in bed, since she'd never had anybody else, but it seemed good enough for her. When Lefty gave up professional baseball, Lou was disappointed. She knew he would never have comparable successes at anything else, and she was right. He didn't feel good about himself, and he lost some of his cockiness; but he was making it OK in the real world, and he was home now and was good with the kids. She loved him, but she thought he was a little fragile, so she protected him a bit.

The great advantage of having Lefty off the road was that Lou now could go back to work. She had always loved nursing, and she got a wonderful job in the office of the plastic surgeon who had removed a scar from her chin. She really admired him, since beauty was very important to her, and he could create it. Her doctor was a funny-looking little man, nothing exciting unless he had a scalpel in his hand. She had no idea how she ended up in bed with him. It just happened. It was awful. It really made her appreciate Lefty. She knew it would never happen again.

She didn't know whether to tell Lefty or not, but she'd never kept any secret from him, and he had told her about a little affair he had had, so she told him. He was upset, and he insisted that she leave her job. She did, but she resented it.

This little affair was just an accident, but she understood why Lefty felt as he did, and she was guilty enough to realize it was necessary. But after she gave up the job, and despaired of getting another opportunity quite so good, she began to resent both Lefty and the surgeon. She didn't care about the surgeon, so that didn't matter, but her resentment of Lefty festered. She had certainly loved him at the time she had that silly little affair, but now she wasn't sure. He kept acting as if she didn't love him anymore, and she finally began to believe him. Now he was the enemy of her happiness. She came to therapy raising the question of whether she should get a divorce.

Myth #4: *The affairee was sexier than the spouse.* Since an affair involves sex, it is often assumed that the affair is about sex and the object of the affair is a champion sexual athlete. Of course, that is sometimes the case. But in my practice, I've noticed that it is about as common for the infidel to acknowledge that sex was better at home. And affairs may not involve very much sexual activity at all. A few affairs, like that of Carly, continue for years after one inept sexual encounter, as if the sex, however unsatisfactory, were obligatory to produce a bonding that would enable the friendship to proceed on a basis of limited intimacy.

Affair partners are not chosen because they are the winners of some objective sex contest. They are chosen for all manner of strange and usually nonsexual reasons. Affair choices are usually far more neurotic than marriage choices. When one is chosen to be an affair partner, one should not feel complimented. When I compare cuckolds and affairees, I try to understand the crucial difference that seems so important to the infidel. I find no consistent pattern. I certainly have not found a pattern of affair partners being better-looking than marriage partners, or nicer, or more accomplished. Some are more dependent, some less. Some are more emotionally involving, some more restrained. One woman chose a lover for his primitiveness—he didn't seem superior to her as her husband did. A man chose a woman who shared his excitement for waterfalls. Men with domestic wives seem attracted to career women, and men whose wives are involved with careers seem attracted to domestic types. Women with successful husbands choose the shepherds, while the nymphs frolic with the stockbrokers. The choice of an affair partner seems based on the other person's *difference* from the spouse rather than *superiority* to the spouse. The point of difference may diagnose a problem for which the affair is seen as a cure. The problem could be sexual, most likely is not.

Affairs are sometimes alternatives to the marriage, efforts at finding a partner to assist in escape from a marriage. There are people who can't tolerate the unpartnered state. They must find their next mate before they can leave the current one, no matter how awful or dangerous the relationship. The new rescuing relationship does not have to be very sexual to establish the bond that produces the partnership. The most important characteristic of such affairees is their immediate availability.

In romantic movies of the damsel-in-distress genre, the delicate gothic heroine could not escape her insane homicidal husband by herself. There had to be a hero to assist her in her escape, even if he was just a passerby—the heroine must not be left unpartnered. Joseph Cotten served this function for Ingrid Bergman in her escape from Charles Boyer's efforts to convince her she was insane in *Gaslight*. As Vincent Price terrorized Gene Tierney in *Dragonwyck*, the sturdy family doctor, Glenn Langhan, came to whisk her away from all this unpleasantness. In the more sophisticated genre of film noir, preoccupied with the evil within the hearts of all of us, the dissatisfied wife would find a horny chump to seduce so he could assist her in killing her husband. Lana Turner rang John Garfield's bell in *The Postman Always Rings Twice*. Kathleen Turner turned up the thermostat for William Hurt in *Body Heat*. These women preferred men who were dumb, mean, violent, and disposable.

More often people are not seeking an alternative to their marriage, but a supplement to it. They just want a friend for whatever they aren't getting at home. Some people don't realize they can have friends of either gender without having to sexualize the friendship or keep it hidden or see it as a threat to their marriage. So they sexualize the friendship, and turn it inadvertently into something quite different from its original function. The sex was not the purpose for the relationship but merely the seal of the friendship.

To my subjective eye, affairees have not tended to be a startlingly good-looking group, or even more attractive than the cuckolded wife or husband. There are certain times when appearance seems to be important to the infidel. Even then, the desired appearance may not be beauty. Instead, the betrayer may choose an affair partner who connects with some forbidden sexual fantasy. The betrayer then becomes obsessed with the fantasy, and may prefer to limit contact with the real person who is the object of the fantasy. It may be a rather idiosyncratic fantasy, one that would have little meaning for anyone else. For example, in *Cabaret,* the musical about decadence in pre–World War II Berlin, the emcee sings an ode to his love for a woman who is quite clearly a chimpanzee in a dress, munching on a banana. The song is called "If You Could See Her Through My Eyes." We are not shown what the emcee's usual partner looks like.

I saw such a case. Crystal called me first. It did not surprise her that Chip had left her—he'd threatened it for years. It was the timing that surprised her. He had blamed all his marital dissatisfaction on her obesity. Crystal had felt betrayed by that, since she'd been a bit plump when they had met and married, and hadn't really put on that much weight through the years. But he would avoid her sexually, drink too much, stay away from home, and talk interminably about other women who looked better to him. Recently, Chip's mother had moved back to town, and had helped Crystal with diet and exercise. Crystal had lost a great deal of weight and she looked marvelous. She went around in great-looking new clothes, getting lots of attention. And it was right at the height of her newfound beauty that Chip got into an affair and left her. The shocking thing was that his affairee was even fatter than Crystal had been before her diet.

I then saw Chip, who cheerfully told me of his great romance. He showed me her picture. She was, by even the most Rubenesque standards, fat. I tried to understand why Chip had spent all those years complaining that his wife was fat, bullying her into losing weight, only to leave her for a woman who was even more overweight. Chip was not somebody who was good at understanding things: he only knew what he felt and what he wanted. It did not begin to make sense until Chip brought in his mother, a former beauty queen. This aging glamour girl had devoted her life to her appearance, and had deserted her husband and children in her search for a man who would fully support and appreciate her great beauty. Chip had spent his life with intense emotional confusion about his feelings for his mother, and whether the girl of his dreams was a glamorous beauty like his mother or someone softer and more nurturing, like the grandmother who had actually raised him. Faced with the reality of his prodigal mother returned in all her skinny glamour, he found himself desperate for the warmth of a more comfortable woman. Crystal had just become too beautiful to make him feel secure.

Myth #5: *The affair is the fault of the cuckold.* The irresponsible belief "You made me do it" is often accepted by both the betrayer and the betrayed. Despite all the therapeutic effort that goes into teaching patients that they are responsible for their behavior, many therapists believe that affairs are an exception, and they can only be brought about by collusion between the marital partners. In a slightly modified form, "You're part of this too," the belief is sufficiently widespread to be a cornerstone of marital therapy. There seems to be some therapeutic advantage to declaring an affair to be a collusive effort, but that is almost a paradox. It quite obviously is not actually true.

One person cannot make another have an affair. Affairs, almost by definition, require the physical absence of the spouse who is being betrayed. I have seen one martial partner try to make the other have an affair, and rarely has this succeeded. Each one of the swinging couples I have seen through the years began the swinging when one had an affair and was then determined that the other would do so too. Far more frequently, the betrayer tried to coerce the betrayed into having an affair and faced refusal. It is a hard thing to force.

Moe refused to have an affair. He suspected his wife of infidelity when he found the costumes from Frederic's of Hollywood, and the bills that showed she had sent a fur-lined jockstrap to her recently divorced old high school boyfriend. All those nights at that motel near her old hometown, when she said she was visiting her mother, but her mother knew nothing about it. And then her behavior changed so. Nonetheless, Moe tried to believe her when she insisted that she was not being unfaithful, but that he was becoming paranoid like his uncle and needed to see a psychiatrist, who would surely recommend that he have an affair to help him relax.

I didn't recommend that Moe have an affair, though his wife urged me to do so, insisting that the marriage would not survive unless he had an affair. She pushed harder. He refused. She insisted, then demanded, then threatened. She began to bring strange women to the house and put them in bed with him. He would get out of the bed and sleep on the couch. She installed a hot tub, and installed buxom ladies in it with him. He would politely get out and get dressed. She finally filed for divorce, claiming mental cruelty because "he acted morally superior by refusing to commit adultery." I emerged from dealing with this harrowing case with the firm conviction that no one can force someone else to be unfaithful.

It is certainly easy for one marital partner to make the other wish to be somewhere else, or to be with someone else. But the unhappy partner could choose divorce, murder, an argument, therapy, or whatever instead. The dissatisfaction in a marriage may or may not be a joint effort, but the decisions about how to deal with an intolerable situation are clearly individual. When adulterous couples come in to therapy, the one doing the betraying may be complaining that the one being betrayed has, in some way, caused the affair, but this may be the first time the problems have been emphasized. Even when the problems have been argued about for years and blamed for the affair, there may be considerable reluctance to solve them during the affair.

The relationship between the affair and the problems blamed for the affair becomes increasingly confusing. It is often difficult to believe there is any relationship. It may well be that the decision that there is a problem in the marriage is made after the affair begins. This decision has one useful result—the cuckold can't withdraw into a position of moral superiority. There are few more helpless positions than that of blamelessness. But the decision that the problems caused the affair turns responsibility for ending the affair to the betrayed spouse. It may be useful to consider the affair as an effort to call attention to a problem in the marriage, but just as telephones stop ringing once they are answered, affairs must stop before the problems can be approached.

It is very difficult for people to work on a marriage in which an affair is going on. Affairs usually stop once they are revealed. Sometimes, though, the affair comes out into the open and still continues despite all efforts to stop it. The continuation of the affair proves that it has an existence independent of anything about the marriage. Affairs, once begun, have a life of their own, and it seems foolhardy for the betrayed spouse to pretend to have any influence over it. Efforts to stop an ongoing affair seem only to strengthen the attachment.

In general, I don't find it helpful for a betrayed spouse to take responsibility for any part of the affair. The one being betrayed can't make affairs happen, can't make the betrayer stop, and can only make him- or herself available for solving whatever problems there might be in the marriage, though those are going to be grotesquely distorted and exaggerated as long as the affair is continuing or being defended.

Myth #6: *There is safety in ignorance of a spouse's affair.* Affairs are complicated and have a certain message value. One message might be that the betrayer wants out of the marriage but doesn't want to take responsibility for that position, so would like to offend the one being betrayed into threatening divorce. That sounds far-fetched, since people willing to be adulterous would not seem finicky enough on matters of protocol to let vital life decisions depend on who brings up a subject for discussion. I have encountered an occasional marriage in which one partner seems to be saying, "If you object to my behavior in any way, then leave me or I will leave you." These partners didn't leave, but they were effective bullies until that threat was challenged.

Ignorance of affairs puts people in the position of not having to acknowledge problems or do anything to solve them. If the affair ends, the sexual, emotional, functional, and intimate relationship will be between husband and wife. Many—sometimes I think most —people prefer not to be happily married, to retain some limits on the intimacy and "togetherness." They work at maintaining just the right distance in the relationship. The affair may be an aid to that distance. Although the spouse's affair may create an undesirable state of distance, the end-of-the-affair reunion and postaffair problem solving might produce an even less desired state of excessive closeness. The danger of bringing an affair into the open is not that the infidel becomes more likely to leave, but that the infidel becomes more likely to *stay*, and try to get close.

Ollie came to see me alone. Laura, his wife of many years, was again leaving evidence that she was in another affair. Ollie had gotten good at hunting for affairees, and had even identified the man with whom Laura was presently involved. The other times, he had revealed the affair, thrown a temper tantrum, demanded that she give up the affair, and then gone through the reconciliation process, with fancy trips and fur coats as part of his courtship offerings to her. He knew she was expecting him to bring it all out into the open. But he was too angry with her to go through this process again, especially right now during his busy season. Ollie realized that if he didn't acknowledge knowing, then he wouldn't have to reconcile with Laura right now, devote all that attention to her, reassure her that she was forgiven and that he loved her. He just wasn't ready to get that close to her, and take that much time from work. Ollie would rather have left Laura in her affair until it was a more convenient time for him to go through the forgiveness process. What he really wanted to ask me was whether he was commiting some sort of infidelity by not revealing to her that he knew of her latest affair.

It must be kept in mind that affairs thrive on secrecy. The conspiracy and adventure and tricks produce an alliance in the affair, while the lies and deceit increase the discomfort at home. All of us feel bound to those who share our secrets, and uncomfortable with those to whom we are lying. The power of an affair may be in its secrecy. The weakness of the marriage may be in its avoidance of issues.

Myth #7: *After an affair, divorce is inevitable.* Certainly, an affair is a crisis in a marriage. After any crisis, the marriage may become better and it may become worse. There are people of such distrusting, perfectionist, or romantic natures that they find it difficult to live in a blemished marriage, or elsewhere in a real, imperfect world. Once some defect has been discovered in their world, they can suffer indefinitely, whether the adulterous spouse stays or goes. There are marriages in which the betrayer remains on probation or under punishment for decades after the affair.

Adultery, however common, is a major offense against a marriage. But I can also recall marriages in which a spouse was punished for decades for (a) parking crooked in front of the church at the wedding, (b) failing to arrange to get the wife into the Junior League, (c) saying a four-letter word, (d) leaving dirty socks on the floor, (e) having an overweight mother, (f) spelling imperfectly. It would seem that people who are determined to be unhappily married can find justification, whether the spouse becomes unfaithful or not.

Bud believed that he would have to divorce Bette if he acknowledged knowing what he knew. He didn't want to divorce Bette. They'd been together since high school, and he'd grown accustomed to her. They didn't talk much, and they never went out together anymore. He had always preferred playing with machines, and he had a wonderful computer he'd trained to do amazing tricks. He had made lots of money selling video games when they were hot, had sold his business for over a million dollars, and had retired before he was thirty. So he stayed home and tended the children, the computers, and the investments. He wanted Bette to stay there with him, but she tried it for a while and realized that Bud was a nice man, but an awful bore. She didn't remember being so bored with him when he had his business, but then he wasn't around very much. She tried to talk to him about it, but he wasn't good at talking. She decided to go to work. He didn't think a millionaire's wife should be working as a cocktail waitress, but that's the only thing she knew to do. She made it very clear that she didn't care what he said about it, but he wasn't much of a talker and wasn't going to say anything anyway.

Bud was uncomfortable with Bette's job, though he didn't say so; he didn't like to talk about feelings. Instead, he went to the club and spied on her. He suspected that she was having an affair with the manager of the club. He was wrong. It was the bartender. Bud didn't know what to do. He was afraid to tell her what he knew. So he just got quieter and quieter. This went on for months. Bette became more brazen, and made little effort to hide what she was doing. She was growing increasingly disgusted with Bud, and finally told him she was going to leave him. He didn't say anything. She asked if he wanted to know where she would be. He finally spoke, and said he assumed she'd be at the bartender's apartment. Then he started crying, and told her more of how he felt than he ever had. He even asked her to give up her affair and stay with him, and he would do anything, even go back to work if she liked. Bette insisted later that she had not thought she was doing this just to get a response from Bud. She thought she was in love with the talkative bartender, but once the conversation with Bud began, she didn't want the bartender anymore.

She never returned to the job at the bar. She and Bud came to therapy instead, and Bud learned to talk while Bette dealt with the intimidation she felt from Bud's financial power. She realized she didn't know him very well, had no understanding of his vulnerability, and didn't feel needed by him. He did learn to talk a little, and they stayed together. He was glad he had risked saying something about the affair as she was walking out the door. He even thought it might have been easier if he had mentioned it earlier.

I have not noticed the expected connection between happiness in the marriage and the decision to divorce. Miserable marriages stay together, and slightly flawed ones break apart—it seems to have more to do with individual expectations than with objective "happiness," if such a thing can be measured. Some people trade cars when the ashtrays are full or the "new" smell fades, others hold on to machines that are mechanically faulty, often in the shop, and unable to start on cold mornings. Some people divorce after an affair, some remain married and punitive and miserable, and others use the affair as a crisis from which to produce a more satisfactory marriage, one either more or less intimate, more or less exclusive. Therapy, which seems so ineffectual during the affair, can determine the outcome of the postaffair marriage.

Whatever the problems in the marriage before a crisis of infidelity, the problems after the affair are quite different and far more serious. The affair brings its own problems, God knows, but also brings urgency to the preexisting problems. In my experience, in my practice, couples therapy is crucial after an affair, and can reverse the prognosis for the marriage. Certainly many marriages do end in the wake of an affair, but far more end in an effort to maintain the secret of the affair.

I have very rarely seen a couple in therapy divorce because of an affair that is now over. It happens routinely in marriages that are not in therapy. (We must remember that everybody has therapists, professional or nonprofessional experts on problem solving, and some of those don't really believe in marriage.) I certainly see people divorce over repeated infidelity or romantic affairs that drag on long after they are known, but most of the postaffair divorces are instituted by infidels, not cuckolds, who express bewilderment about how to return to marriages they feel so guilty for betraying.

Honestly, it is safe to talk openly about affairs. It saves lives and marriages to do so. So I would substitute a quite different set of generalizations about infidelity, and this book is really about these generalizations.

1. Infidelity is not normal behavior, but a symptom of some problem.
2. Affairs are dangerous and can easily, and inadvertently, end marriages.
3. Affairs can occur in marriages that, prior to the affair, were quite good.
4. Affairs involve sex, but the sex is not usually the purpose of the affair.
5. No one can drive someone else to have an affair.
6. Affairs are fueled by secrecy and threatened by exposure.
7. Marriages can, with effort, survive affairs if the affairs are exposed.

3 / Guilty Secrets

"Why can't women play the game properly? Everyone knows that in love affairs only the man has the right to lie."
CLIFTON WEBB IN *THREE COINS IN A FOUNTAIN,*
WRITTEN BY JOHN PATRICK

"I suspect that people lie about their sex lives more than any other subject."
"DEAR ABBY," MAY 31, 1977

Inherent in much of the popular psychology of recent decades has been the absurd idea that acting on one's impulses is mental health. From that perspective, the forces that interfere with one's sexual freedom become the forces of evil, the devils of sexual freedom. These twin devils are guilt and jealousy. In practical application, the embodiment of guilt and jealousy becomes one's spouse, the person with whom one contracted not to do the very acts one is trying to achieve the freedom to do without arousing guilt or jealousy.

Infidelities, as I'm defining them here, don't have to be sexual. If an agreement has been made with one's marital partner that one will not drink, or smoke, or gamble, or spend money, or spend time with certain people, then to do so secretly would be a betrayal of the relationship. The seriousness of the betrayal varies. The greatest threat (the most serious betrayal of the trust) would ordinarily be a sexual infidelity. But getting together secretly for lunch with an old lover might well be a greater threat than visiting a whorehouse and sampling all the wares. To lunch openly with the old lover or to do scientific research in the whorehouse might not be an infidelity at all. The infidelity is not in the sex, necessarily, but in the secrecy. It isn't whom you lie with. It's whom you lie to.

Yet we have common assumptions: (1) Dishonesty is necessary between men and women. Men and women look at things so differently, they just wouldn't understand the truth if they knew it. (In other words, your mate is disorientingly foreign.) (2) Dishonesty protects people from getting hurt. Dishonesty is honorable, even noble, if it keeps people from having to face things that are unpleasant. (In other words, your mate is pathetically delicate.) (3) The danger of infidelity is in getting caught. If it is kept secret, then nobody will get upset. (In other words, your mate is dangerously unstable.) Each of these three beliefs, however innocent or seemingly noble in concept, undercuts the marriage by implying that your mate is too different, too delicate, or too frightening to understand you, and therefore must be kept at a safe distance.

One way of assuring distance is to disorient the other person, and of course the classic way of disorienting someone is to give him or her a little piece of crucial misinformation. A little lie will create distance. Was Goldie Hawn right in *Cactus Flower*, when she said that "a man who lies cannot love"? That may be an overstatement, but I think it fair to assume that someone who is lying to someone else is not trying to bring about closeness, intimacy, or understanding. Lies can bring temporary comfort or peace to a relationship (and permit quick getaways), but at the cost of ultimate distrust, misunderstanding, and distance.

DISHONESTY AND GENDER

There seem to be different *codes* of honesty, depending upon whether you are a man or a woman, or whether you are dealing with a member of your own sex or with a representative of a sex you consider "opposite." As a rule, male friends, business partners, and athletic teammates deal with one another in a manner that is aimed at increasingly efficient teamwork, which benefits both parties.

Competition (outside of certain clear boundaries) would be a detriment, even a betrayal. It would be unacceptable for a man to sabotage a business or athletic partnership because of some personal emotion. Dealings between people who are on the same team are quite different from dealings with the competition, with opponents, and with outsiders. Dealings between partners are, of course, fair and according to the rules, but also honest. Honorable dealings require that both parties agree that the rules have been followed and that things have been settled fairly. This obviously requires honesty. Men of more or less equal status don't seem to have much trouble being honest with one another. Those men who deal with other men dishonorably, even if their lawyers and accountants can demonstrate that they have followed the rules, and even if they themselves consider their behavior to be fair, are just not gentlemen, and they cease to be considered socially respectable.

Of course, whether a man is a gentleman or not concerns only his dealings with other gentlemen. There are exclusive clubs that discriminate quite cruelly against men of lesser social standing. Men who cheat on their golf cards are not admitted. But men who cheat on their wives or their income tax are welcomed. Mythology has it that there is honor even among thieves. The book *Men in Groups* by Lionel Tiger explores all of this, and everyone who has ever been male understands it. Central to all the conventions of male honor is the sense that females are the ultimate outsiders, that males must band together to protect themselves from females.

Is there the same sort of honor among women? I can't say for sure, having never been a member of an all-female group, but I regularly have the experience of being the only male in a group. It used to be that the only male in the female group would get all the attention. In recent years, the only male in the female group may get all the criticism. In either case, it is clear that women treat men differently from the way they treat one another. Freud complained that women don't have the same concepts of morality that men have. Women have been thought to put emotional attachments ahead of the rules of the game, and to consider relationships more important than fairness. Women have even been said to consider romance more desirable than honor.

It is assumed that women in our society, having had to rely on males for advancement, would be likely to view one another as competitors in a contest that is too life threatening to be played by the rules. This seems to be changing rapidly, especially as women take their identity from something more than their relationships with men. Distrust between females as potentially unfair competitors seems contaminated by sexual jealousy and envy.

Still, women do manage to form wonderfully open friendships with one another, a thing men have great difficulty doing. Male homophobia prevents much intimacy and emotional sharing, no matter how many physical activities are shared. Men are terrified of getting emotionally close to one another, as that is not manly, and might even cause suspicion of homosexuality. In fact, *anything* that brings males close together can be highly suspect. So men strut around growling at other men in order to reassure themselves and one another. Men are the constant objects of one another's attention, the focus of one another's displays of heterosexuality. But they can't risk closeness to other men.

The masculine ideal requires men to keep their distance from women as well as from men. Truly masculine men are not supposed to need closeness to anyone, except for sex with women and games with men. (Real men don't have sex with men or games with women . . . women are the sexual playing field on which men compete with one another in sexual display.) Men who achieve the masculine ideal become very lonely creatures, and the closest most men get to intimacy is sex. Sex and intimacy can become horribly confused. For men, the sex seems safe; it is the intimacy that is dangerous. Real men cannot be honest with women—they are the enemy.

Anytime men start being honest, and opening up their innermost secrets, what they reveal is their sense of imperfect masculinity, their failure to live up to the masculine ideal. Actually, almost anything that is human would be a failure in masculinity. Men recoil from other men who reveal weaknesses, and the increased distance is protection from male-to-male closeness, which is the real danger. Women, though, might not recoil from a man who reveals weakness. A woman might pounce upon the revealed imperfection and adore it or exploit it, but in either case leave the man dependent upon the woman and unfit for continuing the game with the guys. Or so it is thought.

Little boys are carefully raised to be emotionally aloof and distant. They can be punished at amazingly early ages for showing "unmanly" emotions. Carol Gilligan in *In a Different Voice* attributes this to the mother's realization that her son must leave her to grow up and must go forth to compete in a masculine world that operates according to competitive rules of fairness rather than emotions and attachments.

So men are taught to be honest about facts with other men, and not to mention emotions. And men are also taught that it is neither necessary nor desirable to be honest with women. There is even a code of honor among men that requires that men who know of one another's infidelities keep this from their wives, who might spread the forbidden knowledge.

I have reason to believe that little girls may be taught to deal dishonestly with little boys. It has been my impression that girls, prior to puberty, tend to identify with maternal power over children, like Margaret in "Dennis the Menace," and become the defenders of the rules. Then at puberty, little girls realize that they must behave in a "feminine" or passive-compliant fashion if they expect to be accepted by boys. The ideal feminine role requires indirectness, deceit, and concealment. Young girls are put through the humiliation of being taught that it is best to tell men only what the men want to hear.

In the eighth and ninth grades, boy-girl relationships are exercises in deceit. Many boys and girls who get good at the game keep playing it into adulthood. At that junior high age, boys and girls swap rumors and myths and fantasies about the nature of the "opposite" sex. They can be fairly open with members of their own sex in their exploration of these strange foreign creatures. But they can get little information from the enemy species. Like their forebears who for millennia believed that females had more ribs, adolescents believe one another and don't count the ribs.

PROTECTION FROM HONESTY

When people are dishonest with one another, they may tell themselves they are protecting one another from hurt. It has been traditional for men to believe they were supposed to treat women as delicate, and protect them from unpleasantness. "A gentleman never offends anyone unintentionally," my grandmother used to say. A gentleman may betray, desert, or even murder a lady, if required, but he must never disconcert her, or put her in the position of having to deal with some unpleasant reality. When little boys go out and do boy things with their fathers, they are told not to bother the womenfolk with this, since women don't understand the way "us boys" are. (In my Southern youth, I was taught that gentlemen must not relax in the presence of ladies, and certainly must not tell them anything that might ruffle the formality of their carefully arranged posture. While this seems absurdly Southern and old-fashioned, I still encounter traces of it throughout society.)

Men, routinely, have been taught that women react emotionally to things and just don't understand the realities of the world, and particularly the realities of "man"kind, so it is the job of men to censor reality in such a way as to protect women from things they wouldn't understand. A classic rule between fathers and sons is "Don't upset your mother." The pattern of men lying to women begins early, and is maintained. Some of the (male) reporters who hid the stories of various presidential infidelities have explained that they did so to protect the government. They have gone on to explain that women react too emotionally to this sort of thing and would not understand that "boys will be boys."

Women can be just as protective of men, pretending to see them as powerful heroes, while protecting them as if they were small children. A woman may convince herself she is boosting the man's ego when she protects him from various realities, such as the state of the budget or the various crises of the day.

There are women who lie to their husbands about their orgasms. They insist they have orgasms when they don't, even when nothing has gone on sexually that could conceivably produce an orgasm. If the husband believes the lie of the orgasm (and to some men, women are so foreign that they really would believe this), he is likely to continue to do the clumsy things that don't work, and the couple will be trapped in a sexual pattern that is increasingly unsatisfactory. The woman here is doing what she has been taught to do—she is telling the man what he wants to hear. By doing so she is disorienting him, destroying their sex life and eventually their marriage. She is right in believing it would upset him if she told him, but he might have some suspicions already, and while the news would be traumatic, it might well be a relief. But if she doesn't tell him, she will grow increasingly resentful. As her resentment toward him grows, he won't understand what it is about; he will have no clue as to what he is doing wrong.

DISHONESTY AND POWER

Another carryover from childhood is the fear of being made powerless by admitting fault. Parents seem to be always shouting things like "Who spilled that milk?" to powerless children who are busy saying "It's not my fault." Some parents are wise enough to stop crying over the spilled milk, and even punish children for the lying. Most parents seem instead to punish children who admit wrongdoing, while being sufficiently unsure of their own rights or judgment to go ahead and punish a child who has not confessed. Children are taught to lie, assuming correctly that they will be dealt with more leniently if the parent is unsure of guilt. The school officials react the same way, unwilling to punish a child who refuses to confess, since the parents of a punished child may well side with the child and create problems for the school. Misbehavior may not be punished at all, but confessing will be. Adolescent movies, such as *Ferris Beuller's Day Off*, extol the virtue of lying to adults. An adolescent hero is the one who can lie most convincingly. The ideal is to look totally innocent, while denying everything. The American public, in 1987, briefly lionized a lieutenant colonel who acknowledged lying while denying wrongdoing, a confession so confusing that the society applauded the absence of guilt as if it were proof of strength.

An adult, trained to admit nothing, identifies a confession as an act of weakness, which puts one under the power of another. In this carryover from child-parent experience, the one who admits wrongdoing loses power, and the one who denies wrongdoing gains power. It is too much trouble to prove that someone is lying, so you don't exact retribution from the liar, you just cross that person off. In minor traffic accidents and the like, it may well seem preferable to be crossed off by strangers than to pay retributions. In lying, one is identifying the other as one's opponent, even one's enemy. A lie should always be followed by a quick getaway, because everything that follows the lie is too awkward and false to tolerate.

In marriage, retributions are cheap compared with enmity and disrespect. In marriage, intimacy is developed through confessions, explanations, and soul searchings. But of course intimacy involves equality, and people who are telling lies are not seeking any aspect of intimacy, especially equality. Liars are hoping for an advantage, which will be produced by disorienting and distracting the other person. The liar is stepping outside the relationship.

The lie may be a greater betrayal of the relationship than the misdeed being lied about. It takes very little misinformation to disorient and destroy a relationship. I often point out to people that if I gave them detailed instructions on how to go from Atlanta to New York City, and I threw in only one left turn that was a lie, they would end up in Oklahoma.

DISHONESTY AND GUILT

People can lie about practically anything. And they do. But I, like "Dear Abby," doubt if there is anything about which people lie more consistently than sex. I'm sure this is influenced by the fear of the other gender, and by our insecurity, particularly the genital kind, which makes us feel relatively impotent in this area. I have known few people, even those who display their sexuality with great bravado, who did not feel sexually inadequate.

We are taught to feel guilty about our sexuality. Our parents talk about sex in euphemisms instead of the "right" words, they may make nervous jokes about sexual matters, and they become frightened when children don't seem frightened enough about sex. Not knowing how to tell us that we must get sexual experience and practice, they tell us to hide our emerging sexuality from them. This isn't just their incestuous threat, it is their real misgivings about whether they know enough about it to tell us anything useful. And of course they aren't quite sure whether they believe what they were taught about sex and sin and virginity. So they tell us to keep sex secret from them. We may even be punished if we make them aware of our sexuality.

One result of taking our sexuality underground at puberty is that we have clumsy experiences and learn badly. We can also end up feeling guilty for feelings and experiences that are quite normal, even universal. But we naturally assume that if something must be kept secret, then it must be wrong. Ever since Adam and Eve saw their nakedness and were ashamed and cast forth from the Garden of Eden, we have hidden ourselves behind fig leaves.

Parents may teach their children to handle their sexuality with "discretion," that is, to do the polite thing and lie about it. Children raised this way can end up feeling that lying is good but sex is bad. After marriage, the object of the guilty fear shifts from the parents to the husband or wife. It now becomes one's marriage partner who must be lied to, i.e., kept discreetly disoriented. Obviously, whomever one must hide one's guilty secrets from is the enemy.

Of course, sex is not the only thing about which people feel guilt. The Baedeker is packed with possible guilt trips one can take. There is only a limited amount of guilt anyone can feel at one time, so the people who have decided to feel guilty about frivolous matters may then feel no guilt over those things that really do hurt other people. I've known patients who devoted their lives to bemoaning some sexual impulse or some long past sexual experience, and, while wrestling with that guilt, behaved rudely or insensitively to the real people in their lives now. Some would be so wracked with old guilt that they barely noticed what they were doing in the here and now. Over the years, I've come to think that the people who feel guilt most intensely are by no means the people who behave most responsibly. The converse might even be true, that people who feel guilt most are least likely to consider the effects of their actions on others. It is as if guilt becomes the alternative to behaving responsibly.

Children who have been sexually abused frequently grow up keeping it secret because they blame themselves for it. Often they feel intense guilt, and they may punish themselves in various ways for a lifetime, while they inflict enormous pain upon husbands, wives, and children who try to get close to them. A recently popular psychiatric diagnosis is borderline personality, which really means a person who is so totally narcissistic and self-centered that he or she bounces back and forth between intense love and intense hatred of people. Love must be perfect, or these people will exact revenge (the Glenn Close character in the film *Fatal Attraction* might be considered a borderline personality). Often, such people are believed to be suffering from the guilty aftereffects of childhood sexual abuse. They feel so much guilt that they lash out against their loved ones by inflicting harm upon themselves. They often make suicide attempts, which can be quite devastating to anyone who cares about them. People who feel sexual guilt from adult experiences of their own choosing can behave in much the same way. I once treated a man who liked to have sex with prostitutes on his way home from work. Then when he got home, he would feel a bit guilty and would handle the guilt by accusing his wife of not liking him enough, and then abusing her verbally or even physically.

There are people who have been trained in an extraordinary form of guilt—guilt for what they think or feel. Some people feel guilty for their sexual fantasies, or their sexual attractions to passing strangers. Such people are missing one of life's safest pleasures, of course—basking in the titillations one will not act upon. People who can't enjoy innocent sexual attractions are dangerous—these are the people who are at risk for violent sexual perversions. Since they feel the guilt over their *thoughts,* they can relieve the pressure of the thoughts by acting out the fantasies, and then erasing the trigger for the fantasies by eliminating the object of their sexual attraction. Few notions have been quite so dangerous as the concept that lusting in one's heart is the same as doing it in the flesh.

Not many people are improved by guilt. Most are at their absolute worst when feeling guilty. Guilt is uncomfortable, and guilty people can experience fear and anger, and misunderstand the source of their guilt. They can identify the source as the person they feel guilty about hurting. In a bizarre switch, when they feel guilty, they lash out at the person they are hurting at the moment.

This strange phenomenon—at the root of the crisis of infidelity —is a carryover from adolescence. It works this way. The child does the normal sexual things that have been driven underground by the parents, and alternates between guilt over the defined misdeed and anger at the parents for defining something so pleasurable as a misdeed. The concept of "naughty" results, the word meaning something like "deliciously wicked" or "delightfully sinful," and leading ultimately to the confusion between that which is fun and that which is forbidden. The notion then arises that whatever is forbidden must be fun. Therefore when one is feeling either pleasure or guilt, the appropriate response is anger at whoever caused the confusion between the two, whoever is witness to the guilty deed, and whoever's suffering is fueling the guilty one's guilt.

It is commonplace for guilt-ridden people, after an infidelity, to distance their unsuspecting mate, whose love makes the guilt-ridden feel even guiltier. The greater the discomfort, and the more trusting the mate, the greater the distance needed to protect the infidel from being overwhelmed by guilt. At the same time, the infidel will seek out the only person who can relieve the guilt—the affairee who was an accomplice in the act, the one who can assure that no wrong has been done. The infidel and the affairee are thus trapped behind imaginary enemy lines, hiding from the poor trusting cuckold who gets somehow turned into the source of the painful guilt. The guilt therefore undermines the marriage, and fuels the affair.

DISHONESTY AND SCANDAL

Our confusion and conflict about secrecy and guilt, about what should be made public and what should be kept private, came to a head during the extraordinary spectacle of public sexual scandals in the spring of 1987. Gary Hart, front-running presidential candidate, followed in the wake of Jim Bakker, top-grossing TV evangelist, by coming to ruin over an extramarital affair. Jim Bakker knew very well what he had done wrong, and had been paying blackmail money to keep it from being exposed. It is noteworthy that while his stock in trade was religious forgiveness for whatever human failings people come up with, he could reveal his wife's former drug addiction for fund-raising purposes, but his little affair was too dangerous to be exposed. To confess would be dangerous and facile, but once the secret was out and it was clear how much anguish it had caused, followers were reminded that "forgiveness is divine." There was a problem with all the other revelations that came forth in the wake of the disclosure about the sexual encounter. Once the little affair was out in the open, it looked far too insignificant to bother with, but the financial shenanigans in the cover-up, like those of my great-uncle Jos, were alarming.

A year later, Jimmy Swaggart, the rival evangelist who had been accused of blowing the whistle on Bakker, was himself defrocked for sexual misconduct. Swaggart, a rather sweaty evoker of visions of hellfire and damnation, had proclaimed that he had had no sexual partners but his wife, and called forth God's vengeance upon those who were not so pure. Prostitutes in New Orleans described him as a pervert who came weekly, not for intercourse, but to watch pornographic acts. The public was left with the impression of a man obsessed with sexual guilt, struggling against the impulses he was hiding, and protecting his "morality" by not quite "doing it."

Gary Hart's background was in a similar fundamentalist religion, and his thinking was also influenced by this strange belief that it is the sex that is wrong rather than the dishonesty. Hart dared the press to follow him and investigate the charges that he was a "womanizer" (an interestingly sexist term). He was caught, yelled foul, and denied that actual sex had taken place, as if that were the issue. He totally ignored the embarrassment and betrayal of his wife and his supporters. His supporters were devoting their time and money to his campaign while he was lying, hiding, and playing cat and mouse games with the press over his sexual daring. As these alarming character flaws and errors in judgment, loyalty, and priorities were noted, the poor man, trained in sexual guilt, thought it an appropriate defense to insist that he hadn't actually "done it" on the occasion under observation. And he received considerable sympathy from people who thought he had done something wrong but reasonably normal and had then been left, by the press exposure, in an impossible position.

Gary Hart, who emulated Jack Kennedy in many ways, apparently assumed that if Kennedy's infidelities could be protected by the press, so could his. He was wrong on several counts. Kennedy's behavior would not have been tolerated had it been exposed at the time. The times were different. We still idealized presidents back then, and the press was careful not to disappoint us with any unsavory reality. The post-Watergate presidency is no longer granted immunity by the press. The downfall of Nixon marked a change in the attitude of the press toward our errant leaders. We may not have had better presidents since then, but we have observed them more closely.

Gary Hart's scandal tested societal attitudes. As the story unfolded, a few editorialists seriously questioned whether a man's behavior toward women was a factor to be considered in assessing his abilities as a "leader of men."

By contrast, a woman's behavior toward men, even the fantasies she evokes in men, has been the sole determinant of how her character is assessed. It is interesting that some of the women involved in these recent scandals have gone on to exploit the affairs for their own purposes. It seems clear that these affairees are not asking the press or society to go out of its way to protect their honor and their anonymity. Anybody's sexual secrets could now become news. Careers are made and careers are broken by this news, and by our disorienting repulsion/attraction to whatever seems "wicked."

What, however, did we think Gary Hart should have done? Some people believed that he should not have been unfaithful to his wife, others thought he should not have pretended to be married to her when he was clearly living a single's life. Once he did whatever he did, some people thought he should have handled it more discreetly and lied more effectively, and others thought he should have been more honest about it. It became clear that we are not all in agreement about what should be kept secret and what should be revealed. Not knowing how such things should be handled, we'd rather not be faced with them.

KEEPING SECRETS

Even if we are fairly clear about what we should tell newspaper reporters or financial contributors, we are confused about what we should tell our husband or wife. This is, hands down, the most-asked question from audiences and patients when we are discussing infidelity. They ask, "Surely you don't mean that I should tell my husband everything? That would upset him, he would never forgive me, the marriage would be over." Or "I can't tell her this. She would (a) die, (b) kill me, (c) leave me. Disaster would befall us, etc." And I have to tell them that, yes, they should tell their marriage partner everything—even the big one, the secret of infidelity. To date, I have not had anyone die or kill anybody or even get a divorce over the revelation of a secret infidelity if the infidelity is now past. I'm sure it happens, but it must not be very common. By contrast, all hell breaks loose over infidelities that are continuing, or those that are known but lied about.

Q. "Are you trying to tell me that other people actually tell husbands or wives the truth?"

A. Yes. Most people do, most of the time. Some marriages in the past, and most modern marriages, begin openly and honestly and have continued to accept and encourage revelation of the things that people are uncomfortable about. Others begin with secrets and an attitude of protective secrecy but face some crisis that strips away the secrecy and leads to a determination to keep things honest and open. Of course, there are still many marriages in which various things are kept secret, and it would be a break with the usual patterns, perhaps with the family traditions, for the partners to become close enough to start revealing things about the past or the present.

Q. "Won't it upset my partner to start telling the truth?"

A. Certainly, in those marriages that are built around protective dishonesty and polite secrecy, the revelation of a disconcerting piece of reality might seem a betrayal of the accepted pattern. The first few times the curtain of politeness opens, there might be a crisis. As I've seen it, people are never comfortable living in a state of disorientation, but they take to honesty like a duck to water. It causes ripples and even waves, but it quickly feels natural.

Q. "My husband or wife is much too crazy to be told the truth."

A. If you've been lying to your partner long enough, your partner is bound to seem rather crazy. People who are lied to become dependent, anxious, delicate, and overreactive. They can even become paranoid, and believe they are being lied to even when they aren't. Your partner may seem a great deal saner after being better oriented to reality.

Q. "Maybe there's a way to present things that will make them more acceptable?"

A. Sure, we all censor things and present things with the slant we prefer, and that's an effort to disorient the other person just enough to let us get our way. We really have to ask ourselves why we want to disorient our partner, why we don't trust the other person to share the decision or reaction with us.

Q. "What's the difference between telling part of the truth and telling all of it, maybe withholding just a little?"

A. Any effort to disorient your partner is a power play that will eventually hurt the relationship.

Q. "What if the affair is over, and didn't really mean anything anyway?"

A. Over for whom? Didn't mean anything to whom? If you know it would mean something to your spouse, then the secret of it means something to your marriage (and you know it), so the secret will affect you in the marriage.

Q. "What if it happened a long time ago?"

A. Then it must have been very hard on you and your marriage to keep it secret all this time. It would certainly be apparent that the affair was no threat, but the secret has been a barrier. The revelation of it is a reaching out for intimacy.

Q. "I wouldn't actually lie if I'm asked point blank, but I don't have to bring it up, do I?"

A. The difference between a lie and a secret is a technicality. What I'm talking about is how two people can share a life in which they understand each other and all the reality they deal with. Couples may have an agreement that they will maintain a certain level of distance. They may agree that they won't reveal things unless asked directly. This leads to a weird and stilted relationship, based on cautious distance.

Q. "My partner doesn't want to hear things."

A. Your partner may not want as much intimacy as you do. Or maybe he or she does. You may be trying to hide the guilty secret with an overdose of words or details. Reveal the guilty secret as directly as possible, and fill in the details later. If your partner is determined not to *hear* the secret, he or she then has the option of pretending your words were not said, or simply forgetting the conversation altogether.

Q. "Shouldn't I wait for the perfect time and place to bring up the subject?"

A. Many people break bad news in fancy restaurants, hoping to encourage a polite response. Others wait until they get to a therapist's office. There's never a right time for bad news, but some times may be worse than others. I wouldn't tell an upsetting secret to someone who is drunk and holding a gun, but why would you be married to a gun-toting drunk anyway? If you seriously believe your partner is out looking for a reason to kill you, run for your life.

Q. "Do I need to tell my partner about things that happened before we met?"
A. Only if you want to be understood or to stop feeling guilty.

Q. "Do I need to tell my partner all of my thoughts?"
A. Absolutely not. That would be terminally boring, but the better your partner understands your complicated state of mind, the more comfortable you'll be with each other. Comparing emotional reactions with each other is the stuff of most good conversations. We all have an emotional jungle inside our heads, and most of our thoughts aren't worth the proverbial penny, but we're likely to make too much of those thoughts and feelings that make us feel guilty. We all want reassurance about what's inside us, and we achieve closeness when we open up. Your partner may well be uncomfortable with some of your emotions, so these have to be put into a perspective that will make you both more comfortable.

Q. "What about my sexual fantasies?"
A. Once both partners realize that everybody has all manner of sexual fantasies, and that neither of you is going to act on them, you can enjoy them privately if you like. You don't really need to share them unless that would in some way be a turn-on for both of you. (Does everyone realize that erotic dreams are not likely to be about one's familiar partner?) Most couples like to experience pornography together, though they are frequently turned on by quite different things. But some don't. If your fantasy repulses your mate, keep it to yourself—but by all means keep it if it works for you. Your fantasies are there to turn you on, and you should have whatever fantasy works for you.

Q. "Aren't there secrets that keep the good tensions alive?"

A. Some flirtation, some sense of mystery can be titillating and intriguing, but too much of it makes people nervous.

Q. "But surely some things should be kept secret? Like how much things cost?"

A. Couples play strange games with money, hiding it from each other and telling all manner of lies. In traditional single-income marriages, there are men who have no idea how much groceries cost, and women who have no idea what sort of savings and investments they have. He makes all the money; she spends it all. He therefore becomes frugal and controlling, and she becomes devious and extravagant. These couples are conducting a strange guerrilla warfare with money. If he can stash away money, it becomes his; if she can spend it, it becomes hers. It's bad for their finances, but even worse, it's bad for their relationship.

Q. "Modern couples don't handle money in such sexist ways."

A. People of any generation can lie about money. I recently worked with a couple in which the wife, who handled all the money, kept telling her husband how well their investments were growing. He decided to quit his job and start a new business. She encouraged him. When he got things set up and came to her for the money they had in savings, she told him it was all gone. He panicked and demanded to know what had happened. She said, "I don't want to talk about it. It just makes you upset."

Q. "If I start saying the things I haven't been saying, all hell is going to break loose."

A. If the two of you have been keeping a lot of things secret, all hell *is* going to break loose when you start bringing these things out into the open. That's right. Honesty, after a period of discreet deception and cautious politeness, will certainly be attention getting, and may well trigger some full-scale crises. And then things can start getting good in the marriage. But that's what you have to do to make marriage open, honest, and intimate.

Q. "Do you mean I have to be totally honest, reveal everything, keep nothing secret in order to make my marriage work?"

A. No, you don't have to. But I present a model of total honesty as an ideal, since it is the most likely model for keeping problems small, manageable, and useful. Try it your way if you must, but keep in mind that your secrets and your lies are probably unnecessary and will damage the marriage more by being kept hidden. It really is possible to have an honest marriage, and it might be considered. Monogamy, as a state of honesty and intimacy between two equal partners, has not been traditional, but I strongly recommend it.

Even if what I'm advising is too frightening for you, and you choose a model of marriage that falls short of total honesty, I would suggest that when you lie (or keep secrets, which can be the same thing), you try not to lie to yourself about what you're doing. Dishonesty in marriage may be a power play, may be a symptom of guilty fear, or may indicate an attitude of gender antagonism. Dishonesty is the enemy of intimacy, and it is not likely to be good for marriage. Dishonesty creates distance. Of course, that may be what you want.

4 / Jealousy and Infidelity

"If you love something, set it free.
If it returns, then it was meant to be.
If it fails to return to thee,
Then stalk it down and kill it."
WALL PLAQUE AT FILLING STATION

"We don't give up jealousy. We give up passion."
NANCY FRIDAY, *JEALOUSY*

Jealousy is surely the most misunderstood of human emotions. Closely related to love, it is sometimes considered the "true" test of love. The absence of jealousy can be as disturbing as its presence. And even moderate jealousy can frighten, offend, or irritate the person on the receiving end.

Some people are unable to tolerate even a twinge of jealousy. Those who fully intend to be faithful and want intense intimacy can perceive a partner's jealousy as evidence of distrust, therefore insulting. The message as they receive it is that they still have not earned sufficient trust, despite trustworthiness over time.

Other people are monogamous but feel they need their independence. A partner's jealousy becomes possessive then, interfering with personal freedom. These people feel tied down, held back, and clung to. They don't want to have to think about that other person all the time. A friend told me of an intrusive lover who said, "I don't want to control you. I just want to know where you are and what you are doing all the time."

71

Finally, there are people who don't believe in monogamy and sexual commitment, and think that their extramarital activities are normal, and none of anybody else's business. To them, jealousy seems a frightening and probably sick intrusion. When an infidelity is discovered, they make little distinction between a partner's reproachful frown and a machine gun attack—the point is that no one has claim on their sexuality, so any degree of jealousy must not be tolerated. Such determined sexual independence seems to be incompatible with the nature of the human animal. Humans naturally mate and they naturally guard their partnership through the mechanism of jealousy.

HOW NORMAL JEALOUSY WORKS

Jealousy can be a normal, appropriate, and even necessary emotion. It is the awareness of distance and interference in a bonded relationship. We all experience it. It develops as we sense that our partner is no longer as closely connected to us as we'd like. It may signal that something else (or someone else) has come between us and is loosening the bonds.

Jealousy is useful if it occurs in a bonded relationship and if it calls forth behavior that brings the couple closer together. For example, the two of you go to a party and you notice that your mate is nowhere to be seen. Appropriate and healthy behavior would be to notice the absence, then to seek out your partner and make the kind of contact that reaffirms the partnership. Couples do that constantly, many times a day. They notice distance and reach out to breach it. That would be appropriate. However, if the jealous partner raises hell with the other for having stepped into the other room, for seeming more interested in some other activity, or for talking with a third person, that clearly would not bring the couple together. If jealousy is expressed as anger and attempts at punishment, then it isn't working right. It will produce distance rather than closeness.

A person who is feeling twinges of jealousy detects delicate signals. It is not unusual for one spouse to recognize the other spouse's attraction to a third person at about the same time (or even before) the attracted spouse recognizes it. It is hard to explain how this works, but the jealousy must be answered by closeness, which intends to reduce the jealous response.

Freud, in "Certain Neurotic Mechanisms in Jealousy, Paranoia, and Homosexuality," said that "jealousy is one of those affective states, like grief, that may be described as normal. . . . If anyone appears to be without it, the inference is justified that it has undergone severe repression and consequently plays all the greater part in his unconscious mental life."

In marriage, jealousy is a necessary sensitivity to distance or to disorientation. More than the accustomed distance or less than the accustomed honesty in marriage is a threat, and implies problems that should be examined. Jealousy can be excessive, of course, part of a crazy marital interaction, but jealousy in and of itself is a useful defense against marital entropy. Little squirts of jealousy may glue a relationship together, and prevent any natural tendency toward drift.

When there is drift, jealousy can be a subtle measure of distance. Jealousy may be a subliminal awareness of a lie. People who are truly intimate know when they are being lied to, even if they can't precisely identify what the lie is.

A lie will make one's mate feel distanced. The mate who has been distanced will automatically attempt to breach that distance. If the effort at contact is blocked, then the increasingly jealousy mate will focus on whatever is blocking access, and will attempt to remove it.

Jealousy probably contains an element of dependency and fear of abandonment. It may be the adult equivalent of the fears of parental abandonment that we all experience in infancy. As we grow older we do become more self-reliant, less dependent than we were as babies, but unless we become hermits, we remain dependent on our central relationships. We live quite normally with the fear that we could be abandoned by our partners. And if there really is a threat, we will react to it.

JEALOUSY AND LOVE

Is the intensity of jealousy a measure of the "trueness" of the "love," as so many people think? Intense jealousy, in the absence of dishonesty or actual infidelity, may indicate all manner of things, but love is way down the list. While the absence of jealousy may be indicative of loose bonding in the relationship, the presence of intense and alienating jealousy may be symptomatic of either a crazy relationship or a psychotic individual. Of course, if the object of the jealousy has been unfaithful and dishonest about it, a jealous rage would be the normal, natural response, while calm acceptance would imply detachment from the relationship.

People who have recently been unfaithful themselves (and are ashamed of that) may be the most likely to demonstrate unprovoked jealous rages. Someone who is frightened and guilty, producing distance to protect a secret while feeling anxiety and crying out for closeness, may display disjointed and disorienting jealousy by asking for closeness and distance at the same time. Any response from a partner would increase the anxiety in one direction or the other.

Marriages in which jealousy is most intense may be those with the highest level of possessiveness and the lowest levels of intimacy. In marriages such as these, one partner reveals so little of what is going on that the other must be constantly snooping around and testing, just trying to stay oriented in a relationship without clear road signs or maps.

I have not noticed that jealousy is different for men than it is for women. Where the wife is expected to carry the relationship, to be alert to the state of it, she may seem to be the more jealous partner. It was once thought that women were flattered by their husbands' jealousy and wanted more of it, while men resented the control implied by jealous reactions and wanted it to stop. But that was when husbands worked away from home and more wives had their jobs at home. Now, when both are likely to be working away from home, those particular differences may no longer apply. Most people, male or female, are flattered by jealousy in low doses, but resent it when it begins to interfere with daily activities (which may necessitate some level of distance). Overcontrol through jealousy can be obnoxious.

JEALOUSY AND SELF-ESTEEM

Excessively jealous people often feel unworthy. Their sense of unworthiness, coming primarily from within, could stem from a secret (childhood incest, a past affair), a flaw much criticized in their family of origin (being less smart or good-looking than another sibling or parent), or a failed previous marriage (few people get through a divorce with their self-esteem unscarred). People may feel more jealousy during periods of failure or loss. As we age, we may lose a certain sense of security and imagine we are on the verge of being deserted by our partner. When people suffer the loss of a job, the death of parents, the children leaving home, they may feel lost and want to bring their partner closer. If greater closeness is not convenient for their partner right then, jealousy can result. A classic example is the crisis of the empty nest, when the children have grown and gone, and the couple are left to provide each other with the totality of their emotional needs. With the dependency thus heightened, each can feel that the other is too distant and imagine an affair.

People who feel so bad about themselves that they think they could never find anyone else to put up with them are likely to bond desperately. They may even try to reduce their partner's self-esteem in hopes that they will make the partner bond to them with equal desperation. This effort is not only destructive, it is likely to backfire. One man, who had never gotten over the shock of landing a beauty queen as a wife, felt he didn't deserve such a prize. He spent years convincing her of her many deficiencies, and even had her believing that she had become ugly. She finally began to turn to other men for reassurance.

An excessively dependent person, wallowing in self-pity, may resent a more confident partner, and may go to war against the sources of the spouse's confidence. Partners of the petulantly jealous may have to forgo career, education, hobby, friends, relatives, and even children, all in an effort to reassure the jealous one of a singularly high place on a list of priorities. The jealous one attempts to force the other to sacrifice self-confidence and its sources to equalize the marriage. Insecure husbands may be terrified as their wives find jobs and activities and relationships that make them more confident and less dependent. Such threatened men may force their wives to drop out of school, to quit jobs, and even to give up friendships. One such husband would not let his wife go to her family reunion because he knew she had a female cousin who was a lawyer, and he feared the cousin might infect her with feminist notions of going to law school herself.

Jealousy is the perfect tool for those people who are so angry and frightened that they must protect themselves from intimacy, and yet can't acknowledge that the anger to which they are so sensitive is coming from themselves. If they can arrange for a spouse to be unfaithful, they can then justify their anger and distance for the duration of the marriage. And none of it is their fault. If, however, the spouse is uncooperative enough to remain faithful and still try for intimacy by constantly overcoming all unworthiness, the spouse who is determined to be a victim may have no option but to imagine an affair.

Overall, though, it would be misleading to assume that jealousy is an expression of low self-esteem. People who are investing themselves in a partnership are going to feel protective of that partnership and are going to experience jealousy when distance enters the partnership. No one could be or should be secure enough to be immune to jealousy.

PROBLEMATIC JEALOUSY

Jealousy can, of course, be in error. There may be errors in direction, in intensity, in expression, or in appropriateness.

The jealous spouse may sense an attraction to someone else, but may exaggerate the degree of the attraction, and may start a campaign to protect the marriage from someone who is no threat at all. Sometimes the attraction is actually there, or there has even been some flirtation, but nothing so concrete as consummation. Thus, the jealousy is accurate, but vigorously denied because the suspected offense has not quite happened yet, and therefore technically there is no infidelity. One man, vigorously insisting that he had not been unfaithful, despite his wife's accusations, finally turned to me and asked, "Does oral sex count?"

The jealous one feels jealousy, and it is accurate, but the accused one insists there is no guilt, saying things like "Nothing happened." Although accurate physically, this may be dishonest emotionally. If the accused does show guilt, denies it, and then becomes defensive and distant, the jealous spouse is likely to respond with hostile and controlling dependency. The accused really should examine whether the jealous spouse may be on target. The jealous one is threatened by a specific relationship. While he or she may be asking for physical explanations for an emotional reaction, the question "Are you having an affair with so and so?" is not a simple yes or no question. What is actually being sought is an exploration of the accused one's state of mind. The jealous one may need more closeness in the marriage, and more caution in the suspect relationship.

Jealousy may well be mistaken without being wrong. The jealous one may be reacting quite sensitively and accurately to a partner's distance, even though the cause of the distance might be something other than the presumed rival. People who are accused by a jealous spouse, whether in error or not, might be defensive in a way that increases the distance in the marriage. In a sense, the distance becomes a reaction to the jealousy itself (though the effort to treat jealousy by distance would be a singularly uncaring approach). When one spouse feels jealousy, and there really is no attraction to the suspected rival, the couple can join forces to seek a more accurate explanation for the distance between them. That can be a productive search. The most important thing about jealousy is that it is easily softened by closeness and honesty, and inevitably aggravated by distance.

Jealous people may feel threatened by relatively asexual friendships. Much of this jealousy is fleeting and disappears as soon as the spouse gives reassurance. Honesty can reduce jealousy. I have even seen a situation in which the intensity of jealousy has been reduced by the revelation that an affair actually had taken place and was now over, with an explanation of what the unfaithful person did not find satisfactory about this particular affair partner. When someone feels jealousy over a particular relationship that can't be brought to an ending, such as the relationship with someone at work or with an ex-spouse with whom one shares children, it doesn't always help to deny sexual interest or to defend the relationship. What seems to help is an honest appraisal of one's degree of sexual attraction, and the reasons that attraction would not be acted upon.

INAPPROPRIATE JEALOUSY

Jealousy may feel frighteningly inappropriate and intrusive when one person feels a "coupleship" and the other does not. Such an imbalanced pattern occurs regularly, and inevitably destroys the relationship. An example would be someone who is dating and begins to show jealousy toward a partner who has not yet begun to think in terms of couple. While a partner who is somewhat insecure and unaccustomed to being loved may be flattered by jealousy, more secure people tend to be frightened off by jealousy that begins too early. The very popular and very terrifying movie *Fatal Attraction* (without alluding to AIDS) heralds the end of the sexual revolution and the beginning of the AIDS era, in which a casual sex act can have deadly consequences. The film centers on a brief extramarital affair, after which the affair partner, Glenn Close, refuses to disappear. Instead, Close insists upon intruding herself into the lives of Michael Douglas and his family. Even before the horror aspects of the movie begin, the true horror is in Close's assumption that her sexually charged weekend with Douglas gives her claims on his time and attention, and above all the "right" of jealousy.

Jealousy can seem bizarre and frightening in a relationship that is now dead, such as a marriage that is over. Ex-spouses may claim all manner of justifications for having an interest in one another's new relationships. The horror literature abounds with stories of ex-spouses who are crazed by jealousy and exact revenge on their replacements, with dead mates dragging the survivors into the grave. This is such a familiar fear, it feeds comedy as well. James Thurber's classic cartoon has the former wife crouching atop the bookcase as her ex-husband introduces a guest: "That's my first wife up there, and this is the *present* Mrs. Harris."

Of course, the jealousy can go in the opposite direction. Another famous story of horror, Daphne du Maurier's *Rebecca*, the basis for one of Alfred Hitchcock's greatest films, concerns a young wife who is so envious of the grace and beauty of her husband's dead former wife that she becomes jealous of her, believing that her husband is still in love with the dead Rebecca, and attempts to turn herself into the wife he actually loathed. Obviously, our heroine was suffering from some envy of the glamorous, however loathsome, Rebecca.

There are those who are so frightened of betrayal that they want to control a partner's thoughts and fantasies. Such people are actually made jealous by their partner's sexual dreams or thoughts, by passing glances given to attractive passersby, or by masturbatory fantasies or even memories of past relationships. One woman briefly left her husband when she discovered that he had gone to a strip show while at a convention. She feared that he would now be able to think of some other woman in a sexual manner, and she could never be sure that all his thoughts during sex would be about her. Men who want to marry virgins are perhaps seeking the same security from competition.

Private fantasies are necessary for normal sexual and emotional functioning, and they need not be shared. The situation of the moment is not always sexually stimulating, and we must reach back into our memories and fantasies to achieve sexual arousal. These fantasies may retain more of their necessary aura of unreality if they are kept private. The failure to recognize the need for privacy in fantasy can threaten a relationship. The fantasy is not a threat to the relationship, but the jealous one's preoccupation with the private thoughts of the other may indicate that there is not enough openness for the jealous one to know how to please or make contact with the other. Such jealousy may indicate that the jealous one is being closed out in various ways. Many men and women prefer solitary masturbation, alone with their fantasies, to anything that could go on between the marital partners. Some of the appeal is the self-sufficiency of the activity, and its utterly fantastic nature. It can come to replace the marital relationship, rather than supplement or stimulate it, and thus can arouse strong and appropriate jealousy.

CRAZY JEALOUSY

Some people get reassurance, and a feeling of being loved, by arousing their partner's jealousy. They may even feel they are not loved if their partner does not go crazy over them on cue. Most people manage to play their games of jealous love without having to go crazy, but sometimes jealous rages have to approach homicidal levels before the desired result of impressing an insecure partner is achieved. Such people can stage scenes in bars, endangering the lives of innocent bystanders who are seduced into this marital foreplay.

Really crazy jealousy, according to Freud, can be rooted in either *projection* or *competition.* Jealousy that is rooted in *projection* occurs when the jealous one has betrayed the relationship, or would like to do so, and protects against guilt by coming to believe that the other is the faithless one. This is believed to be the common mechanism by which philanderers, and other infidels, suffer from wild, often violently intense jealousy, which is at its most intense when the jealous one is being most unfaithful. Jealous infidels may assume that their mates are equally unfaithful, and may even justify their own infidelities as "fighting fire with fire," or "leaving before I am left," or just "doing it first, so it won't hurt so much when it's done to me." It has seemed to me in my clinical practice that the most intensely jealous people were being unfaithful themselves.

More commonly, neurotic jealousy grows out of *competition* and envy. Freud described this, and Melanie Klein made much of it in *Envy and Gratitude.* Klein traces envy to the childhood rivalries that are made so intense when there is only a single parent to be possessed and perhaps shared. Certainly losses have a cumulative effect over time, and each loss in life makes the next loss all the more desperate. People raised by a single parent have automatically experienced the loss of the other parent, and thus grow up with a sense of deprivation that makes envy more likely. Of course, in what we have come to consider traditional families, most children in our society have been raised mostly by a single parent, the mother, while the father was the more or less absent breadwinner. But children growing up in a family full of children have to experience an enormous amount of jealousy and envy as they compete for whatever parenting they can get.

However people come to be envious, they tend to turn love into something excessively possessive. The envious seem to believe that others have been loved too much while they have been loved too little, and they use jealousy as their currency in their effort to swap their anger for someone else's love.

Jealousy and envy are often confused. While jealousy is normal and necessary under certain conditions, envy is a rather unpleasant emotion. Envious people (all of us, to some extent) want more. They not only want what other people have, but they want the other people not to have it. They go through life feeling they have been deprived and therefore deserve more than their share. Such people can never be loved enough. Not surprisingly, they have little love to give.

I once saw such a man. His wife was urging him to show more love for his son. He was already quite envious of the amount of love his son was receiving, and he refused to give any love to someone he thought was getting more than his share. He said, "How can you expect me to love anybody else when no one has ever loved me —the only people who ever tried to love me either gave up or pissed me off." His wife thought he was jealous of their son for coming between the couple. What this man actually felt was envy, and his envy was creating a wedge between him and his wife.

The truly envious are often extremely competitive, and assume that others are competing in the areas where they feel most insecure. They can assume that their mate is attracted to whatever they envy in others. I recall a man who assumed his wife would be attracted to a man with nothing much to recommend him except a golf swing the husband envied. More than once, I've seen women with slim, athletic bodies who envied more zaftig women, and assumed their husbands were attracted to big-breasted women.

DESPERATE BONDING

Most marriages outlast their initial passion, and work nicely on a basis of mutual dependency, habit, respect, and allegiance. The commitment remains voluntary. Such a comfortable marriage can be blown away by a sudden burst of passion. And the insecure jealous ones, wherever their insecurity comes from, may not trust the voluntary nature of the other's commitment. Under such conditions, the possessive partner may try to make the relationship involuntary, perhaps through guilt or fear. He or she may try to make the partner dependent, too dependent to leave, or may try to make the other feel too guilty to leave, perhaps by threatening suicide and the punishment of guilt through eternity. Or the threat may be more mundane and immediate, the threat of violence or even homicide. These threats are common, though rarely acted upon, after an infidelity. Coming up at other times, such threats may seem bizarre. They are efforts to end the voluntary nature of the relationship and maintain bonding through intimidation, to clip the wings emotionally. Once the relationship is based on such threats, the threats are hard to relax.

I've seen several marriages that had been held together by the intimidation of a suicide attempt. The marriage with such a history was always uncomfortable, on both sides, since it seemed involuntary and inescapable. Despite the myth of the Sabine women, in reality, people don't take well to being held captive, whatever the bonds that tie them. Several novels and films have sought metaphors for this desperate, involuntary effort at holding loved ones hostage. In the 1964 Japanese film *Woman in the Dunes,* a woman sets a trap in some isolated sand dunes, and captures a hapless entomologist whom she holds prisoner as her husband in her isolated shack at the bottom of a sand pit. In John Fowles' novel and film *The Collector,* a lepidopterist captures a young woman, adds her to his collection, and tries to make her love him enough to accept her state of captivity. None of these involuntary relationships worked out in the long run.

When jealous people carry on long and loud about their betrayal, they run the risk of getting themselves seen as the problem. Their partner is already trying to escape the relationship, and their punitive possessiveness makes things worse. I think often of the woman who noticed that her husband's jogging clothes were not sweaty when he came back from his evening run. Suspicious, she followed him to his secretary's apartment, where she found him hiding, stark naked, in the secretary's closet. He glared at her and informed her, "You do not see me here. You have gone crazy and imagined the whole thing." He then took her to a psychiatric hospital where he tried to have shock treatment administered for her jealousy. The woman was finally able to leave this destructive man, but the pattern is not uncommon: people will define accurate jealousy as craziness in order to protect themselves from the anger that would come if the truth were known.

There are people who dedicate themselves to overcoming jealousy. The hippies of the late sixties somehow assumed that jealousy would disappear if everything, including relationships and sex, were shared communally. That didn't usually work, and the communes that attempted it generally failed. The urge toward pair bonding and the resultant jealousy were among the reasons.

Swinging used to be considered a treatment for jealousy. (You'd think that swinging, in an AIDS-sensitive society, would be only a terrifying memory, but, believe it or not, people still risk it, and swinging clubs still exist.) One aspect of swinging clubs seems to be the sexual democracy of the organization. Whoever comes to the party must be served. It is considered quite rude to show sexual preferences for one person over another. Everyone present must demonstrate a willingness to be sexually involved with anyone else. At the point at which sex is absolutely impersonal, it is said that jealousy disappears. That point is rarely reached.

The only really helpful response to jealousy, whether it is normal or jealousy that has gone awry, is to reaffirm the bonds of the partnership. If the bonds are indeed being broken—by infidelity, distance, or dishonesty—then the jealousy will quickly turn into desperation, despair, and rage. The solution to jealousy is trust, and trust is not an act of faith but the state of a relationship. It takes both people and it takes time.

5 / Monogamy and Its Discontents

"Marriage is like life in this—that it is a field of battle, and not a bed of roses."

ROBERT LOUIS STEVENSON, *VIRGINIBUS PUERISQUE*

Swimming instructors who teach drown-proofing have learned that drowning occurs when people are afraid of the water and struggle to stay above it. If they went ahead and immersed themselves in the water, they would find they could float securely, breathe comfortably, and relax totally. The effort while in the water to keep from being engulfed by it is exhausting and ultimately fatal.

In a similar way, marriage can be frightening, far more frightening to most men and many women than warfare. Many drown rather than surrender themselves to it. They try to protect themselves from it, or win at it, and are therefore doomed to failure at such a simple but completely engulfing state as marriage.

People have reason to fear marriage. Every marriage is a disappointment. Everyone who marries expects to be adored, pampered, and served or supported in style. They expect their status to rise, they expect the world to envy them. They expect to live happily ever after. When this doesn't happen, they are disappointed, and they do whatever they do when they are disappointed—they pout, or they cheat, or they fight, and they make life even less wonderful.

People marry, over and over again. As the divorce rate rises, the remarriage rate rises accordingly. Almost everyone marries, and almost everyone who divorces and can do so remarries. We read that the institution of marriage is in trouble, yet a higher percentage of the population is married now than in the past, most of them married to their original spouse, and the spiraling divorce rate is finally beginning to fall. Richard B. Stuart details this data in his book *Helping Couples Change*. Stuart collects the data to remind us that people who can't maintain a marriage don't have a very good time of it in other areas either. People yearn for a good marriage, and suffer without one. Unfortunately they assume that the defect is in the institution or in their partner, rather than in themselves. So they change partners and start the process again.

What is the problem with this, our most basic institution? Is the permanence of marriage frightening? (I forget who said "Without divorce marriage would be unthinkable," but Hugh Hefner quoted it.) Is monogamy unnatural? ("Higgamus piggamus, man is polygamous. Hoggamus poggamus, woman's monogamous" supposedly dates back to medieval times.) Is marriage a female plot to enslave men economically in exchange for sex? (Men historically have complained that this was the case, and male liberationists tell dirty jokes that make that point.) Is marriage a male plot to enslave women in exchange for children? (Feminist literature sometimes reads human history from that point of view.) Are men and women inherently incompatible (gay liberation)? Should we return to the jungle (Tarzan and Jane)?

THE NATURAL STATE OF MARRIAGE

Is marriage natural? There are people, particularly philanderers, who insist that marriage is a perversion of their basic nature. What is natural for human beings? Which of our animal relatives do we most closely resemble: gibbons, gorillas, orangutans, or chimpanzees? The gibbons are so monogamous that they chase off all intruders, including their own children. Gorillas are polygamous; dominant males maintain harems of females, while other males do without and offer constant threats and harassment to the harem. Orangutans are solitary and antisocial, but occasionally meet in the forest. Chimpanzees are promiscuous; the females live in communes with the young, while the males surround the group and intermittently raid and mate with the females. We all know people who follow each of these patterns; they find their pattern as natural for them as it must be for their primate models.

I haven't the foggiest notion what was natural for the prototypical human being, nor does anyone else. The most important thing about human beings, the reason for our success, is our amazing adaptability to whatever conditions we find ourselves facing. Males can and must adapt to the wishes and needs of the more biologically important females. Since males exist to serve the females, as sperm donors, nest builders, protectors, competitors, warriors, trophies, or companions, males will do the females' bidding—not immediately, perhaps, it may take a generation or two, since no one female can overcome the influence of all the other females. Obviously, the female with the greatest influence over a particular male is his mother. But the process of adaptation can go awry when mothers have so much power over young males that men then spend the rest of their lives running from women, believing that their masculinity is at risk unless they are escaping or defeating female control.

Humans have a capacity for monogamy, even a tendency toward it, but we aren't bound to it. Unlike the inescapably monogamous birds and gibbons, who languish and die if they lose their mate, humans have an escape clause. We can survive our mate, if we must, and live on to raise our children and take on other partners. Our strength is our flexibility and our adaptability, and we can do whatever we must—we're not bound by our instincts. Whether we are monogamous or not will depend upon the societal support for the institution, the effectiveness of our individual training for it, and how well it works when we try it.

The human animal may be ideally suited for monogamy, but it doesn't always work out that way. It has been working very badly of late; the question has even been raised that perhaps the human male is instinctually polygamous, and thus human history is a cruel joke consisting of a permanent struggle between the basic nature of man and the needs of women, children, family, society, and civilization. This is a depressing view of things, but one that has found its way into both the feminist and the male liberation literature.

Whatever our natural state, we've been at the mercy of some pretty unnatural social forces for quite a while now. In our efforts to make monogamy work, we have much to overcome.

THE DEFECTS OF MARRIAGE

Monogamy, however natural, requires a better class of human beings, people who haven't been warped too badly by some societal forces that have made us defective as partners in monogamy. These defects include our exaggerated stereotypes of what is male and what is female, our belief that all will work out if the "chemistry" is right, our romantic expectations, our isolation into nuclear family units, and our amateurish sexual skills. Of course, there are some people who aren't the raw material from which a good husband or wife is made—they're just not fit for marriage.

Gender Differentiation

"Women! A mistake? Or did He do it on purpose?" asked Jack Nicholson in the 1987 film of John Updike's *Witches of Eastwick.* When Nicholson, who tells us he is just "your average little horny devil," asks that question, the (male) audience roars and cheers.

The foremost problem with marriage is that it takes place between one male and one female, the two equal, slightly differentiated halves of the complete partnership. I know sex is necessary, and it is nice too, but the idea of gender has gone too far. By gender, I don't mean sex or those thoughtfully designed sexual organs that fit together so well. I mean all those things that human society has attributed to the two sexes, the roles that males and females have been expected to perform, the character traits that have been encouraged for people with different genitals, the mythology about what is male and what is female, or how males are supposed to behave and even feel, and how that differs from the ways in which females are supposed to behave and even feel.

Gender may not even be necessary. Most forms of life manage to get along quite nicely without separate genders. Viruses, amoeba, jellyfish, and the like have only one gender, which reproduces asexually and creates offspring identical to the "mother." Plants, with some exceptions, have separate "male" and "female" elements on the same flower, or at least on the same plant. I don't know whether asexual life is less painful, but it is certainly less complicated.

We males may get carried away by our arrogance and assume that we are the standard, or the important gender, as if we came first, like Adam, and women came from us, instead of the other way around. Women have the crucial biological function. Males seem to exist primarily to provide genetic variety. Males are ambulatory sperm donors, permitting the offspring to vary genetically from the mother. If the mother and children are lucky, they can find some other function for the male, but it is by no means assured. Beavers, birds, and a few apes have produced useful males. Whether the human male is useful is a matter of recent debate.

The actual biological differences between human males and human females are minimal, despite thousands of generations of selective breeding based on preferences for the most gender-differentiated specimens. Gender arrangements have ordinarily been justified from the observations that males have stronger muscles than females. When females are encouraged to develop their muscles, the differences are largely erased. Male Olympic records are only 3 percent better than female. A long time ago, Johnny Weissmuller won five gold medals and set Olympic swimming records. He went on to play Tarzan in a dozen movies—a symbol of natural masculinity—and to marry six times. Meanwhile, his swimming records were all broken by women.

We have also accepted the pretense that females are inherently delicate and males inherently powerful. These two myths—Male

Power and Female Delicacy—clearly serve to keep females from scaring males away. Human males, like monogamous birds and polygamous antelopes, are showy; they put on as much display as needed to attract females. (Human males are a little bigger and a lot hairier, but most specimens of either gender are not really very spectacular when unclothed.) Most of the differences between males and females are culturally determined and serve to foster these twin myths. Every difference that could be found between them, plus many differences that do not exist, has been used to support this show of male power and to keep female power from showing. A female's status has derived from her male's competitive authority. Traditionally, her status has depended upon his show of masculinity, so she has had to exert control in a feminine manner, one that wouldn't cast doubt upon his masculine display.

Each little boy and girl has been raised to be one half of a couple, and therefore an incomplete human being. Children are prepared for the extremely important courtship rituals by being molded into the stereotypes of their gender—dressed in pink or blue from birth, and treated roughly and physically or delicately and emotionally from the start. Boys (made as they are of snakes, snails, and puppy dog tails) are taught to be active, assertive, anti-intellectual, nonverbal, risk-taking, etc. Girls (made of sugar, spice, and everything nice) are taught to be passive, helpful, constricted, emotional, self-sacrificing, etc. Anyone who becomes a complete person after such training does so by accident.

In our world, the far extremes of gender differentiation are much admired and sought after by the opposite sex. The ideal adolescent boy is both hunter and prey for the ideal adolescent girl, and, of course, vice versa—there is no setting in which they are allies, much less partners. Those who achieve their gender ideal have nothing in common with the ideal members of the "opposite" sex.

Gender training does not prepare anyone for a sharing of life's experiences with people of another gender. Instead, it leads to an impersonal dance in which each performs his or her expected, gender-based role, and does so automatically, independently, and impersonally. Not only does each restrict behavior to that gender ideal toward which each is still striving, but each expects the partner to do so as well.

Even more disabling, people think of their partners as "a man" or "a woman" rather than as a fellow human being, and they expect certain behavior based upon that distinction. If their partner does not live up to their gender expectations, they may go beyond confusion and disappointment, and become indignant, as if they had a defective piece of machinery on their hands. They may even become frightened, as if they were being forced to behave inappropriately—as if cooking a meal or bringing in a paycheck were tantamount to a sex-change operation. They recall that the most undesirable fate of all is to be imperfectly "masculine" or "feminine." Heroes and heroines have always been perfectly gender trained; comic second leads are funny because they aren't quite right for their gender. Lives of shame and ridicule await those who don't fit the stereotype, or those who deign to mate with them.

Those qualities and talents that people develop for success at courtship render them unfit for marriage. The problem with marriage begins at the beginning. Marriage cannot become personal enough to work until the dehumanizing gender boundaries are breached.

Belief in Chemistry

A second problem inherent in marriage is that few people are trained at it, or even think they need to be. They are told, "When the right one comes along, you'll know, and it will happen, and you'll live happily ever after." Society somehow conveys the impression that marriage works by magic if it is between the "right" people, and if it doesn't work, that means it was between the "wrong" people, who just weren't right for each other.

People are not taught the skills necessary to maintain a relationship. Young people are, or at least used to be, taught domestic skills, how to be a house "wife," how to be a handy "man." Some of them may even be taught how to ingratiate themselves with their elders, how to be popular with their peers, how to win friends and influence people, how to sell refrigerators to Eskimos, or how to attract and seduce the opposite sex. Much of this training leads to hiding one's feelings and avoiding intimacy in order to control the reactions of others. Such impersonal interpersonal skills may make for a successful courtship, but are likely to assure an impersonal marriage.

There is, unfortunately, no marriage-training process accompanying marriage. Both people enter the marriage with patterns and expectations based upon their own previous family experience, usually the parents' marriages, which were kept somewhat private from them. If the parents' marriage was openly conflictual, it would be difficult for the children to absorb helpful instruction as to what works and what doesn't. If the parents went through several marriages, the children might learn something about the impermanence of relationships, or even a few specific pointers about what to watch out for. But the children of divorced families seem more likely to divorce in their own marriages. They may not learn how to solve marital problems, but they do learn how to escape them.

Theoretically, people who have been married before should be better at marriage than novices. They are older and wiser and are making more mature choices with appropriate caution. However, the divorce rate for second marriages is actually higher than for first. Clinicians notice how frequently people marry the same person over and over again (Henry VIII married three Catherines and killed two of them, Johnny Carson has divorced Joan, Joanne, and Joanna). It makes one think that people don't learn from their own marriages.

So people go into marriage bright eyed and bushy tailed, no matter how many marriages of their own and their parents they've suffered through. They hope this one will be different because they have finally found the "perfect" person. They've found someone who is either just like or totally unlike their parents or whomever. Then they can react in horror when they find some quality that reminds them of their mother or their first husband or their second stepfather. They have not learned that marriage partners are not made in heaven but are the product of on-the-job training.

Romance

A third problem with marriage is romance, which seduces people into expecting too much. Romance is wonderful and smells like a new car and fades about as fast and has nothing to do with real life. Most people of marriageable age have not learned the difference between love and romance. Some never do.

A romance, according to Webster, is "a fictitious and wonderful tale," therefore "an experience embodying the quality of picturesque unusualness." Obviously such experiences, however exciting, are not quite sane. However picturesquely unusual the bottom of the Grand Canyon or the top of Mt. Everest or a day at the circus, few would choose to live there. Yet society has decreed that romance should be the basis for choosing a partner for life. When people are "swept off their feet," especially by a romantic, i.e., picturesquely unusual stranger, the intensity can be so exciting that they sign on for life.

They are in-love, personalizing this romantic excitement, and hoping marriage will make it permanent. In-love is, of course, a form of temporary insanity. Psychoanalyst Lawrence Kubie describes being in love as "an obsessional state driven in part by anger." Still, romance is much treasured by medieval poets, modern songwriters, and young lovers of every age. Since the intensity of the romantic excitement is directly in proportion to the picturesqueness and uniqueness (therefore the inappropriateness of the relationship), the least workable matches are the most intense.

When the romantic excitement fades and the poetry becomes prosaic, or the inappropriateness becomes impractical, someone feels cheated or misled. Suddenly the magic is gone, and with no magic, the lights go on and all is revealed. Many people want the magic of romance more than they want to be married. You can't have both—one is fleeting, the other forever. Some try to keep the magic alive by avoiding the mundane world of practical reality, and instead stirring up startling and disorienting experiences to provide a picturesquely unusual setting for the increasingly mundane relationship. This may hold things together, but the cost is someone's or everyone's sanity.

Sexual Ignorance

It used to be assumed that men would somehow become sufficiently sexually experienced to teach sex to their inexperienced brides. Such an expectation is, among other things, naive. Little boys, by having their genitals on the outside and having their sexual arousals more obvious, learn to arouse and pleasure themselves early and often. (Girls, having their genitals on the inside, may not learn masturbation quite so early, so overtly, and so mechanically. And it is not at all rare for women to grow up without ever learning to masturbate at all.) Boys, after learning to pleasure themselves alone, or with the other boys, go on to learn how to pleasure themselves with a female, perhaps someone professional, perhaps someone expecting little if any pleasure, or perhaps someone equally inexperienced—not just inexperienced in heterosexual relations but inexperienced in sexual arousal and pleasure, someone unable to teach her partner how to give her an orgasm. These experiences cannot possibly teach the young man anything about sexual give and take, and can do nothing to educate their partners except about the selfishness of naive men.

The sexual double standard, as Simone de Beauvoir details in *The Second Sex*, is a vestige of a patriarchal society in which women were property, valued for their child-production function. Virginity was a form of prenuptial birth control, assuring that women were not pregnant by someone else before marriage. This led to sexually ignorant women, and sexually incompatible marriages.

The cult of virginity produced another problem even more severe than sexual ignorance. Little girls were taught (and not so long ago) that men who desired them sexually were insulting and degrading them. A girl would "know" when a man truly loved her, as he would make no effort to have sex with her. Girls were encouraged, in effect, to marry men who were not sexually attracted to them.

Even today, there are women who believe that a sexual overture from a husband is an invasion, even an insult. The man must make everything else right first, as she would be selling herself too cheaply if she agreed to have sex with an imperfectly loving husband. Such women may believe that it is inappropriate for them to be sexually assertive. They may even pride themselves on how little pleasure they get from sex, and may treat the sex act as a sacrament. Men from this tradition may feel justified, even compelled, to go outside the marriage for relaxing sex. Such men, who might think of themselves as considerate, take their sexuality outside the marriage. For these men, women are either madonnas or whores. Patriarchal monogamy, when it institutionalized these sexual double standards, seemed to require the institution of prostitution for stabilization.

Some men take seriously this role as the "sexual expert" of the marriage, and treat it as a performance. They end up having performance needs rather than sexual appetites. When they can't perform sex as well as they think a "real man" and true sexual athlete should, they give up on sex, perhaps entirely, perhaps only within the marriage. Similarly, women who believe that their sexuality lies in their appearance, may avoid sex when they don't think they are as beautiful as they once were or as someone else is now. The fairy tale does not specify, but one can imagine what sort of sex life was left for Snow White's stepmother once the mirror ceased telling her she was the fairest of them all.

Sex *is* important in marriage. It can be the glue when things are drifting apart, the lubrication over the rough spots, the cushioning for the bumps. But if sex is used as a reward for getting everything *else* right, the marriage loses its flexibility and stability. Of course, sex only provides those functions if there is sexual exclusivity. Sex has no fastening function in those marriages in which the couple gets around to having sex with each other when the preferred partners are unavailable.

Marriage is not for everyone. Marriage undoubtedly reduces the variety of adventurous experiences, particularly sexual adventures and the opportunities for sexual variety. Sexual hobbyists don't do well at marriage. Nor do those who fear they will lose their sexuality if it is not constantly aroused by new partners.

At the other extreme, marriage doesn't work well for those who are determined to remain sexually inhibited and amateurish. Sexual openness and honesty can solve almost any sexual problem. And most people seem to like sex, some of them quite a bit, once they get the hang of it. In general, those couples who keep in regular practice are more sexually adept, more sexually comfortable, and closer to each other. Couples who have sex infrequently, and after days or weeks of awkward conflict and flirtation, may never get comfortable enough with it either to enjoy it or to let it make the relationship safe, close, and special.

Then, of course, they have to get beyond that antisexual gender training. In a trade-off between love and sex, women-who-fear-men put them through a romantic process, having them face various ordeals to prove their love before sex can take place. In the classic fairy tale, Sleeping Beauty was surrounded by a bramble forest that Prince Charming had to hack through before he could awaken her with a kiss. In Wagner's *Siegfried*, Siegfried has to brave the magic fire before he can be rewarded with Brunnhilde's love. The usual ordeal is that the man must pay attention and say romantic things, especially "I love you." There is a special nerve in the human woman-who-fears-men, that runs between the eardrum and the clitoris. If a man says "I love you," it short-circuits the brain.

By contrast, men-who-fear-women think that love and romance are dangerous and lead to entrapment, whereas sex is a victory over women that proves a man's masculinity is still standing free. A man may find impersonal sex reassuring, and may even want to degrade his partner by having her get herself up or comport herself according to his fantasy of a whore. For men-who-fear-women, the most impersonal, least romantic sex is the most reassuring.

It is therefore not unusual to see a couple where the man-who-fears-women wants his wife to dress up in sleazy costumes, go out in public without her underwear, or put on a show for him, even with other men. In milder form, he might expect her to make all the sexual overtures or require her to pretend that whatever gives him sexual pleasure makes her orgasmic by proxy. (Pornography has been written primarily by men and for men-who-fear-women. It has no relation to the mutual enjoyment of sexuality.) The wife of the man-who-fears-women might prefer sex that is friendly and considerate, and comes after a period of just being together and musing about the details of living. She might prefer that the sex be quite personal and face to face, while he would want it animalistic and impersonal.

If a man-who-fears-women marries a woman-who-fears-men, they may have very bad sex, or they may have sex that is mechanically good and emotionally bad. Yet they may develop a ritual of alternating romance and pornography that works OK if each knows he or she is faking it but doesn't realize that the partner is faking too. Whatever they are doing, it isn't personal. This may not matter to them, since neither expects what goes on between males and females to be personal or friendly.

Isolation

We have a hell of a time reconstructing the prehistory of mankind and figuring out what manner of animal we are, but the human animal in its natural state seems to be a small group hunter, living communally. While monogamy seems to be natural, the nuclear family (just the couple and their young children) as a totally separate and independent functional and emotional unit is not natural, and therefore must be worked at.

The nuclear family as the societal ideal is fairly recent in the world's history. As a unit it is now isolated from the extended family, and from the small community or neighborhood of people who share a common culture, know one another personally, and concern themselves with one another's lives. The extended family and community offer support, buffers, and constraints that bolster the vital institutions, including marriage. The human animal does not tolerate anonymity, and when cut off from community and family, becomes easily demoralized.

A nuclear family cannot provide all the functions required by its members. This is obvious for instrumental functioning (getting all the necessary jobs done), but it is equally true for emotional functioning. Whatever made us decide that it was good for people's mental health to break away from the constraints of family and community and to give in to our impulses, especially the sexual ones? That trend has been a disaster. It has put all the burden on marriage, and particularly on wives, to provide cultural continuity, restraint, stability, and whatever else the community of friends and relatives used to provide. Expectably, the experiment has failed.

Occasionally I return to the small town in which I grew up and hear stories of how my old friends' lives have turned out. Those who have stayed in the town provide thick padding for one another, and few have divorced, though all have problems that everyone else is aware of. Those who have left the town are the topic of morality tales and warnings, and have about the same divorce rate as the population at large. I don't know whether my old friends still in the hometown are better off staying together under community pressure, but they seem to think so.

When the partners in a couple depend exclusively on each other for everything, the deficiencies of each will become both apparent and important, and the talents of each will be less respected and more taken for granted. In a state of such interdependency, dissatisfaction will be greater and conflict more likely. But conflict resolution will be more difficult, because distance becomes unbearable since the couple is already isolated. To outsiders, who are not a part of the community or family buffering system, it may seem reasonable and efficient to discard or exchange marriages as one would other pieces of defective or outdated equipment. What's worse, when people don't have family around for buffering and intimacy, they may be tempted to establish the necessary intimacies outside the marriage, as they are needed.

Defective People

Some people just don't do marriage well. Those who should not marry. include the obvious ones—those who don't care enough about other people to form partnerships, for instance, psychopaths, and people who abuse substances or become violent when they don't win each point. But marriage is also difficult for the people who want it most—the immature, the unhappy, the miserable, and the romantic.

Depressives, who find life painful and exhausting, alcoholics, whose lives are not their fault, obsessives, who must have everything just their way, paranoids, who can't be wrong, phobics, who must be forced to face life—these people may want to be married, so someone will take care of them and protect them from having to do it for themselves, but they aren't likely to want to give as much as they want to receive. Give and take is difficult for such people. One has to be fairly healthy to make a marriage work, yet people often marry because they are not healthy and marriage seems a way to avoid personal wholeness. Family therapist James Framo points out the confusing literature on marriage, in which "it has been said by some that no one ever cured himself of a neurosis by marrying and that the neurotic problems of the two marriage partners are cumulative; on the other hand, others say that a marriage by virtue of its being unhappy can mask or prevent the emergence of a neurosis, or that the marriage relationship may embody compensatory mechanisms for seriously disturbed partners." Even married people would do well to make themselves as sane as possible as individuals, rather than copping out by expecting a spouse to make things right.

When they marry, people usually give up some closeness to their same-sex friends and even more to their opposite-sex friends. They must forgo the patterns of early adolescence, when they played at being grown-up with their friends, while their parents took care of the realities of life. After marriage, they become the real grown-ups. They may even have to establish adult-to-adult relationships with their own parents. They don't have to run away from home, though. Marriage is for grown-ups.

I am amazed at what defects some people will tolerate in marriage and what defects other people won't. In dealing with marriage, it must never be assumed that people want a partner to be competent, much less sane. Some people, particularly men who are afraid of competent women, seem to seek out and value incompetence in a mate. Some even make sure that that incompetence is never overcome. Such people are puppeteers, and their mates are dolls in what Ibsen described as *A Doll's House*. Grown men may marry cute young girls. Men or women may marry people who barely speak the language, who can't hold a job, and who are socially or culturally inept. And then they try to keep their spouse from becoming equal. They really value the incompetence, and defend against any threat to it.

We naively assume that people want equality in their marriages. Unless people grow up with it, equality is an extremely sophisticated concept that requires emotional security and maturity and differentiation. Instead, I fear that many people see marriage as a contest, in which one partner wins and the other loses. They can't see that either they both win or they both lose. They want to be the one who wins at the marriage, or at least doesn't lose. To that end, they tolerate glaring defects in their partners, defects that produce an aura of dependency, proof that they are needed more than they need. But they may not tolerate defects that seem to give their partner an advantage. People can tolerate great stupidity, cruelty, and even psychosis in a spouse, but may not tolerate thoughtlessness or nonchalant independence. The partner who can most easily escape the marriage has the upper hand, and has nothing to prove by leaving.

People who try to protect themselves from monogamy by making only a partial commitment are sure to find the totally engulfing state of marriage terrifying. Those who expect marriage to make them happy and healthy (with no effort on their own part) are in for a lot of frustration—for themselves and for their partners.

MARRIAGE AND HAPPINESS

Romance fades. Those who depend upon the reassurance that comes with each new romance find something missing in marriage. Dependence on romance is evidence of a hysterical character. There is little to distinguish a hysteric from a psychopath—both rely on the feelings of the moment, both have difficulty thinking of long-range consequences, and both avoid reality. Romantics think of weddings, not of marriage. Marriage is too realistic for romantics.

It cannot even be assumed that people want to be happy. Many people arrange to become and remain unhappily married—it is a cherished state in our society, as it grants one maximum freedom and plenty to talk about. Those who admit to being happily married are considered socially subversive—they make everyone else feel ashamed.

Sometimes I think the most sensible thing on the subject of happiness was said by Beatrice Arthur in the film *Lovers and Other Strangers*. Her son had decided to get a divorce. She kept asking why he would do such a thing. He told her it was because he wasn't happy. She kept trying to explain to him that marriage was not supposed to produce life's happiness. She pulled forth all her wisdom as she said gravely, "Don't try to be happy, Richie. It will only make you miserable."

Those words, on the face of it, seem absurd. But this is an important message—happiness cannot be a goal in itself. Happiness, like sweat, is a by-product of hard work. It comes about when one is working toward some other goal; it comes more reliably when two are working together toward some goal. A happy marriage comes about easily and automatically if people will just get all the way into it and then let it happen as they experience together the transitions and crises of life—and whatever time and space throw at them.

6 / The Turning Points
of Marriage

"Ah, so you are married! Well, there is nothing so nice as a new marriage. No psychosis yet. No regressions. No guilt complexes. I congratulate you and wish you have babies and not phobias."
BEN HECHT, *SPELLBOUND*

"Seldom, or perhaps never, does a marriage develop into an individual relationship smoothly and without crises; there is no coming to consciousness without pain."
CARL G. JUNG, *CONTRIBUTIONS TO ANALYTICAL PSYCHOLOGY.*

Marriages usually start off well, and the couple appear to be in it for the duration. The defects that were apparent to all the friends and relatives haven't developed into anything serious. Then it somehow ceases to work. The marriage becomes more distant, or more conflictual. Nothing very dramatic has happened, the marriage just isn't quite working anymore. Typically, one partner suspects the other of having an affair, and at such points the suspicion is often correct. But the crisis, while quite different and infinitely easier to resolve without the affair, is still a crisis.

In the course of a life and a marriage, there are turning points, periods of transition and crisis at which things change. There is an instability at these turning points, and all manner of problems may erupt. It is at these times that a marriage—and even before that, a relationship—is most at risk for infidelity. The turning points that are most dangerous include these: "falling in love," "prenuptial panic," "the end of the romance," "the adult world," "parenting," "the dropping off of sex," "reaching the summit," "the empty nest," and "the facts of life."

Falling in Love

Someone measured and found that couples talk to each other most on the third date and in the year before the divorce. There is a crisis in all courtship relationships around that third date, when one partner begins to feel an attachment first. If the other has not started to have romantic notions yet, the relationship may begin to get confusing, and quite sticky. Someone has to acknowledge first that what is being felt may be "love." The saying of "I love you" is terrifying, the not saying it is also terrifying, and the not hearing it in return is grounds for suicide. Insecure people may fall apart early in a relationship as they fear their need for love is not going to be met. They are not particularly concerned with the quality of their own loving or the needs of the other person, but only whether the other will give them the love they feared they'd never get.

Insecure individuals who are out there dating can drive themselves and everyone around them nuts as they wait for the loving response they feel their lives depend upon. They often operate as if the entire "opposite" sex gets together daily to determine the insecure ones' relative desirability, and their date will react to them according to their official rating. So if a particular person does not fall in love with them on this day, they are doomed to a life of loneliness and degradation forever. Any sane person who gets a whiff of this desperation is likely to cut and run. Most people do grow up and are never again so panicky about the question of whether they are loved, but some feel the same insecurity daily and need regular reassurance that they are indeed loved, no matter what they have or have not done.

Prenuptial Panic

If a couple do get past the "third date panic" and fall in love more or less at the same time, they will eventually get close to marriage.

At this point, just before getting married, most men and increasing numbers of women will suddenly stop the courtship and consider the implications. He (usually) may overtly or covertly "cool" the relationship for a while. It would be unlikely that both partners will experience this cooling at the same moment, so she will be jarred by it. The cooling is an effort to step back and see if he still owns himself, still can control his own life and destiny and particularly the distance he puts between himself and his loved one. Obviously, if his fiancée reacts to his coolness by panicking and pulling him tighter, his experiment has failed and he realizes he is losing himself in the relationship, and he may back away even more deliberately from his loved one.

The woman who panics when a man gets a bit distant is accurately known as a "good-bye girl." That is changing. A woman's life need not center on marriage anymore. Increasingly, as it becomes apparent that marriage is a better deal for husbands than for wives, it is the woman who fears marriage and the man who is eager for it, so the woman creates distance and we see "good-bye guys." The more insecure these guys are, the more they hover over younger, more dependent, and more unsuitable women and try to control them, until the women get frightened and back off.

The End of the Romance

Typically, the romantic haze continues to disorient the couple until they have been married for a while. If the romance has cooled before the marriage, the wedding may still take place, but one or both partners may recall that they "knew it was wrong." Some people never really feel a great deal of romance about their marriage, and never think they should go through a whole lot of romantic disorientation. For them there is no crisis. But for most, the loss of that bright, shiny romantic glow is a bit sad. They begin to notice that their spouse is less wonderful than they had thought. They don't feel the sexual intensity. They may even be bored. They may be irritated by the human frailties of their partner, even by the simple humanness. They might prefer to spend an evening with their friends. They may wonder if they have made an error in marrying at all, or marrying this particular person. Sometimes the relationship is good enough for both to acknowledge the End of the Romance, and see it as the Beginning of the Marriage.

If they see the cooling of their ardor as a betrayal, or as a problem, they may try to keep up the romantic atmosphere, which may be irritating to their less romantic partner. There are a few people who panic when the romance ends, and either blame the spouse as defective, or run to a new relationship in which they can hope for a permanent romantic high.

Those who need the constant stimulation of hot romance appear to be dangerously psychopathic, but they seem to have a certain appeal and have no difficulty finding partners to keep life in a continual cyclical uproar. Marriage cannot provide a constant state of romance, and people who are addicted to romance cannot maintain a marriage. But everyone who marries doesn't know that. And some don't learn it after many marriages.

The Adult World

The beginning of the family often comes along with the End of the Romance. At some point, the haze clears and the couple become aware that they are part of something bigger than their coupleship. In the past, many couples were pregnant when they married and therefore acutely aware of impending parenthood. Now, many people have children before marriage; if not before any marriage, at least before *this* one. Those who don't already have children when they marry are very much aware of the decisions to be made about children. Children don't come naturally anymore. With better birth control, children are not automatic by-products of sexual activity. They are chosen and planned, and the process of making all these choices can be disconcerting. And it is not only children who expand the couple into a family. The couple must also become aware of their families of origin and how those families influence the marriage.

When a couple marries, they may not realize that they each remain very much a part of the family that raised them. Now that they have grown up and settled down, they may be expected to take on a set of functions different from those they had while they were running around loose and single. The two families of origin may be very different in patterns and values, and in their expectations of the new couple. And the two families are not necessarily compatible with each other (though that can happen and makes it all much easier). Some of the biggest fights couples ever have are over the conflicting expectations of their two (or more) sets of parents over the wedding arrangements. And that is followed in due time with conflict over the plans for the first Christmas or the naming of the children. It is as if the new couple are being forced to differentiate themselves as a new family rather than a branch of the old family. This is a painful amputation, and one filled with crisis. If it is compromised, it merely postpones and aggravates the necessary procedures.

The couple must be able to put their marriage first, without having to break off with their families of origin. They must not let the two original families cut them off from each other, from their parental families, or from their in-laws. Some people delight in setting up tests of love and allegiance through which they recruit one another into family feuds. The jealousies inherent in this procedure can become lethal.

Even if relationships with both families can be kept cordial and correct—better yet, intimate and involved—the couple must still sort out questions of style and values that amount to choosing the patterns of one family over another. This can seem insulting, and cause hurt. Each spouse is required to look critically at his or her own family and own origins to decide what values should be kept and what should be discarded.

Relationships with friends change too after marriage. It is not easy, or safe, to maintain closeness to someone unacceptable or threatening to one's new spouse. It can hurt to have to distance a friend, but it may hurt even more to have to go through life defending a friendship. Marriages need friends who will bolster the marriage—if the marriage and the friend are incompatible, the friend must be distanced. But if all friends are incompatible with the marriage, it may be a good idea to examine the marriage.

As the marriage goes through this pruning stage, it can be isolating and lonely, and it is easy to question whether it is worth it. The answer may well be no. One seemingly popular solution to the problem of the too-isolating marriage is to turn a friendship into a secret affair.

Parenting

The question of whether the marriage is worth it is one that people can't afford to answer if they are busy raising children. That is not an unmixed blessing: parenthood stabilizes a marriage, but parenthood also traps the parents. Becoming a parent is the clearest possible evidence that someone has moved from the child generation to the adult generation, and therefore must give up childish behavior. Our society romanticizes childish behavior and particularly adolescent behavior, and puts the new parent in the unappealing position of having to give up all that is considered fun in life, in order to become a parent and make sacrifices so the next generation can have all the fun. It is not surprising that one or both parents will resent the hell out of a presumptuous member of the next generation for getting to be a child while he or she is forced to be a grown-up. Sometimes both parents will resent adulthood equally, and they will join forces to protect themselves from the child, who may be battered or abandoned or left with others while the couple rebel against the child as they did against their parents or teachers or bosses or anyone else who tried to make them be adults before their chosen time.

Parenting, like sex, tennis, and making up beds, is best done in pairs, and it is the best part of life when the two are working well together. But it usually doesn't happen that way. More likely, one parent will enjoy parenting and center her (usually) life around it, while the other will try to escape from parenting, compete with the child, and feel deserted. The antiparent may find the increasingly mature behavior of the spouse offensively adult and parental, and something to rebel against. When the antiparent is male, he may escape into his work and games with the other boys—there are special clubs for men who play golf all weekend to escape their wives and children. Among the less advantaged, the boys go to bars to drink beer and avoid coming home until the kids are asleep and they are anesthetized. Some may become workaholics or take second jobs. Some have affairs.

Housebound wives may lose any skills they ever had in talking to grown-ups, and may become only mothers, talking daily to their mothers and other mothers, but losing the other facets of their identity, particularly their marriage. A recent movie, *Mr. Mom*, showed a mother returning to work after years of staying home raising children. At her first business lunch, she automatically leans over to her boss's plate and cuts up his meat for him.

The conflict in the marriage may center on one or both partners recognizing that the wife is becoming only a mother. They may or may not notice that the husband is becoming one of the kids.

If it is the husband who throws himself into parenting, he may become the grandmother, supervising his wife in her child care, but taking no direct responsibility, and she might rather do it all herself. He may, of course, become the primary deliverer of child care, and though that is becoming more common, it is still rarely thought of as the masculine ideal, and is downright threatening to many men and to some women. If he does become the nurturing parent and the one who takes care of things, it may be with his wife's blessing and enthusiastic encouragement or it may threaten her. Most often, he is lavishly praised for the least little parental effort, and it is as much trouble to get him involved as it would be for the beleaguered mother to do it herself. Nondomestic men are a luxury that few families can afford, though many men were raised to expect such pampering and feel cheated when they don't get it.

However the couple assign the parenting tasks, it becomes apparent to one or both of them that the nuclear family is just not big enough or flexible enough to support a home, a marriage, a career or two, a child or more, and a nonfunctional prince. Something gets shortchanged. Usually the woman's career, the home, the marriage, and the children are sacrificed to the man's career and his ego. Some couples can afford paid help or have relatives who can fill out the family to functional size, if the husband is frightened of domesticity. But most often, frustration reigns and everyone suffers. This is a societal quandary that has not yet been adequately addressed; the danger is that the couple may think their difficulties are unique, and blame each other for the problems that arise.

As the child grows older, one or both parents may strongly identify with the little tyke, and may react to the other parent as the child does. If the mother yells at the child, the father may experience it as her yelling at him. If the father neglects the child, the mother may feel herself being rejected. If he is authoritarian and seems to put the child down, the mother may feel the put-down. As each parent goes through the various parental activities, the other parent may reexperience his or her own parents, and react accordingly, reviving that childlike sense of being little and helpless in the face of big, powerful grown-ups.

It is a disconcerting experience to watch a lover/playmate suddenly turning into a parent/authority. It becomes even more disconcerting as the child becomes adolescent. Grown-ups remember themselves as adolescents so much more vividly than they remember themselves at any other age, even yesterday. We all identify to a disorienting degree with our adolescent children, and with their struggles with their other parent. This is worst when the other parent is an ex-spouse, but it is bad enough even in the best marriages. People who have had difficulty with their own adolescence, who have never gotten past their rebellion against authority, are likely to rebel against their teenage child's more adult parent, and choose this point in their marriage to start an affair or end their marriage, or encourage their child's adolescent rebellion.

People frequently are not cheating on or divorcing their mate, but someone else. Men strike a blow for freedom by rebelling against their teenaged child's mother. Women erase their young child's neglecting father. Parents, human or animal, will attack anyone who threatens their children, even the other parent.

The Dropping Off of Sex

In the past, couples might marry without regard for their sexual compatibility. Even couples who seemed compatible probably weren't. Sex is usually intense at the beginning of a relationship, even if it is neither efficient nor effective. Actually, many couples have enjoyed their sexuality more during the courtship than in the marriage. Traditionally, boys were required to push for sex, while girls were supposed to hold back. As a result, there was a lot of romancing and pleasuring and foreplay and not much screwing, which was usually a lot more fun and orgiastic for the girl, and for the boy too but he didn't realize it. Once the couple married, there were no barriers, so sex often became frequent and quick, devoid of foreplay, and totally aimed at the screwing—coming, ready or not.

It is not surprising that women were not too thrilled by marital sex, and developed headaches (actual or reported) at the thought. After a year or so, the guy would grow tired of the rejection and the battle and the lack of response, and sex would become only as frequent as necessary to keep the marriage license in force.

Sociologists say that some men are inhibited by women who are comfortable enough to want to enjoy sex. Birth control permits us to separate sex from reproduction and explore it for its own joys. Many women want to explore sex and find their husbands inhibited by fear of their own inadequacy. Men also can see sex as a dirty, rebellious trick that brave boys pull on foolish girls. If a woman wants it, it makes him somehow less masculine, the woman less feminine, and the whole thing an act of servile obedience rather than the desired act of rebellion.

Men, on the other hand, may want to explore sexuality and find their wives inhibited by what they had been taught was ladylike behavior. There are many women who do not believe women should be sexually assertive or adventurous, before or after marriage. Most people in our society are far less interested in sex than they are in maintaining whatever they think is necessary to fulfill the requirements of membership in their gender. Even if their sexuality must be abandoned, they must do what they were told was the gender ideal.

Some otherwise normal people are stark raving mad when it comes to sex. There are people who would risk their marriage or even their life to avoid doing what is sexually requested of them, but would then risk everything to do whatever was forbidden. For them sex is freedom. But it serves another function too, in that it reduces the intensity of their frightening sexual impulses. People who are sexual "perverts" are probably no different in their impulses or curiosities from the rest of us, but they are less imaginative at enjoying their fantasies without *acting* on them. The ideal marital sex is probably between two people who have been turned on by everybody they encountered all day, and saved up all those juices to expend at home, probably without feeling uncomfortable enough about their fantasies to have to spell them out. Of course, it would be nice if marital partners were a turn-on for each other too. If they get good enough at giving each other sexual pleasure, they will be.

Some people consider their sexuality shameful and act accordingly. Rather than sharing and enjoying their fantasies, they keep them secret, and go through a crisis when they are revealed. There are, of course, people who just don't like sex. Some insist that they go for years without masturbating, and certainly without having sex with another person. Others prefer masturbating and would rather not be bothered with someone else's intrusion into their fantasies. It is easier for women than for men to just passively submit to sex, without getting involved. Some men just don't like sex and stubbornly refuse to have it no matter how much the pressure builds. Of course, once the pressure builds to have sex, they can't possibly do so just because that is the way the male equipment works. There are few women who refuse sex completely, perhaps because they have the option of going through it passively, while men don't, or don't think they do.

As men age, many seem to lose their interest in sex, really quite unnecessarily. There is usually no clear physiological reason for this. They probably don't believe this, but they tell themselves and their wives it is because of the wife's aging or some other pet complaint. So the wife, fearing that she is repulsing him, avoids pursuing the poor guy sexually, and everything dries up. Very soon, he thinks of himself as impotent or over the hill. The human penis is an extraordinarily phobic fellow, with a mind of its own and a total refusal to function under pressure. The explanation I use, perhaps not completely scientific but fitting the salient facts, is that male hormones are produced abundantly around the clock when younger, but after the age of thirty or thereabouts they are produced mostly during sexual arousal. Therefore, if older men don't use it they'll lose it. Of course, it is not enough just to have orgasms—the therapy is in the arousal. So couples who are concerned about the man's loss of libido are instructed by therapists to go through frequent and prolonged sessions of sexual stimulation, rather than trying for the desperate quickie.

Sex, perhaps more than anything else about marriage, needs to be released from the myth that there is a difference between males and females. That doesn't usually happen until there is a crisis of some sort. Sex can be better after that.

Reaching the Summit

There are at least three separate crises of middle life, and they are often confused with one another. The "empty nest," when the children are grown and gone, and the couple are alone together, may be the most dramatic. The "facts of life" crisis, the awareness of mortality and the process of growing like one's parents whether one wants to or not, *should* be the most liberating. The "reaching of the summit" and the thought that it is downhill from here on may be the silliest, but in our narcissistic age it is the most popular. This prestigious, but by no means universal, midlife crisis has to do with people, mostly men, discovering that they have limited time to achieve whatever they are going to achieve in life.

This is the point in life when people must take stock. Erik Erikson described the "crisis of generativity," the stage of generativity versus stagnation. Freud described the "success neurosis," when someone becomes depressed just at the point of achieving his life's goal. Bernard Shaw said it best in *Man and Superman:* "There are two tragedies in life. One is not to get your heart's desire. The other is to get it." In either case, people think about things they have avoided thinking about up until now, and consider whether this is how they want to live for the rest of their lives.

At this time, the introspection is followed by a change, perhaps only a renewed surge of ambition. But there may be a change of direction toward something less competitive and more connected with the real world. Of course, there may emerge only a decision to avoid the question for a while longer, until after the young lover, the sports car, and the face lift.

This stage has been called the "male menopause," comparing it with the ovarian shutdown that renders a woman no longer fertile. That comparison overlooks the reality that women after menopause are freer to be sexual, to pursue careers they had interrupted or postponed previously, and to fulfill whatever frustrated ambitions and dreams they have. There was a time, not too many decades ago, when women valued themselves, and were valued, largely for their reproductive function. Then, menopause was experienced as a point of desolate barrenness, and the end of usefulness and sense of worth, especially if it coincided with an empty nest. That has all changed, and most women now think of menopause as a part of the liberation process. Postmenopausal women can be having the best years of their lives, but may be threatening to men going through male menopause and struggling to hold off signs of advancing age in themselves or in their partners. If one spouse decides to settle into a less pressured life, and the other wants to keep up the struggle against age, a severe marital maladjustment occurs. A menopausal man and a menopausal woman may be temporarily incompatible.

Men at the summit of their lives, whether their summit is very high or not, are likely to be depressed and self-centered and very difficult to live with. Their lives have been directed toward achieving success by whatever standards their parents set for success, which did not likely consider their comfort or happiness. They need permission to slow down, level off, and even to coast back downhill. Unfortunately they don't realize that that is the best part of all. If they have the permission, whether they accept that option or not, what follows can be the first comfort these men have permitted themselves.

The Empty Nest

The mythology of the empty nest at its most dreadful assumes a gray-haired menopausal woman, who has rarely left home and never worked outside the home, has served her term as PTA president, has darned socks and knitted sweaters and baked birthday cakes and driven car pools, and has sent her children tearfully off to college or the army or marriage, armed with brownies and good advice. Her husband, who has slept in the other room since the first child left home, plays golf when he isn't working or with his mistress. Her husband's mother is in the spare room gazing at a blank TV, and the children don't write home. She sobs softly when a letter doesn't come, sweetly conspires to make them all feel guilty, considers suicide, and has another drink instead.

The lives of middle-aged women have changed, and the empty nest syndrome is no longer like that. It still occurs, and while it can affect both fathers and mothers, an empty nest is a great liberator for busy people. The problems are most likely for those women who have developed little sense of personal identity, apart from being someone's wife and someone's mother. When motherhood is over, there is very little for them to do. In a society that values youth, they may feel particularly undesirable. Their identity is most dependent on their husbands, just when husbands are most involved with careers, least involved at home, and most attractive to other, younger women.

The woman sitting on an empty nest is in a bit of a quandary. There are two obvious solutions: she can become closer to her husband, or she can become more involved with her own career or activities. But her husband may not want a more intimate marriage. And he may not want her to go in the opposite direction and expect him to take care of himself or entertain himself while she gets her own life going. There are dangers if she goes in either direction.

And she is only too aware that this is the period when her husband is at greatest risk for infidelity. What she may not realize is that she too is at greatest risk for infidelity. If she can't comfortably get her husband more involved at home, and she can't comfortably get him to take care of himself while she pursues her own interests, she may begin to feel that she can keep her courage up with a part-time man.

The Facts of Life

This last period may or may not coincide with the midlife crisis, and while it usually comes later, it may even come earlier. It is a most important and often overlooked crisis, and often a very painful one. At some point in the course of the marriage, people become aware of several realities. They are imperfect, their spouse is imperfect, their children are imperfect, they are not going to conquer the world, they are getting relatively poorer, and older and uglier and shorter and fatter, and less desired by others for any purpose, and it will all get worse.

This seems to occur to people as their parents begin to fail and die and people realize what is in store for them. Or it may occur as they look into a mirror or at their children and realize that they are turning into their parents. So far, they've gotten freer and more powerful every year, and it has all been uphill. Suddenly, they see they've passed their prime. At this point, they have to forgive their parents, if they haven't already done so as they became parents. If they don't forgive their parents and accept their position as the parental generation, and slowly settle, there is nothing but despair ahead. Geriatric hippies and middle-aged cheerleaders and over-the-hill playboys with gold chains and their hair combed carefully over the bald spot are pathetic. They believe they won't grow old if they refuse to grow up.

As with every other stage of development, one spouse enters it first. The entry may be subtle and gradual, and the partner may not notice. Suddenly, one awakens and finds him- or herself married to a settled, mature, middle-aged person, who is looking forward to growing older rather than struggling to stay young. This realization can be a point of panic. It is often associated with the death or disability of one of the parents, though it can occur with an illness, the death of a friend, or a crucial birthday. Whatever triggers it, it is intimately related to identification with aging or dying parents, and the recognition of the way of all flesh.

The effect on the marriage can be drastic, as the partner who values youth panics at being married to someone middle-aged, someone whose powers are declining. The one who ages first may do so comfortably and naturally, while the youth in the marriage fears age is contagious and wants to get some distance from this horror. Age is not just associated with dying, or even with weakness and ugliness, but with becoming like one's parents. People who are comfortable with their parents seem comfortable with growing into them. Those whose sense of themselves is still of an adolescent in rebellion may rebel against this fact of life. The only way to guard against becoming your own parent may seem to be to escape an aging spouse, either through divorce or through an affair. The alternative may be to recognize the facts of life and forgive your parents.

At each of these turning points of marriage, there may be discomfort and there may be panic. People are forced to see themselves turning with the human life cycle, changing inexorably over time. Or they may just see their own discomfort, and not know what is making them unhappy. At these points, someone may resist the forces of reality and change and choose unreality instead, by having an affair. The danger of affairs is greatest at each of these points of transition.

7 / The State of Affairs
in Our World

"Friendship is constant in all other things/Save in the office
and affairs of love."
SHAKESPEARE, *MUCH ADO ABOUT NOTHING*

"The first betrayal is irreparable. It calls forth a chain reaction of further
betrayals, each of which takes us farther and farther away from the point
of our original betrayal."
MILAN KUNDERA, *THE UNBEARABLE LIGHTNESS OF BEING*

In the movie *10*, Dudley Moore is in bed with Bo Derek on the night of her wedding (to someone else). He asks her why she is doing this, and she says, "Because I want to." Her answer distresses him. He says, "I thought you were special," by which he means, of course, "I thought you thought I was special to the point of being so world-shatteringly extraordinary that you would break your most sacred rule for my sake." She's baffled by the idea that sex should be "special," which offends him so much that he puts on his pants, turns off Ravel's *Bolero,* and goes home. If marriage can't be special, can one hope that infidelity will be?

In pursuing the reasons for infidelity, we have to be specific or we will begin to believe the myths of infidelity, which would render us helpless in dealing with it. There may be as many acts of infidelity in our society as there are traffic accidents, and each needs to be investigated to find out how and why it happened. If people just go around bumping into things and assuming that that is the way things happen, they might be endangering themselves and others.

Infidels are startlingly shallow and naive in their explanations of why they are doing what they are doing. One after another they come in and tell me the same three things, and these three explanations don't explain anything at all.

First, infidels tell me that infidelity is quite natural and that everybody does it. They may even quote statistics on the subject. These people do not believe that monogamy is a (much less the) natural state of things. They have either not been taught or not been convinced that marital fidelity is either natural or possible. They would not consider the idea that an infidelity should be examined and explored as a deviation from the ideal, and perhaps a symptom of some problem in themselves, in their marriage, or in the situation. Zorba the Greek, who was married with children ("the whole disaster"), believed that God would be displeased with him if any woman was left to sleep alone. His multiseductions became a religious duty.

Second, infidels tell me that their affairs don't hurt anybody and are nobody else's business. These people don't think of marriage as an agreement between equals. It would not occur to them that they owed their spouse honesty, that one partner's sexual behavior is the business of the other partner, and should be known. They don't see the secrecy as betrayal, an indicator of distrust of the partnership. They may see marriage as a cat and mouse game, or just as irrelevant. Luciano Pavarotti, playing a philandering Italian tenor in the absurd film *Yes, Giorgio,* varies the philanderer's credo when he says, "I love my wife and children . . . but my private life is my own." Later he says, "My affair is none of your affair."

Third, infidels tell me that they felt a strong attraction for someone else. The thrice-divorced Bertrand Russell, for instance, says in *Marriage and Morals* (1929), "The psychology of adultery has been falsified by conventional morals, which assume, in monogamous countries, that attraction to one person cannot coexist with a serious affection for another. Everybody knows that this is untrue." Russell understood accurately that people feel attractions to one another. What he failed to learn, and what cost him his wives and families, was the same lesson that shoplifters have to learn— one is not compelled to act on one's attractions.

DECISIONS OF INFIDELITY

The human animal is constantly struggling with all manner of impulses, including adulterous ones. The human, if sane, competent, and mature, makes decisions about whether or not to obey the impulses. The existence of the impulse is not an explanation for why the human made the decision to act on it.

Yet people sometimes do act on their impulses, and then they must somehow justify what they have done. One near-universal human characteristic is the pursuit of some justification for our actions, some formula by which we can say that our actions are not our fault. "It was in our stars and not in our selves," "It was God's will," "The devil made me do it," "I must have been out of my mind," "I had an unhappy childhood," explain nothing and solve nothing. Most people, even psychotherapists, can't get past two ideas about infidelity: (1) infidelity is so normal it need not be mentioned, and (2) infidelity is so dangerous that it must not be revealed.

Society, for a couple of decades at least, has been encouraging people to see their sexual adventures as harmless. This attitude must now change, but not because of the alarming divorce rate and the instability of marriage and thus of childhood. AIDS is making casual sex potentially lethal. Still, AIDS spreads.

People who know they test positive for AIDS make the news regularly when they decide to go ahead and have sex with unsuspecting partners. They know they are endangering their partner's life. The legal question is raised of whether their actions should be considered attempted murder. When these people are asked why they did it, they give the same sort of answers that people give to explain their less lethal sexual actions. A drifter with AIDS sells his blood to a blood bank. When arrested, he says, "I needed the money." A male prostitute with AIDS says, "That's what I do for a living." A convict with AIDS keeps trying to bite the guards, saying, "If I'm going to die, I'm not going to go alone." A fourteen-year-old boy with AIDS is jailed by the judge because he keeps having sex with the girls in his class at school. The boy says, "I'm just doing what is normal. It's not fair that I can't have a normal life." A man in Kenya passes AIDS from a prostitute to his wife and says, "I am a man. I have to have sex." An AIDS-infected prostitute in Haiti, interviewed in the August 1987 issue of *Life*, says, "AIDS! There is no such thing. It is a false disease invented by the American government to take advantage of the poor countries." When a prostitute is told that the prostitutes with AIDS are killing the Haitian men, she says, "As for that, everyone is killing everyone else."

These answers tell us quite a bit about the people who lead their sexual lives in ways that inflict pain on themselves and others. Once we get past the level of explaining infidelity by saying "It's natural," "It's unimportant," and "I wanted to," we open up a fascinating exploration of people's attitudes toward sex, gender, generation, honesty, and the nature of human existence.

THE AFFAIRS IN MY OFFICE

I spend my days listening to the details of other people's affairs, trying to understand why they would be willing to risk so much for so little. I can't collect truly scientific data on it, because I'm not in a position to choose my patients—they choose me because they are doing things that aren't working for them. My patients are not a random sample of the society as a whole. They are far more affluent, far better educated, far more concerned with the quality of their lives and relationships than the average. They are also smarter and saner than the average person, otherwise they wouldn't come to me or some other psychotherapist for help. These people are therefore not representative of the population as a whole. But they may be representative of people who come to family psychiatrists with crises of infidelity.

I examined the last 100 adulterous couples I'd seen in my practice. Even my selection of these 100 couples is not a fair representation of my practice, in that I chose only those couples on whom I had some follow-up data. I did not ask the same questions in the same ways each time, and I have undoubtedly biased the manner in which people have told me about themselves and their lives. So these aren't scientific enough to be considered statistics. (Actually, my sample might be 104 adulterous marriages because two of the men had come to me while screwing around on three successive wives each. I counted only the first marriage. Even the process of choosing which to include involves a value judgment.) Still, my experience with other people's affairs may be of interest to you, as it has been to me.

All of these people had come in originally with a problem that included infidelity, though some of them did not know it. Some came as couples, some came alone, some sent their children in first. In these families, at least one person knew there was an affair going on, though other family members might not know what was going wrong in the family. Some of these people did not think of the affairs as part of the problem. (In somewhat the same way that the Trobriand Islanders have sex and have babies but make no connection between sex and reproduction, many in our society have affairs and get divorces and make no connection between infidelity and marital disruption.) It is likely that there are many people out there who have affairs, keep them secret, and consider them normal behavior. They have no idea whether the affairs affect the marriages, for better or worse, as they don't experience crises of infidelity and don't come to therapy about it. And they don't come to therapy about their divorces. Apparently, both infidelity and divorce are part of their expectable routine, but therapy is not.

I have no idea how many adulterous couples I have seen unknowingly for other problems. People may have had many more affairs that they didn't get around to mentioning to me. And it may even be that some of the reported affairs never took place and were "confessed" for any number of purposes in the marital interaction. But the experiences of these hundred couples, and others like them, have influenced how I view the phenomenon.

Observing Infidelity

In these hundred cases, sixty of the initial adulterers were male, forty female. The male/female ratio fits the usual estimated ratio of male to female adulterers. What that means to me is that male affairs are just as likely as female affairs to create the sort of problems that bring people to therapy.

Eight of the cuckold wives and four of the cuckold husbands then had rebound or revenge affairs while still in the marriage . . . openly, angrily, defiantly, and clearly intended as punishment of the straying spouse. Many others, of course, had relationships during periods of separation, and while a few people reacted to sexual activities during marital separations as if they were infidelities too, I didn't count those. There was no ideal consensus on the definition of infidelity, and some couples spent much of their time together debating the matter of what would and what would not be considered an infidelity.

Twenty-five in my sample assumed that everyone had affairs, or at least everyone of their gender. Most of these were males. The few women in this category assumed all men were adulterous and wanted equal rights in the matter.

Only ten, half men and half women, were in sexually dead marriages, though many others thought the marital sex rather routine and unexciting. Many more, thirty of them, again about half men and half women, found the sex at home acceptable but complained of having little or no intimacy. Affairs were thus three times more likely to be the pursuit of a buddy than the pursuit of a better orgasm.

Seventy had more than one extramarital partner. The adulterous men had a larger number and variety of partners, and were more likely to choose strangers. Almost all of the women, and the majority of the men, stuck with people they knew, including co-workers, family friends, and relatives.

Of the thirty with only one affair, half reacted to their one affair with revulsion, shame, or panic. The other half instantly fell in love.

Six of the adulterers had partners of more than one gender. Three of the men had only homosexual affairs, two of the men and one of the women had both homosexual and heterosexual affairs. Both the cuckold and the infidel in these marriages made much of the distinction, seeing homosexual affairs as compulsory and heterosexual ones as voluntary. I'm less impressed with the difference.

A most interesting way of categorizing these cases was in terms of the timing of the initial affair, when it occurred in the course of the marriage. Twenty-three of the affairs began in the first two years of marriage, forty-three between two and ten years, and thirty-four after ten years of marriage. These three groups represented quite different patterns, and quite different outcomes.

Early Affairs

Those who began secret affairs in the first two years of marriage were almost all (twenty-one) men. They didn't seem to like marriage, and they rebelled against it or disregarded it. They may have liked sex, but they didn't like women. They didn't get attached enough to any woman to be faithful to her for very long. They didn't seem to get particularly attached to their affairees. None of those who divorced over these early affairs married the first affairee. Most of the people who married a subsequent affairee have already divorced.

Early affairs are a bad prognostic sign. Most of these people do not believe in marriage, though they do it often. All the people with multiple adulterous marriages began their affairs early. They ran through the whole marriage and divorce process at frantic speed. Most of these marriages were the second or third one for the infidel, and repeated the pattern of the previous marriage. Of the twenty-three marriages in which affairs began early, seventeen ended in divorce. Of the few that survived this pattern, four did so by proceeding as if nothing had happened, with the secret infidelities continuing. Some of these men forbade their wives to mention the matter again, with repercussions if they did.

No man in this sample, and few in my experience, began infidelities early, continued them secretly for years, and then became a faithful husband, to this wife or any subsequent one. And those few who did give up their infidelities did so only after extraordinary and dramatic changes in their lives. In one case, the man had a paralyzing stroke, in another he ended years of intermittent craziness by going on lithium for his manic-depression. It is as if the men who begin their infidelities early are terrified of female control, and must escape it quickly and often. They are, to say the least, poor marriage risks.

Late Affairs

Thirty-four of these affairs occurred in long-standing marriages after a decade or more of marital fidelity. Half of the infidels were male and half female. These were almost all (thirty-three) first marriages—people who believe in marital fidelity don't often divorce. These people treated their marriages with respect and tenacity, and they then did the same with their affairs, usually the first and only sex partner they had had outside their marriage. These were the only people likely to get involved in an affair, get a divorce, and marry the affairee. All but one or two of these people with a history of marital fidelity ended up in stable, faithful relationships, with either the original or the subsequent partner. This group believed in marriage, and they stuck it out. Some of the marriages broken by these affairs were really quite comfortable and compatible relationships. Some of the marriages, and some of the stable affairs and second marriages, were truly awful. But these are monogamous people, and they mate for life with either their first or their second partner.

These affairs were torturous experiences for the infidels, who were often stuck halfway between two partners. Half (sixteen) of this group got divorces, and half of those (eight) married their affair partners. These people are so tenacious about their commitments that half of them actually made their remarriages work. Those who couldn't overcome all the disadvantages of turning an affair into a marriage sometimes gave up and went back to the first marriage. These people took sex personally and didn't change partners comfortably.

Affairs in Mid-Marriage

Forty-three of the marriages were from two to ten years old when the infidelities began. These were almost all (forty) first marriages. The infidels were equally likely to be male or female. Often in these marriages (ten), both partners were having affairs. The marriages were problematic. This group struggled with their marriages. They didn't take their marriages frivolously, and they didn't take their affairs seriously. They tried everything, but they couldn't seem to make their marriages work. Sometimes these people saw the affairs as efforts to escape the marriage, sometimes they saw the affairs as efforts to stabilize the marriage, and sometimes they saw the affairs as efforts to survive the marriage. The emotional energy was still in the marriage. These people might try to fancy themselves in love with their affair partner, but they didn't often feel that for long. The storminess and instability of these marriages keeps the statistics on outcome in flux.

These people were often stuck, not between two equally attractive relationships, but in one relationship they couldn't tolerate and couldn't leave. Fewer than half (twenty) of the couples actually divorced, though they talked about it a lot. Only a third (thirteen) of the time did even one partner remarry, and rarely (three) to the affairee. This group included seven couples who divorced but are either living together or are intermittently together and talking of remarriage.

Overall, fifty-three of the hundred adulterous marriages ended in divorce, but a few still flirt with reconciliation, and forty-seven remain together, though a few are shaky. By contrast, it is rather unusual in my practice for nonadulterous marriages to end in divorce. It does happen sometimes when one spouse is alcoholic or violent, but the percentage is very low.

The Keepers of the Secret

Some of these couples managed to go through their crisis of infidelity, and even made a pass through therapy, without ending the marriage or changing the pattern. There were eighteen marriages in which the cuckold was never told explicitly about the affair. Four quickly divorced without confession or explanation, leaving me and their family disoriented. They seemed to be following their lawyers' advice, to lie and run rather than to admit anything that might be used against them later. Some of those who were in such a hurry to escape then made a try at reconciliation once the financial arrangements of the divorce were secured.

Ten of these marriages belonged to a category assumed to be far more frequent than I find it to be—the sexually dead marriage that is unilaterally "open." The sexless partner gives the still sexual partner implicit permission to take his or her sexual needs elsewhere. These ten weren't able to confess and explain, so they didn't breach the great distance of their essentially sexless marriages. They sometimes tried, and perhaps actually said the words, and the sexless spouse would act as if it had not been said, or forget it before the next meeting. These marriages were determinedly sexless, and the adulterous mate had implicit permission to have affairs, but only so long as the sexless mate didn't have to deal with it or know about it. In these cases, the infidel tried to heat up a long cold marriage, and the effort was rejected. (I might add that it is unnecessary for anyone to make any effort to keep the infidelity secret in these marriages, and the assumption that affairs should be kept secret because this 10 percent of cuckolds does not want to know keeps information from the 90 percent who do want to know. This deliberately sexless 10 percent have their own ways of dealing with unpleasant realities and do not need our help, as they ignore whatever news or information they choose.)

Four amateur adulterers had an affair, experienced it as an individual crisis for which they sought help, knew it had little to do with their marriage, did not confess, did not seek change in the marriage, and returned to the marriage in the expectation of future fidelity. Such people are anxious, don't really trust their marriage, and fancy themselves to be more committed to it than their spouse. They really believe that their spouse is just looking for an excuse to leave them, and the spouse can never provide enough reassurance.

The Happily Married Adulterers

A small number (one in this sample, though I have seen others) are attempting to maintain a sexually intact marriage to an unsuspecting spouse with whom they find no problem, while expecting to supplement the marriage with secret infidelities. Such marriages are sexually active, but emotionally distant. They involve patronizing protection of a spouse perceived as rather childlike. The marriages are determinedly unequal.

The small number of people who are secretly promiscuous and "happily" married may not be as misleading as one might assume. I'm sure it is more than 1 percent, though probably not much. I don't see many couples who tell me that this is what they are doing, and I wouldn't expect to, but I also see individuals who come in alone and tell me secrets with the expectation of confidentiality. I have seen people individually who live this way, assuming the spouse is unaware of their extramarital sex. Yet when I see such a spouse or such a couple, I usually learn that the spouse knows, and would rather have the secret pattern continue than explore changes in the relationship or make some decision about continuing the marriage. These relationships are not very honest and not very flexible, and they are not very equal. So both spouses let the pattern continue, even though they are uncomfortable with it and it destroys the intimacy of the marriage. This is supposed to be a common pattern in many societies and ethnic groups, but the spouse's permission is implied.

I assume that the promiscuous married out there in the real world are like those who come to my office. They must either have explicit or (far more frequently) implicit permission, and live secret lives with little intimacy. They are not likely to seek therapy, except under pressure, and they are not likely to be more open with a therapist than they are with a spouse. Such people, doubting that they could find either sex or intimacy, or permission to seek these elsewhere, arrange to be unhappily married while pretending to be happily married.

The Reasons People Give

What reasons did these people give for having affairs? The question was always asked, of course, and the initial answer was likely to be shallow and naive. The answers became increasingly complex as therapy proceeded, making the information somewhat unreliable.

Some insisted there was no problem, so explanations were unnecessary. Initially, twenty-five assumed everyone had affairs and felt culturally compelled to do so. A few cited ethnic customs, one quoted scriptural demand, and most noted that their parents had been adulterous. All but two of these were male. Five proclaimed themselves bisexual and therefore biologically condemned to promiscuity.

By contrast, some gave quite specific reasons. Twelve people, more often female, said they were reacting to a spouse's affair. The rebound affairs were sometimes actively encouraged or even arranged by the previously adulterous spouse. Ten, five women and five men, were married to people who did not like sex and preferred that the more sexually inclined partner go outside the marriage. The spouses might or might not assist in finding new sex partners. In either case, the spouses knew all they wanted to know about the affairs. This was 10 percent of the total affairs in this sample, a sizable fraction, but far smaller than is traditionally assumed.

Far more often, what was missing at home was not sex at all, but a bonding, engulfing intimacy. Thirty were getting sex at home, and found the marriage tolerable, but complained of lack of intimacy or excitement or romance. Some of this got extremely vague and contradictory. Most had "fallen in love" with someone else *before* deciding there was a marriage problem and seemed to be comparing the marriage with the in-love experience. Their marriage just didn't hold their attention and preoccupy them the way the affair did.

A few thought that they were married to people who weren't good enough for them. Two were married to people they considered intellectually inferior. Four were married to people they found physically repulsive, two of the wives grossly obese, one wife "not pretty enough for a man in my position," and one husband with a bizarrely oversized penis. Far more frequent than the spouse's inferiority was the complaint that the spouse acted superior and made them feel inferior.

Thirteen said they had affairs because they were angry with the spouse. Reasons for this anger varied from "She/he fusses at the kids" to "She/he is only interested in the kids," from "He/she works all the time" to "He/she won't get a job." Some of these disqualified the marriage because "we were too young," "we were too old," "she was pregnant," "she told me she was pregnant and wasn't," "I don't believe in marriage."

Four had not gone much further in their explorations than whether they were or were not "in love." These people, all female, were concerned because if they were in-love, then the infidelity was perfectly acceptable; however, they would have to leave their marriage. On the other hand, if they were not in-love, then they had committed a terrible act, and they were evil, out-of-control people who were in need of help. Their one consolation then was that they would not have to go through the trauma of a divorce. These women saw "love" as a solid, rather than as a liquid or a gas. It was a concrete block that was either there or not there, and it was determinant of everything else in life.

Four more, half male and half female, were baffled by their actions and insisted "it just happened." These people seriously questioned their sanity and stability. They did not consider their infidelity appropriate behavior, wanted to distance themselves from it, and fix whatever was out of order in themselves that would lead them to do such an unaccustomed, unexpected, unacceptable thing.

Politeness emerged as a major reason for male infidelity. Six men described it something like this. "I never went looking for it. She/they came on to me. So I had to do it. It would have been rude not to." These men seemed to believe it would be both impolite and unmanly to refuse a woman sexually, as if it is up to the women to set sexual limits. Some of these people saw the adultery as an act of politeness to someone with whom they felt an unexpected intimacy.

A few were quite specific about the reasons for having an affair. These people, all female, set out to seduce a powerful man from whom they expected quite specific favors. One needed money, one hoped for a promotion, one wanted to get into a social club. Sometimes the spouse knew and encouraged the activity, sometimes the spouse didn't.

Some of the reasons for affairs were rather idiosyncratic. One

woman, believing performance in bed was an indicator of performance on the job, screened her husband's prospective employees.
She was apparently remarkably accurate in choosing which prospective candidates he should hire, but never revealed the process
or the criteria by which she made her evaluations. One young man
had an affair in order to impress his heroically adulterous father-in-
law. One woman insisted she had affairs during episodes of split
personality. A man claimed he was kidnapped by visitors from outer
space and offered sexual opportunities with them. He had felt it his
patriotic and scientific duty to investigate the situation fully.

These people were not, for the most part, mentally ill. Six were
married to overtly psychotic spouses, spouses they didn't want to
leave but with whom there was no possibility of either intimacy or
give and take. They saw the affair as a crutch to help them get
through the day. Only one of the infidels was himself obviously
stark raving mad. Several got into affairs somewhat accidentally
while drunk. Several others said they got into affairs because they
were married to alcoholics. (It wasn't clear how they expected an
affair to cure a spouse's alcoholism, but since they didn't believe
anything would help, they decided to do something that they knew
wouldn't help but would at least give them some satisfaction.)

People with manic-depression, sometimes called bipolar illness,
have mood swings in which they get stuck in a mood for long
periods of time. They may be depressed, and withdraw hopelessly
from life, or they may be manic, the exact opposite of depression,
and embrace life with amazing nonstop gusto. This is a chemical
disorder that is easily and effectively treated, but some people like
the manic highs so much that they don't get it treated. It is fairly
typical of manics to leave home in the throes of some intense
romance, the more ridiculously unsuitable the better. Three of the
adulterers in this sample were manics.

Who were chosen for affairs? Only thirty-one (sixteen women,
fifteen men) of the adulterers limited themselves to a single acknowledged affair, of whatever duration. Some of these involved
only one sex act, others lasted for decades. First-time adulterers
preferred friendly partners. Two men chose houseguests. One man
and one woman chose family members, and sixteen chose close

family friends. Four housewives chose workmen or instructors under their employ. Six had solo affairs with people they knew from their jobs. All but one of those with single affairs chose people with whom they already had established intimate relationships. Amateur adulterers may establish intimacy first, have sex later.

Professional adulterers found their partners everywhere. Those with multiple affairs found partners at work, in the social circle, and while traveling. Two favored prostitutes, two advertised, one found people in bushes in the park, and one called numbers he found on restroom walls. The more affairs people have, the more they seem to want to keep it impersonal.

How did the wife's affairs differ from the husband's? Not as much as one might have guessed. The biggest difference—and it is not an impressively remarkable difference—was that women tended a little more to have solo affairs. The women were more likely to choose people they knew well, more likely to believe they should be faithful, and less likely to cite cultural factors in their motivation. They were just as likely to complain of lack of sex, no more likely to cite lack of intimacy.

I could attempt a generalization that women may expect more from marriage and may be more easily dissatisfied with it, while men expect less from marriage, concern themselves less with whether they are satisfied with it or not, and make their decisions about infidelities without conscious reference to their level of marital satisfaction. While most people recognize that they have affairs because they are not totally satisfied with their lives, men and women experience their dissatisfactions differently. Women rarely located the deficiency that led to the affair in themselves. Men often blamed the affair on their sense of defeat in other sectors of their lives.

The Outcome

Of the hundred marriages in this sample, despite the couple's obvious dedication to the process of straightening out the mess and my best efforts, fifty-three ended in divorce. Contrary to a popular notion, divorce is not more likely if it is the wife who is unfaithful.

But divorce is more likely if both are being unfaithful and there is no one left at home to tend the marriage.

Only one person left because his spouse had a solo affair. This was a messy and unpleasant situation, in which a woman had an affair with her cocaine dealer, became addicted, pregnant, and herpetic in the relationship, appeared with the cocaine dealer around all the husband's colleagues and relatives, and spent all their savings. When the couple did get back together, they really tried to make the marriage work, but too much damage had been done. I think the ultimate failure of this reconciliation came because the wife insisted upon saving hidden mementos of the affair. This was one case in which a little guilt might have helped.

In general, people just don't leave marriages because their partner has been unfaithful. They leave because *they themselves* are being unfaithful, perhaps as revenge for their partner's affairs, but usually not. The decision to divorce was made by the infidel in thirty-seven cases, by the cuckold in only thirteen. In three of these decisions, it was unclear what anyone wanted and what anyone was doing, and the divorce, like everything else in those marriages, just happened, with the right hand not knowing what the left foot was doing. Some of the cuckolds became infidels before deciding to leave, others had chosen their next relationship but had not quite consummated it.

Apparently, it is not difficult to be married to someone who has had an affair. But it is maddening to try to love someone who, by the best prediction, is going to have affairs in the future. It may be possible to stay married to such a person, but only if you hate him or her. Things have to be pretty bad for people to leave a marriage, unless they already have someplace else to go.

PATTERNS OF INFIDELITY

These hundred cases fall naturally into four groups, groups of near equal size in my practice, though I doubt if the four syndromes would occur in equal frequency in the wild. Subsequently, I have noticed that the other affairs coming through my office fall naturally into these four syndromes. Sometimes, as the definition of infidelity becomes more complex, I will see an affair that is unlike anything I've ever seen before. But almost all affairs are just variations on these four themes.

The four groups are (1) Accidental Infidelity, (2) Philandering, (3) Romantic Affairs, and (4) Marital Arrangements. *Accidental infidelities* are those unplanned, unfamiliar sex acts that "just happen," leaving everyone disoriented. Perhaps most initial infidelities are like this, and what happens for the rest of one's life will depend on how the amateur infidel defines the situation. If it feels comfortable and "natural," the amateur infidel may then become a philanderer. *Philandering* is that habitual sexual activity that seems natural to the philanderer, and is motivated more by fear of and lust for the "opposite sex" than by any forces within the marriage or the immediate sexual relationship. *Romantic affairs* are those crazy in-love states that cloud people's minds and make them forget their marriage and family. *Marital arrangements* are efforts to maintain a distance that is required by one of the partners. They range from sexual supplements to flamboyant revenge affairs that keep stormy marriages in a state of intense passion and jealousy. The sex goes outside the marriage, but the emotion is still directed in.

Simply, the four syndromes are divided on the basis of the direction of the emotional energy. Accidental infidels know they are out of order, and may blame themselves or the circumstances as they recoil from the situation. Their primary emotions are guilt and anxiety.

Philanderers are obsessed with gender. Mostly men, they depersonalize both the woman at home and the woman in the bed at the moment, as they have just one more in their long series of victories over the "opposite sex" as a homogenous whole. They are thinking mostly about bodies and genitals, and their primary emotion is anger. It may well be that the philanderers are the predominant infidels out there in the real world, but they are the least likely to come in for therapy of their own volition.

In romantic affairs, the emotional energy is in the romance, and the rest of the world might as well not exist. The emotion here is "love," but the problem is the absence of all other emotions that would be appropriate, and perhaps even necessary for survival.

In marital arrangements, the emotional energy is still in the marriage, and the specific emotions may be quite complex, though there may be some despair about the disjointed nature of the domestic situation. There are many different patterns of marital arrangements, and many are not really infidelities in the sense that they are not quite secret.

Infidelity comes in many varieties, but these overlapping and intersecting patterns represent the most common garden varieties of the phenomenon. These four patterns reveal the state of affairs.

8 / Accidental Infidelity
(It Just Happened)

"Accidents will occur in the best regulated families."
CHARLES DICKENS, *DAVID COPPERFIELD*

People really don't go looking for infidelity, at least not the first time. They stumble upon it. It is nearly always entered into by accident. It just happens.

The word "accidental," according to Webster, means "happening by chance, or unexpectedly, or not according to the usual course of things." I don't mean to imply here that these acts of infidelity occurred involuntarily, but that they were incidents that were outside the usual patterns of behavior, happening in extraordinary situations, or offhandedly and without consideration of the consequences. They happened carelessly. And they take on significance not because of any important reasons for which they happened, but because the participants, particularly the infidel, can't forget them.

When I listen to stories of accidental infidelity, I am sometimes reminded of W. C. Field's famous apology: "I'm sorry I was late for this appointment, but on my way here I was taken unexpectedly drunk." Accidental infidelities too may occur unexpectedly. Unplanned, they take at least one of the participants by surprise.

These accidental infidels do not consider their behavior appropriate. They don't want to leave their marriage, or threaten it, or necessarily bring about any change in it. Their marriage, like all marriages, is boring sometimes, frustrating sometimes, infuriating sometimes, but not to the point that the infidel has seriously considered getting out.

Accidental infidels ordinarily don't expect to continue the adulterous experiences. They don't feel in love with their affair partner; in fact they may find the whole business very awkward. The relationship with the affairee may have been friendly before the sex, but afterward it becomes protective, embarrassing, or downright hostile. The sex has made the relationship too close, too much of a secret alliance, like partners in crime. There may even be a panicky sense of inextricable, and not completely welcome, bonding with the affair partner. Although there may be a clear attraction to the affairee, that is seen as a danger rather than love. If, in the aftermath of such a dalliance, the infidel justifies the act by defining the situation as being "in-love" with the affairee (which sometimes happens in the postcoital confusion), that changes the situation drastically.

The people who commit these accidental infidelities know they are doing it to themselves. They may blame their seductive affair partner for putting them in an awkward situation, but they know they have done something they consider wrong. They may treat the episode as a careless mistake. It happened not because the infidel was mean or perverted or self-destructive or sadistic. These people were merely, for a moment, too curious, too polite, too accommodating, too friendly. They may just have been lucky or unlucky that day. And when they try to explain it, they realize "it just happened."

ACCIDENTS HAPPEN

I find myself thinking of infidelity in somewhat the same way I think of automobile accidents. Some people drive recklessly, not really thinking about the possible consequences; they may even be under the influence of something that clouds their judgment. Some people are just irresponsible drivers, expecting the other drivers to be careful enough to keep them out of danger. Other people are actively suicidal; they've had enough of this life. But most drivers want to live, they generally take reasonable care of themselves, and protect themselves from the usual dangers, yet sometimes they find themselves momentarily distracted. Before they know it, they hear the sound of squealing tires and crunching metal and honking horns. And just as the accident is happening, and it is too late to stop it, they know their lives are now outside their control.

Over and over, as I explore with people their first infidelity, I get the same story: "It just happened." I've heard that line many times, and I've had trouble relating it to anything in my own sexual experience. Yet I do recall my first and only automobile accident. It did indeed just happen. As fate would have it, my first automobile accident also led me through a labyrinth to someone else's crisis of infidelity—which undoubtedly explains why sexual accidents and traffic accidents seem merged in my mind.

The accident happened like this. I had had my driver's license for a week. It was a rainy July afternoon. I was hurrying home in the family car—a green 1948 Hudson—to show my parents what I had bought for myself with my sixteenth birthday money. I'd been driving on country roads since I was thirteen, but not all the way to the big city of Montgomery, twelve miles away, so the drive was not second nature for me. As I turned left across the highway onto the dirt road that led to our house, I was thinking about the enlarger I'd just bought for my darkroom. I ran right into the side of a car headed south. The highway patrolman too seemed preoccupied with my new enlarger. He examined it before he even checked on the other driver trapped upside down in his car. He finally decided that the oncoming car should have had his lights on in the rain, so it wasn't totally my fault, and I didn't get a ticket.

I knew better—I just wasn't paying attention. I can still remember my humiliation as the crowd gathered and everyone tried to pull the poor man out of his car rolled over in the ditch. Traffic must have been backed up for miles, and they all knew, I'm sure, that I had done something really stupid. Fortunately, though both cars were totaled, no one was hurt. I wanted to go somewhere dark and hide, but the highway patrolman invited himself over to have me use my enlarger to blow up the nude pictures he had taken secretly of his girlfriend.

He arrived, with his wife and family of all things, and he came in while they stayed out in the yard. I realized he was blackmailing me, but I did want to see the pictures. To my shock, the subject turned out to be a full-bodied country girl only a few years older than I. I had spent the past summer at the town's swimming pool watching her rise from the water in her skimpy white bathing suit. Now here she was, without the white bathing suit, smiling at my blackmailing highway patrolman, whose wife and baby were sitting in the swing in our family yard!

My loyalties were so divided, my sense of order and propriety was reeling. Thinking about that experience still confuses me— what was I supposed to do? I didn't know, so I just enjoyed looking at that girl in the buff. The highway patrolman was an avid photographer, and he came back a few more times with more pictures to enlarge. He told me the story of how he got into this awkward position, how he had gone to the scene of a fight after a minor traffic accident, and had arrested this big drunk country girl, and how she took off her clothes right there in the patrol car, and how he didn't know what to do, except that he couldn't rightly arrest her after he was out of uniform, and by the time he'd put his clothes back on, he was too confused to know what to do, so he took her home. And then he called her the next day when he realized she had his badge, and it all happened again, and now he was hooked.

I never want to go through most aspects of that experience again, so I'm careful to look when I'm driving, and so far I've not had another accident. I realize I miss some potentially interesting experiences by driving carefully. There are fascinating people in all those passing cars, and unless I crash into them, I'm not likely to get to know them. But one advantage of my business is that the supporting cast in my life is quite a varied and stimulating one, and I don't need any more interesting people than I've already got.

I now drive a 1971 Jaguar XJ6, not very practical, but I'm used to it. It has several significant defects, the most important being a tendency to pull sharply toward the left. In fact, left to its own devices it would jerk over and crash head-on into the oncoming traffic. To prevent this disaster, I have to keep my right hand resting lightly on the steering wheel. It requires no strength or skill to prevent the collision, it only requires a gentle, steadying hand. If I ceased to monitor it, that would be suicidal. In looking at these disastrous accidental infidelities, the issue is not *why* the car was pulling to the left—that is the nature of the mechanism. The question is why the driver removed that steadying hand, and permitted the inevitable to happen.

Let's look at some of the reasons why a driver would take a steadying hand off the wheel.

SEXUAL INNOCENCE

There has to be a first time for everything. No one ever forgets that first sexual experience, though most would like to forget it. The first time is rarely good, and often one of the most humiliating and degrading experiences a person ever goes through.

I'm not sure when is the right time and who is the right partner for a first sexual experience. The idea that sex should occur only after the wedding ceremony was proposed for some time, and now seems to have been discarded. I occasionally see older couples who were both virgins at marriage. Some of them seem happy about that, and others blame various problems on it. In those marriages in which one was a virgin and the other had had some experience, that experience, however minimal, determined who would be the family sexual expert.

Back in the days of the double standard, it was traditional for boys to get their sexual experiences early, often, and either from sexual professionals or from people who were seen as having lower social status, thus "unsuitable" for marriage. "Marriageable" females were often sexually inexperienced; if a girl were known to have had sex, her "reputation" was ruined. Girls were valued for their virginity, and were expected to have no sexual experience prior to marriage. Their greatest asset would be their innocence. Naturally, they would marry quite early.

The glorification of virginity led to marriages of sexual imbalance, between men who might be casual about sex and trained at promiscuity and philandering and women who were amateurs at sex but professionals in the antisexual atmosphere of romance, in which sex becomes so special it can no longer be physical. It is not surprising that when the double standard was in full force, marriage could not be very sexual, and might have to be supplemented from outside. I remember the man from South America who explained to his wife that his infidelities were for her benefit, protecting her from the animal nature of his sex with other women, so he could have pure sex with her. As he put it, "These other women are just parish churches, where I cleanse myself of these sins, but you are the great cathedral, and I must enter you in a state of awed holiness —but only on special occasions." Because of the wife's upbringing, she saw this as a compliment.

When a couple marries young, with little or no sexual experience, they are sexual amateurs. They could, of course, get good at sex—it really isn't that difficult a skill for a couple to master if they practice hard and get their signals straight. But it seems likely that they won't learn to do it very effectively together without practice. What usually suffers in amateur sex is female arousal, and thus female orgasm. The couple, if they know the sex isn't working, are likely to find this frustrating. There will be a fear of incompatibility, a question of whether it might be different with someone else, and a temptation to take a turn with another partner. These doubts lead to questions that are hard to answer safely.

All of that is supposed to have changed, and chastity belts, emotional or physical, are no longer the most practical way to keep our daughters from getting pregnant. Now we're not as afraid that our daughters will bring home illegitimate babies as we are that they and the kids will bounce back on us after their husbands run off with a more sexual woman. So now women are expected to become sexually skilled before they go into marriage. And one hopes these days that every couple going into marriage has already established a high level of sexual compatibility.

Sex is different for those people who have spent their youth giving and receiving orgasms with friendly playmates, so that it becomes a pleasant but not very special pastime. Like those South Sea islanders Margaret Mead used to tell us about, children who grow up developing their sexual skills end up being quite comfortable with sex, quite good at it, and usually monogamous—because the relationship rather than the genitality becomes the part that is special.

There are still couples who attempt to maintain a double standard, and there are still women who are raised to maintain their sexual innocence until they marry a man who believes in a double standard. Such a marriage is, on the face of it, sexually incompatible, so some go into it expecting to have their sexual adventures later and elsewhere. Either men or women deprived of sexual experience prior to marriage may forever distrust what they are getting and may forever wonder what they are missing.

CURIOSITY

Curiosity can be a significant drive for innocents. But curiosity can drive the experienced also. Even those who have had vast experience may think it wasn't enough or was the wrong kind. People vary in the amount of sexual experience it takes to satisfy their curiosity. The same curiosity that can kill a cat can certainly seduce a human being. The curiosity grows, to the point that the curious innocent may be easy prey for passing seducers. People who missed out on such things earlier may drive themselves nuts until they can experience a threesome, an orgy, a professional, a giant, a dwarf, something homosexual, something animal, vegetable, or mineral—whatever they might have missed. Of course, some people may require each of these things, or all of them in various combinations, or even some really kinky stuff in hopes of discovering what the sexual excitement might be that drives other people to such risky behavior. The issue is not necessarily that the sexually curious are sexually dissatisfied, but that they are preoccupied with the notion that there must be something even better than what they know already. After years of marital fidelity in a sexually stimulating society, the curious, whatever their sexual training, may want to find out what they are missing.

People ask me if there is an age at which the curiosity is most likely to reach the level of overflow and lead to accidental infidelities. Certainly, in my generation, we have associated this with midlife, when there is so much awareness of having reached the summit, of having gone over the hill, and of losing the chance to turn back and see what has been missed. It seems to me that younger generations, having had more sexual experience earlier, don't have much sexual curiosity as they age. They've been to the orgy and they don't need to go back again. The highs they are more likely to seek may be the emotional ones. They may want a touch of romance before it feels too late.

A man had been faithful throughout his marriage. He liked sex, and he thought what he was getting at home was as good as it came. There was certainly nothing wrong with his marriage, or indeed with any other aspect of his life. But he had been hearing stories from his buddies about all their sexual carryings on with the women at work, and even with prostitutes at the hotel next to his office building. He wondered if he might be missing something. Anyway, it was Christmas, the time of year when he had to face the fact that there was no Santa Claus, and he was feeling a bit deprived. At the annual office party, a woman noticed that he seemed a bit down, and she offered herself as a gift of Christmas cheer. At first he felt embarrassed and wanted to escape, but then he started getting curious. He thought it over for a few minutes, and watched the woman leave with one of his friends.

He doesn't recall making a decision to do what he did next. It just happened. He walked to the hotel next door. There he asked the concierge for a prostitute. One was quickly provided and took him to a room, where she performed her services with great deliberation, efficiency, and speed, leaving him feeling like a real chump. He put the room, the woman, and even the tip on his credit card and went to a movie for the rest of the afternoon. He told his wife about the movie, but she didn't find out about the prostitute until the American Express bill arrived. She carried on a bit over the next few weeks, and he decided that next Christmas he'd get himself a compact disc player instead. His curiosity had passed.

POLITENESS

Years ago, a friend from college called me in a panic. He was living in another city, but he had to see me right away, and he couldn't talk with anyone else. He got to my office, in the midst of an anxiety attack. I couldn't imagine what would be this traumatic. He had always been the calmest of people. I suppose the primary quality I'd always associated with this large, handsome friend was his politeness. He had been much pursued by women, and could never tolerate the idea of doing anything to displease a woman. He had married the woman who had pursued him most vigorously, and he had remained passively pleasing while he enjoyed her eager attention.

He had gone to a business meeting out of town, and had had too much to drink and had woken up in bed with a strange woman. He had no idea who she was or what had happened the night before, but the young woman was acting very familiar. She grabbed him, and behaved as if she expected a sexual response. He made a halfhearted effort to excuse himself, but she acted as if his withdrawal would have hurt her feelings, so he did as he always did: whatever a woman asked of him. The sex that resulted was not good sex, but it got better over the next few days. The better the sex got, the worse my friend felt. This was not what he wanted to happen.

To his relief, my friend learned that the strange woman was married and had no intention of continuing the relationship past that week. So he escaped. And then he started thinking about the meaning of this. He'd been married ten years, had three children, considered himself satisfactorily, if not ecstatically, happy with his wife. He'd never been unfaithful before, and had certainly never expected to be. What was wrong with him? Was he out of his mind? Was he in love with this other woman? Was he unhappily married without knowing it? Or is this what men do? As he anx-

iously described this extraordinary happening, as he anxiously out-
lined the possible explanations, I realized that these were questions
he needed to be asking his wife, and I sent him home to ask her
to go through the crisis with him.

The crisis did not turn out well. He did go home and tell his wife
what had happened, and she comforted him and they were close,
and that felt good. They realized they needed therapy. I did not
see the couple, and they said the reason was that they lived so far
away. But I knew the wife feared that I would be on my friend's
side—a common error people make in choosing therapists, assuming that a therapist who cares about you will support the point of
view of your blamelessness, even if such support will mislead you
and wreck your life. People have friends to tell them their lives are
not their fault; therapists, at least good therapists, have to deliver
the bad news.

Instead they went to a therapist in their city, a man who spent
the next few years convincing my friend that his desire for further
infidelities was normal and should be respected, and convincing his
wife that she was too possessive and controlling and therefore
responsible for his behavior. In other words, his infidelity was
normal, but her fault. Needless to say, that led to an impasse, and
eventually to a divorce. The therapy had turned this friend, who
had suffered a common household accident, into a philanderer.
And it had turned his formerly outspoken wife into someone who
was afraid to trust her own reality testing. It has been years since
the divorce. She has not remarried. He has done so several times.

I saw my friend recently: he has had things done to himself to
make him look quite young. His experiences with open marriage
have failed. He's just gone through another divorce. I told him I
was writing this book, and owed a lot of what I know about infidelity to him. He wanted me to tell everyone how frustrating it
makes life to treat one's sexual impulses as if they took priority over
the rest of reality. He thinks he handled the postaffair crisis badly.
He knew he was doing something nutty, letting his politeness take
priority over his commitments, but he found appealing comfort in
his therapist's idea that his behavior was normal and that he could
do it without consequences if he convinced his wife that his affairs

were her fault, caused by her trying too hard to stop them. It was a wonderfully seductive formulation, and he bought it, but it turned out to be very expensive.

Such extreme politeness as that of my friend may seem to belong to another time and place, but I still encounter it with surprising regularity. Many people just don't know how to say no to anyone who seems friendly to them. Though the young woman from *Oklahoma!* who "cain't say no" is far from unique, it is perhaps even more common for males than females to be unable to resist a sexual advance. Little boys used to be taught to be sexually aggressive, as if it were socially required that a gentleman offer his sexual services to a lady, in much the same way in which he would offer her his arm as they walked together. It would be tantamount to insult for a man to neglect to make a sexual pass at his date. Many men even felt compelled to call upon any recent divorcées in the neighborhood to offer their services as handy man and sex partner. Italian men, I understand, have developed these offers of sexual services into an art form, and while it seems to be good for keeping the tourists happy, it is not intended to be taken seriously. The woman is expected to accept the compliment but decline the services.

But there are women who don't decline the polite offer. Some of them are normal women who want sex. Others are "bimbos." The bimbo is the woman too dumb or naive to know she is supposed to resist sexual advances. She is the fantasy object of insecure philanderers, the joke in *Playboy* cartoons. Bimbos are most at home in light comedy, but they exist in the real world too. We usually think of bimbos as being single, but we may think that way because the bimbo can't seem to remember whether she is married or not. They accept sexual offers rather too easily, and sometimes even accept offers that have not actually been made. These round-heeled women are not philanderers, they aren't pursuing these experiences. They just don't resist them. They are merely being agreeable. They're not sure of their worth as people, view themselves as objects for the pleasure of men, and fear they would not be desirable for any purpose other than sex.

If a naive woman assumes that an invitation has been extended, she may accept it, leaving the man in the awkward position of either having to follow through on his offer or admit he was merely trying to pay a pleasant but empty compliment. His manners may be good enough to help him escape gracefully, or he may find no polite option but to follow through.

JUST LUCKY

Some men tried as adolescents to develop their skills as seducers of women, but were never very good at it. Even as they tried, they just never made it as sex objects. They couldn't get laid often, but they found they could get married. They may still feel that their masculinity has not been sufficiently massaged. The world in general has not found them sexually desirable and has not pursued them. They suffer as a result. Such men may be suckers for sexual flattery. When a woman comes on to them, they become disoriented to time, place, and situation, and are transported back to that earlier period when they announced their sexual availability to the world and got few takers. They feel so lucky when a woman likes them that they take a holiday from their usual sanity.

When a man who has gone through life feeling that he is sexually unattractive "lucks up" and has a brief fling and suffers some unpleasant consequences, it comes as a surprise. He may feel no guilt, since he didn't "go looking for it." It may not be his fault, since "she came on to me." The underlying thesis for these men is the classic convention that the decision about sex should be made by the female, and if he should be chosen, he's lucky.

There may be women, married or single, who fall into this category too, women who do not often get chosen for sexual advances, and who deeply appreciate the flattery of the offer. Such people, male or female, may be lecherous, but they aren't philanderers because they lack the talent for it. Of course, if they were attractive enough to be the object of others' sexual attention, that might make them even less likely to have affairs. The offers might be sufficiently flattering so they would not have to test out the sincerity of the invitation by accepting it. People who are considered physically attractive get quite enough sexual offers and learn not to take them personally as compliments. So it is only the sexual beggars who find such an offer "lucky."

Zinnia was plain. She'd never had a date before poor Mervin came along and married her. He wasn't very exciting, but she was sincerely grateful to him. She'd never had sexual flattery from any other man. She didn't really need it, but it would have been nice. She watched the goings on at her office, and she noticed the flirtations. She was very sensitive to them. And she was particularly sensitive to the realization that no one flirted with her. When one of the salesmen brought a flower to each "girl" in the office, he gave her one too. As he gave her the flower, he touched her hand. She said, "Yes. I will." He asked, "Yes, you will what?" She said, "Yes, I'll go to bed with you." He looked stunned and delayed his response a moment too long. She looked as if she were about to cry. He assured her that he wanted her, and he made good on his unmade offer that very night.

FRIENDS IN DEED

Politeness offers less of a problem with strangers than it does with friends, co-workers, neighbors, etc., people with whom one does have a real relationship that one values and wants to keep. Once someone is a friend, and now a friend in need, one has an obligation. How far does friendship obligate us? In *The Big Chill*, Mary Kay Place can't find a suitable man to impregnate her, so she asks best friend Glenn Close to lend her husband, Kevin Kline, for the procedure. The beatific Close does so. We are not given a chance to see how the relationships are affected by this act of friendship, but I left the theater uncomfortable about all the possible complications.

In *Hannah and Her Sisters*, Woody Allen has discovered that he is sterile, but his wife, Mia Farrow, wants children. So they invite over their closest couple friends and request a sperm donation. It is a scene of excruciating embarrassment and, I think, far greater emotional accuracy than its counterpart in *The Big Chill.*

Sometimes the circumstances don't permit people to hold a family conference to determine the limits of friendship, and people have to decide on the spot just how much they are willing to do for their friends in need. These situations don't quite fit the definition for infidelity because they aren't secret, but they do raise questions about the limits of friendship. Off the screen, most of these favors are requested from individuals rather than from the couple.

A common pattern of accidental infidelity occurs when a man and a woman who have worked together or known one another socially for some time find themselves talking more intimately than usual. One or both are married, and they would not have seriously considered having an affair. But then, perhaps some crisis has occurred in one of their lives, maybe her boyfriend has just been arrested, or her dog got run over by the milk truck. Anyway, she feels unusually needy, and collapses on him, making him feel like St. George slaying the dragon. The usual formality is breached, and they talk about things they haven't talked about before. He may even tell her about the time *his* dog got run over. This is not their usual efficient, socially correct conversation. She starts crying. He holds her. It isn't clear whether he says something that makes her think he is recommending sex as therapy for her plight, or whether she mistakenly assumes that is what he has in mind. He doesn't know how it happened, but they are suddenly passionately kissing, and she is just too vulnerable to push away.

He may indeed have made the suggestion of sex. There are men who have had so little experience with intimacy that it feels dangerously sexy when it occurs. These guys may never have had a female friend or confidante, and may think of women only in sexual terms. If a male friend were baring his soul, the guy might suggest that they go work out or have a beer, but since this is a female, he doesn't know anything to offer except sex.

Little girls are taught to say no. Little boys are not. It would be unmacho as well as unfriendly for a gentleman to say no to a lady, even if in sexual situations he knew such a word. Men who can't say "No, thank you" gracefully are at risk for pity affairs with depressed women who have recently lost a lover and need reassurance of their attractiveness.

These pity affairs with old friends are awful, since there is no way to stop them. The desperate one just gets more and more dependent, more and more demanding. There may never be another sex act, yet the affair, i.e., the secret relationship, continues. Getting out of such an affair with a suicidal friend would be tantamount to murder. These St. Georges and Georginas don't really feel in-love—it's more like in-pity. But it is a nice feeling, a feeling of power and goodness and virtue. And when the affair is exposed, the friendly one may be rather baffled at the spouse's anger over this innocent, friendly act of mercy.

ONE OF THE BOYS

Some people, mostly males, are team players. They do whatever the other boys are doing. These are guys whose primary relationship is not with their marital partner, but with their buddies, and their loyalty to their "mates" interferes regularly with their marriage.

These men have a few characteristics in common with philanderers, especially their strong gender loyalty, but they aren't angry with what they see as "the opposite sex." And they don't philander regularly. They are just willing to have sex with a stranger if their friends goad them into it. They may even perform sexually in front of one another, or take turns with the same woman. But they aren't really homosexual at such times; they're at that stage of early adolescence at which boys seem obsessed with comparing penis sizes. They're just Good Buddies.

Typically, the Good Buddy will go out of town on business with a philandering co-worker or boss, and will go along with the companion's hobby of flirting with women. When women come in pairs, the Good Buddy helps out his friend by taking care of the extra woman. Knowing that the Good Buddy would prefer being faithful to his wife, but also knowing how ingratiatingly passive the Good Buddy is, his friends may amuse themselves by persuading or hiring some woman to seduce him. They may arrange to get him drunk, or do whatever they have to to put him into embarrassing situations. The Good Buddy, unlike the philanderer, does not seek out situations to humiliate women. He's just trying to keep his friends from humiliating him.

Good Buddies don't seem to feel much guilt about their occasional infidelities. They know these dalliances have nothing to do with their marriage. Yet the wife must not know about them, because she might then require him to choose between her and his friends. He, in his own sneaky, early adolescent way, would choose his friends. She knows that and is already complaining about it. But he doesn't quite trust his friends, and he lives in the fear that they will in some way leak the news of his sexual exploits, so the secret binds him even closer to his buddies.

These men may someday grow up and become able to decide for themselves whom to have sex with and for what audience, but they might just as easily become philanderers. The secrets of these intermittent dalliances are doing great damage to whatever marital intimacy such immature men can establish. They are already seeing a wife as the enemy, since the wife is in a custody dispute with their friends. The other women are just shuttlecocks in this badminton game.

GOING CRAZY

People who say that they must have been out of their minds to get into an affair may be literally accurate. Those who would not otherwise be unfaithful can have an affair during a psychotic episode. Schizophrenics are not likely to be sexually aggressive, but may be taken in by people who are sexually exploitive. Depressives are expert at driving away those who are trying to get close or offer assistance, but a depressed person may collapse helplessly upon an amateur rescuer who may try everything, even sex, in the effort to be helpful. But it is most likely that a manic psychosis will involve an infidelity. Manics typically have a "great" romance during each manic episode, and the partners for these great romances can be astounding in their inappropriateness. One classic example would be Don Quixote, who mistook the gross servant girl Aldonza for the lovely lady and chaste maiden Dulcinea, and paid extravagant court to her. In *Man of La Mancha,* this is a corrective therapeutic experience for Aldonza, but signifies to even the most casual observer that the old man is daft.

I recall one successful businessman, happily married for decades to a wife he liked, who was subject to manic episodes beginning when he was about forty. During his first episode, the only overt symptom was an affair with a five-times-married alcoholic prostitute and part-time drug dealer. He bought her clothes and a car, and announced wedding plans. She was baffled by this, and while it flattered her at first, she began to find his intense energy exhausting, and finally called for help—even though she realized that when he recovered he would no longer want her. On lithium and back with his wife, he agreed that his loved one was inappropriate, but when he got off his medicine and had another episode a few years later, he tried to go back to her. She knew immediately that this meant he had gone crazy again, and called for help right away. This thoughtful woman and the man's long-suffering wife worked out a way to cooperate in getting the poor man help.

People who are going through crazy episodes seem to have much appeal as affair partners for professional and amateur rescuers. Many men and many women feel a protectiveness akin to love for those who seem vulnerable and needy. These are dangerous attractions, since people who are down will in time either recover and leave you, or get worse and take you with them, or stay the same and either blame you or frustrate you. Dependent people offer a romantic appeal for those who are insecure enough to be flattered by such desperation. Such relationships rarely work out. The doctor-patient relationship works only to enable the patient to recover and no longer need the doctor—it is not the basis for a permanent relationship.

These episodes of going crazy and relying on the sexual kindness of strangers can, if they occur too frequently, begin to look more like adventurous vacations than like fits of incompetence.

Vicky had never met a stranger. She was a successful portrait painter and a hostess of style and charm. She was a social leader whose life centered around the cocktail hour. She and Al had been happily together and faithful for almost twenty years. Vicky's disappearance was shocking. Her reappearance three days later was a relief, of course, but the circumstances were disturbing, especially the fact that she had spent those days in the company of their recently divorced and defrocked alcoholic priest. Vicky and Al decided it was an aberration and chose not to talk about it. Several months later, Vicky disappeared again for a day, and was brought back without explanation by a cab driver, whom Vicky praised for his great kindness. Al worried, but said little.

When Vicky disappeared with a basketball team of men half her age and twice her height, Al finally decided she would have to give up alcohol. He thought it wiser to accompany her to the A.A. meetings.

HAVING A BAD DAY

Someone may be temporarily needy, lonely, isolated—just having a bad day. At such moments, they may be quite vulnerable. They may just need a smile, or a compliment, or a hug, and they may get more than they intended. In Beth Henley's Pulitzer Prize winning play and film *Crimes of the Heart,* the three Magrath sisters have worried for years over why their mother hanged herself and the cat when their father ran off with another woman. They eventually come to the understanding that she had been having a bad day. Likewise, when the youngest sister Babe shoots her husband for being rude to her fifteen-year-old black affairee, and then makes three suicide attempts, her behavior is explained as having a bad day. The unscientific concepts of biorhythms or astrology are efforts to calculate when people will have their bad days. When a woman is having a bad day, perhaps showing anger at her husband, she may be told she is suffering from PMS (particularly if her husband is a gynecologist). I have no doubt that a male equivalent of PMS is in the offing, so men too can apply a name to any unattractive behavior when they are having a bad day.

People do have bad days. Sometimes this is an appropriate reaction to a set of ridiculous circumstances, and sometimes this is a ridiculous reaction to a set of appropriate circumstances, and sometimes I'm left with no explanation, though I trust the hormones more than I trust the stars. It just seems that we human beings are needier at some times than at others. If we are needy on a day when our spouse has a surplus of nurturance, all goes smoothly, but if we are needy at a time when we are alone, or out of favor at home, or when we know our partner to be unavailable to us, we are at risk. People need safe friends for their bad days. The need to be close to someone who loves us is too easy to confuse with a mating urge, and I fear we are at our least wise and least discriminating when we are having our bad days.

Accidental affairs are most likely to "just happen" when people are having a bad day—or so they tell me.

DIGGING OUT OF THE WRECKAGE

After an accidental infidelity, there is likely to be panic. First, there is the fear of being discovered. The great effort is to prevent this incident from affecting the marriage. If the illicit relationship continues, it may be because of emotional blackmail, offering whatever the affairee wants to keep the thing quiet. If all the emotional energy is going into keeping the secret secret, the amateur adulterer may have little attention left for other aspects of the crisis. He or she may want to reveal it to the spouse, especially if the experience was unsettling. But exposure might alter the marriage, and that would not be safe—the marriage is fine just as it is.

The accidental infidel is thus alone with the memory of the episode, not wanting to talk it over with the friend in need, the strange professional, the passing stranger, or the Good Buddies who may have arranged it. So the amateur infidel must sort this out alone.

The usual explanation for the incident is "I must have been out of my mind." People call therapists after these episodes. They may diagnose themselves as manic-depressive if that runs in their family. They are correct in realizing that the sudden or episodic onset of sexual adventurism is a classic symptom of manic psychosis, but it is also a symptom of just having a bad day. Accidental adulterers may decide that they are alcoholics and quit drinking, which may be wise. People who go out to bars and drink are at risk for sexual accidents, of either the polite, the Good Buddy, or the curiosity type. When someone who has previously been monogamous suddenly begins to have affairs, he or she might be wise to consider whether alcoholism or drug addiction is involved, or whether this is the beginning of manic-depressive cycling.

Whatever the specifics, many fear they can't be trusted out in the world. After a dalliance, some develop agoraphobia, and become too panicky to leave home. Most people with agoraphobia are not recent infidels, but it happens often enough for that to become one of the classical explanations of the phenomenon.

If the amateur adulterer commits an accidental infidelity and is frightened by it, and decides "I must have been out of my mind," then all is well. If, though, the infidel decides "I must be in-love," disaster lies ahead. It may be almost as awful if the adulterer decides "I must be unhappily married" or "This is a wonderful activity. I must make it my hobby and do it more often."

There is an enormous temptation for the infidel to keep the secret and avoid the crisis. When the infidel decides not to mention the accident, but not to repeat it, there may be some strain on the marriage, and some inevitable loss of intimacy. If, on the other hand, the infidel decides to reveal the episode, it will most likely lead to conflict and emotional interaction, and perhaps therapy, and will result in increased intimacy. Does everyone realize that?

My recommendation to people in this situation is, almost without exception, to report the accident, to take full responsibility for making the mistake, to apologize profusely, and to avoid even the slightest hint of blaming the betrayed spouse. This may well trigger a crisis, and it is the natural tendency of human beings to avoid such crises, but the alternatives may well be worse. People who feel guilty tend to blame others for their misdeeds; they want to dump the problem on someone else and somehow establish that they themselves are blameless. Your confession will, of course, make your partner unhappy, anxious, and distrustful, and maybe even guilty for some real or imagined deficiency that might have led you to do this. Your job, in confessing, is to relieve your partner's guilt and anxiety. No one made you do what you did, you did it yourself, and unless you appreciate that, you're out of control and shouldn't be let out in the world loose.

My recommendation to cuckolds under these circumstances is to go ahead and feel whatever you feel: angry, upset, frightened, insecure, and insulted, and to express this fully until it is perfectly clear to your unfaithful partner how much this has hurt you. Then, if you really care about your marriage and its fidelity, you will take on the admittedly unfair burden of bringing the marriage closer together. Your impulse may be to punish and to distance and to pout. Your best interests most likely rest with pulling your errant spouse closer, appreciating the risk of the revelation, and making the marriage more intimate. Your friends, especially as they tire of hearing about it, may tell you that your pride requires that you kick the wayward one out. Your pride has been hurt, and there's no repair for that, but if that's your top priority, you have a bigger problem than your mate's infidelity.

Accidents happen. The only thing more dangerous than deciding they are too frightening to talk about is deciding that they are too horrible to overcome. Honestly, I have never seen a cuckold permanently end a marriage over a single dalliance. I'm sure it happens, but it must be quite rare. Reporting these accidents is not terribly dangerous. But, by contrast, I have regularly seen a single perfectly accidental dalliance, kept secret or handled badly, lead to a life of philandering, or an intense, inappropriate romance, or the decision that the marriage is incurably flawed. Thus the inevitable sequence of events leads from a meaningless act of carelessness to more infidelity, and gradually to the tragedy of an unnecessary divorce.

9 / Philandering:
The Battle of the Sexes

**"I've got those 'God-why-don't-you-love-me-oh-you-do
I'll-see-you-later' Blues!"**
"BUDDY'S BLUES" FROM *FOLLIES* BY STEPHEN SONDHEIM

**"What most wives don't realize is that their husbands' philandering has
nothing whatever to do with them."**
PHILIP BARRY, *THE PHILADELPHIA STORY*

Philanderers are the foot soldiers in the war between the sexes.
"Philanderer" means, literally, "a lover of man," and the term
might accurately imply either "lover to mankind" or "lover of
masculinity." Philanderers are characterized both by their broad
sexual range and by their concern with gender. Philanderers are
those people who require a steady change of sexual partners. They
use this sexual supporting cast to protect themselves from making
and keeping a commitment to just one partner.

Philanderers are obsessed with their gender. They take gender
and its stereotypes quite literally, and are uncomfortable in any
situation in which they aren't displaying and even exercising the
attributes of their gender. Philanderers are mostly men, and are
most comfortable in those societies that worship masculinity. Such
societies permit, or even encourage, a double standard by which all
that is masculine is declared good and all that is feminine is declared subordinate. Such societies don't expect or encourage monogamy, which requires gender equality.

Philanderers fear women. Women, through their sexuality, have the power to define the sexuality of men. Philanderers handle that fear by believing that women are the "opposite" of men, are less important than men, and should exist primarily to serve men in various ways, most crucially through sex. Masculinity is the determinant of status and security in life, the most important of virtues. Masculinity can be achieved in two ways—by competing with other men and by exerting sexual dominance over women. A man who is not defeating men and screwing women is not enhancing his masculinity and is losing status. The greatest loss of status would be to come under the control of a woman. Escape from female control is an affirmation of masculinity.

Such men recoil from the idea that a man would give a woman enough control over him to determine such personal matters as whom he has sex with. Philanderers can't believe in monogamy and marital fidelity, or even in negotiating a marital arrangement. They may come from a religious or ethnic background that supports their belief that God Himself created Man in His image and has commanded him to keep women and their dangerous sexuality under male control. These men don't believe that a woman should, or safely could, be an equal life partner with a man. Male domination may be an article of faith for them, or it may just be an obsession.

Philanderers may be hostile and cruel to women, using seduction to humiliate them, or they may be intimidated and frightened by women to such a degree that they use seductions to tame them. Or they may merely see women as belonging to a different species of animal. Even those who think they like women, and are friendly in their seductiveness, can depersonalize women by treating them as if they were replaceable and exchangeable. These men may have some awareness of the female person, but they are primarily aware of the female gender. They may like women the way the fox likes the chicken. Of course, they do notice the body even if they don't notice the person inside.

I understand that in Jules Feiffer's original script for the film *Carnal Knowledge,* the opening line had Jack Nicholson saying to his prep school roommate Art Garfunkel, "Remember when we were younger and we didn't like girls? We still don't. We just like sex."

Philanderers can be charming and friendly—briefly—with their affairees, but it is nothing very personal. At the same time, a philanderer is far friendlier to his affairees than to his wife, who embodies all that is dangerous in women; she stands between him and the multiple seductions that he needs to reassure himself that he has power over women rather than women having power over him. Guy Marchand, the philandering husband in *Cousin, Cousine,* asks his sister-in-law to intercede for him with his wife, who is displeased over his latest round of affairs, and is retaliating by carrying on an overt affair herself. He says, "Please help her understand that a man has no way to prove he is a man except by sleeping with other women." As he says this, his hand moves up his sister-in-law's thigh. When she moves his hand and laughs at him, he hits her.

In popular culture, philanderers are seen as comic—bad little boys trapped in adolescence, trying to establish their manhood and defying their mama at the same time. In male liberation literature, philanderers are portrayed as tragic, as normal polygamists misplaced in a sick, monogamous culture. In women's liberation literature, philanderers are seen as villains, dangerous evolutionary throwbacks, creatures who have not quite differentiated from the chimpanzees. But whether we consider them to be in the wrong stage of development, the wrong culture, or the wrong species, we generally suspect there is something wrong with philanderers. They, on the other hand, regard their activity as quite normal. They believe they are envied and admired. They assume that every other man does as they do, or would like to do so if he could. They may assume women do the same, or would like to. They are often unaware of their anger toward women, they protest that they "love" women, and they consume them regularly.

PHILANDERING AND PATRIARCHY

In order to understand philandering, we have to realize that to these men, women are not quite people. They are prizes or property —things over which men compete, sometimes for ownership, and at other times simply for access. In our culture, the ideal for some men seems to be to experience women without having the expense or bother of owning them, to receive their services without having to give anything in return. Philandering is an outgrowth of the same societal forces that have rigidified gender arrangements and have produced polygamy and its variant, the double standard.

Male domination has been part of our history, has been supported by religion's "head of the household" concept, and has been central to the social arrangements of quite a few ethnic groups even in modern times. Philanderers create problems for themselves and others by refusing to question and reconsider what they have been taught. But they can't do that; they have been carefully programmed not to receive any critical message from a woman.

The explanation for gender arrangements that appeals to me most appears in Gerda Lerner's book *The Creation of Patriarchy.* Lerner decides that humankind was monogamous, with essentially equal genders, throughout prehistory, and that patriarchy is a fairly recent phenomenon. She dates it to perhaps five thousand years ago, and the invention of warfare. As she sees it, economic forces molded our ancestors into polygynous, slave-keeping warriors with different functions and different lives for men and women. The religions that began during those periods supported such a patriarchal system. So even now, we are stuck with vestiges of it.

The full expression of male domination is seen in cultures that practice polygyny, such as the Arab world today. There, women are legally considered to be one-half a man; it takes two female witnesses to contradict a male one. Sandra Mackey in *The Saudis* describes a society in which male domination is legally protected. Baby girls are weaned early, ignored, and taught that their main purpose in life is to give birth to baby boys. Boy babies are nursed, pampered, and served by all females, who calm the little boys by masturbating them. These boys grow up (if that is the term) without sexual restraints. Women must avoid arousing their uncontrollable appetites, so are covered and veiled. Adultery, defined as the misuse of female sexuality, is dealt with by stoning.

Monogamy in which there is male domination or a double standard is not really monogamy, but a variation on polygyny. Philandering males try to have the benefits of both monogamy and polygny, without the responsibility of either. Such men are rather like the Saudis. They fear women and attempt to escape them or neutralize them or defeat them. Their real interest is the competition with other men. They aren't very good at marriage, which doesn't bother them much, but may be hard on their wives and children. Philanderers may be seeking situations in which they can act masculine, because they feel their masculinity is insufficiently appreciated at home. Or they may merely be practicing their gender skills on a new audience.

THE LIFE OF A PHILANDERER

I have an acquaintance, only a few years younger than I, who is an eager, proud, dedicated philanderer. He belongs to a club at which I work out, and while we are fighting with the Nautilus machines and the effects of time and gravity on the human body, he tells me his exploits. In twenty years of marriage, he has had sex with approximately one thousand women—if we use his arithmetic, based upon the formula of one new woman a week. He has made money in real estate, and despite his humble origins, he could now do almost anything his heart desired, but he has found no activity that appeals to him quite so much as "chasing pussy."

He began this activity three days after his wedding, as he felt bored with his new bride, and couldn't get his mind off one of the bridesmaids. He left the honeymoon early in order to pursue the bridesmaid, which he did successfully. Actually, the marriage brought no change in a pattern that had gone on since the age of fourteen, when he had his first girlfriend and then started sneaking around with her best friend. He goes now to singles bars, where he does not drink but buys drinks for women there. Within an hour he can find some woman who will meet him in the parking lot, or spend a few minutes with him in one of the houses he's showing, or accompany him on a trip somewhere.

He makes it a rule never to see the same woman more than twice. He adopted this rule for himself after he had the bad experience of beginning to like one of them—a woman who worked for him, and who came by his office each afternoon for a quickie. He tells a joke: Q. "What is a romantic?" A. "A romantic is a man who suffers from the delusion that one woman is different from another."

In recent years, my acquaintance has noticed that sometimes he doesn't want to go through with the sex. Once the woman has agreed, the game is really over. He doesn't actually turn down the sex that is offered, though. He lives in fear that someone might think he was gay, and believes they would if it were known that he had turned down sex with a woman.

This man refers to his activity as "tagging" women. He has "scored" a victory by seducing them, or by making them care about him more than he does about them. But the concept of tagging also implies that the woman is now marked and filed for storage and will never have to be dealt with again.

Why, my acquaintance asks, would any man want things different? He is fairly relaxed, though unceasingly competitive with men, and he is well liked by the men he knows. Around women who have not yet been tagged, he is tense and becomes stiff and formal, going through excessive rituals of good manners. He plays a little game that he hopes he never wins: he acts as if he is looking for a woman who is "better" than his wife, and he hopes he won't find one, because he wouldn't want to go through a divorce, with all the expense and bother. And anyway, he'd never find a woman as dumb as his wife, who hasn't suspected a thing in all these years (or so he thinks). He sees himself as a very lucky man. He has three children and has never had to change a diaper, go to a teacher conference or the pediatrician, or drive a carpool. He's had all the women he's wanted, never has to see any of them again, and is the envy of other men at the bars he frequents.

He derides Gary Hart for getting caught. He talks a lot about President Kennedy and his affairs, and about the polygamous patriarchs in the Old Testament, and about the Mormons, though I would not think of my acquaintance as a student of either history or religion. He *has* brought me cartoons from *Playboy* from time to time. He protects himself successfully from the belief that there is something wrong with what he is doing. At the center of his life —and the life of other philanderers—is a determination to establish that he is a normal man. He is not concerned with the fact that he is a human being, but with the fact that he is a *man*, and the greater his difference from women, the greater his victories over women, the more clearly he is a man.

A philanderer wants power over others, and that desire for authority can lead him to become either a street fighter or a tycoon. Politicians, who want the most power over others, seem to be particularly susceptible to this way of looking at things. (Politicians, like philanderers, think of populations rather than individuals. They must depersonalize.) Highly successful men are usually highly competitive people who never get enough of anything. They compete with one another in every imaginable arena (and some that are truly amazing). They may notice that their competitors are notorious philanderers, and they too may want to do what the big boys do. The daughter of a notorious philanderer told me that her father and all his friends and all the presidents he admired were constantly having affairs. When she came to marry, she had decided to find a poor, unsuccessful man. Perhaps, she reasoned, an unsuccessful man would stand a better chance of being faithful.

Actually, philanderers are even more likely to be unsuccessful in other areas of their lives. Philandering is time-consuming, often expensive, and likely to interfere with more productive pursuits. So philanderers, despite their basic competitiveness and aggressiveness, are likely to set up roadblocks to their success. When success has been expected and failure arrives instead, these men have a hard time facing the folks at home. Competitive men who feel like failures often prefer the company of women they regard as inferior. In Woody Allen's *Interiors,* the failed husband of a successful poet seduces his sister-in-law, and tells her, "It's been such a long time since I made love to a woman I didn't feel inferior to."

A philanderer may get along well with family members other than wives. He may have been adored and pampered by his mother, so he is not necessarily hostile toward her. His father, very likely, had escaped the family in some way, either by leaving, withdrawing, or chasing other women. So our man sees masculinity as escape from female control, either because his father achieved it or because he believes his father wanted to escape and couldn't. He wants women to serve him—masculinity and male domination are equated with safety and happiness—but they can't control him, or act like his equal. They scare him too much for that.

A philanderer may be right at home with other men. He may go out with the boys a lot, and he may also slip into alcoholism if their accustomed activity is drinking. He relaxes in the company of men, with whom he attempts to feel equal. He might like to have some unthreatening women around the edges of the group, so that he and the other guys can impress one another with their skills at flirtation or seduction, or at putting women down.

This is the basic pattern. There are also a few variations for us to look at.

CHARMING PHILANDERERS

Philanderers can be very attractive, with well-polished social skills and talents. There is a refreshing innocence to their guiltless sense of entitlement and the childlike pleasure they take in doing whatever they like. Some are so seductive that few could resist them. Their confidence comes from having been loved well and often. Women may frantically pursue them, and the more successes these men have, the more desperately certain women want to test out their famed expertise. It is as if the entire female world were lined up awaiting its turn.

The prototypical philanderer is Don Juan, or in Mozart's opera,

Don Giovanni, one of the great charmers of all time. In the opera, Giovanni has raped Donna Anna and killed her father. He is now hiding in the bushes with Zerlina, the peasant girl he has seduced from her own wedding. Donna Elvira, his wife or whatever, is chasing him, trying to get him back. His manservant Leporello entertains Don Giovanni's frustrated pursuers by cataloging his conquests. "In Italy six hundred and forty, in Germany two hundred and thirty-one, a hundred in France, in Turkey ninety-one, but in Spain there are already one thousand and three!" Leporello's admiration for his master is boundless. Giovanni is his servant's hero. Leporello, an unsuccessful amateur seducer himself, particularly admires Giovanni's lack of discrimination. "He doesn't care a fig if she's rich, if she's ugly, or if she's pretty, so long as she wears a skirt." At the end, the stone statue of Donna Anna's father begins to drag Giovanni off to hell, telling him to repent, to change his mode of life. Giovanni refuses, saying that he will never be accused of cowardice. Giovanni would rather die than come under social control. His masculinity, as he defines it, is more important to him than his life.

A particularly charming philanderer explained to me, "All women are beautiful to me, each one I haven't had is a mystery and she obsesses me. I just can't stop looking at her and listening to her move and breathe, and I smell her and even taste her. All I want is to know her and to give her pleasure. I will make her feel good—I'll tell her anything she wants to hear. It won't take long, and then I'll be out of her life forever."

THE FRIENDLY PHILANDERER

The friendly philanderer does not appear to be hostile toward women, or exploitive of them. He is a helpful nice guy rather than a seductive charmer. He does not want to humiliate women, overwhelm them, or, on the surface, have his way with them. He humbly offers himself for their pleasure. His attitude toward them is one of awe. He finds them frightening, and he wants to please and satisfy them. He may develop his sexual technique to such a degree that he barely experiences his own sexual pleasure. He can train himself into ejaculatory incompetence, so that he can pump away all night without feeling a thing, and without coming to orgasm. He is, in effect, sacrificing his own sexuality for the hope of bringing a female goddess under his control.

These men are excruciatingly anxious to please these powerful females. Such a man might be just as charming and accommodating to his wife as he is with every other woman. He might make a special effort to please a woman no one else seemed to want. Some of our notorious world-class lovers have had this reputation for sexual generosity. Some of these men become professionals, though the market for their skills is not great and most retain their amateur status.

There is no overt hostility here, so a sexual artist like this might seem to be different from more hostile philanderers. He experiences the power of women, and fears it. He is attempting to pacify and tame it rather than escape from and degrade it. He really does like women, and even if he finds them interchangeable, he's careful not to let the women feel depersonalized.

The wife of such a man may be awed by his sexual expertise and thoughtfulness, and then devastated when the sex fades out of the relationship. He uses sex to overcome his fear of women, but it is a performance, and he might hope that in time he and his wife could be good enough friends to do without the sexual exploits. He'd just like to be comfortable with a woman, and not have to donate his sexuality to pacifying the bitch goddess. Like the more hostile philanderer, the friendly philanderer is not quite comfortable with friendly sex among equals.

The prototypical friendly philanderer would be *Zorba the Greek*, who feels a responsibility to see that no woman sleeps alone. He says of his philandering, "You make fun of me that I love women. How could I not love them, such innocent, delicate creatures. A hand on their breast and they give you all they've got."

HEROIC PHILANDERERS

Real Men are too tough for mere sex. For them, the sex must involve an element of danger. While most men don't function well sexually when they are anxious or endangered, there are a few who find danger sexually exciting. They basically believe that women are dangerous and out to possess, control, and thus destroy them. The greatest danger for them would be to relax and become comfortable with a woman, so they are safest when the relationship is at its most hostile and overtly threatening. Any sexual encounter with a woman is dangerous for them, an act of extreme heroism. Probably all early adolescent males experience their first sexual encounters as heroic flirtations with danger. Some never get past that stage.

James Bond is our current heroic philanderer. He seems to risk his life regularly by bedding down the women who have been sent to kill him, and giving them such sexual pleasure they will betray their allegiances for him. His most famous conquest was Pussy Galore, a fascist lesbian assassin whom he converted on all counts. The women he seduces are universally dangerous, but they usually get killed as a result of their involvement with him. He shows a quarter second's regret over each woman's death. Bond will risk his life in any way, for any cause. What he won't do is go to bed with Miss Moneypenney, the safe, "wifely" sex object.

PSYCHOPATHIC PHILANDERERS

Philanderers are not always nice guys. However delightful they may be out in the world, they can become monsters at home. At home, they sense most intensely the danger of letting a female get control of them.

I know of a retired army officer who had been in an affair for many years with the wife of his rich best friend. After the friend's death, he married the widow, and let her support him, while he began other affairs. His latest conquest was his bride's niece. The wife learned of this while she was away from home, and called her husband to confront him. She fussed. He explained that he would not permit a wife to fuss at him, and would punish her by breaking her china while she listened. He broke the china. She told him she would leave unless he saw me. When I heard the story, I clumsily referred to the china breaking as an overreaction. Whereupon the man stood up and informed me, "If you don't understand why I had to break that china, then you don't understand anything about how to handle women. The next thing you'll tell me is that she had the right to criticize me for who I slept with. I'm not going to put myself in the hands of a pervert like you." He walked out and, I am sorry to say, she followed.

In his dealings with women, a philanderer might appear to be a psychopath, even though he might well be a man of honor and morality in his dealings with men. Such men may be much admired, may even be elected president. They may be vigorously pursued and extravagantly admired by women, even when—or perhaps because —their philandering is notorious. Women may throw themselves at such men. How could anyone object to their pleasure? After all, women like it, and "what wives don't know won't hurt them." These men are monsters only to their loved ones.

Certainly psychopaths—men who like to break rules, who like to take advantage of others—will probably also be philanderers. But there really are men whose character seems impeccable in every other way, yet who seem bewildered by the theory and practice of marital fidelity. They enjoyed their promiscuity when they were single, though it was optional, but now that they are married they seem compelled to philander. These men may feel no shame or guilt about it. They would feel ashamed of themselves if they didn't do it. Some of them are such people pleasers they may try to please you by telling you they feel guilty, but they don't.

THE HOSTILE PHILANDERER

This type of philanderer can't seem to see commonality with a woman because he is too preoccupied with the differences. So he becomes obsessed with female genitals and breasts. He is not necessarily oversexed, though he may like to see himself that way. He's obsessed with his own genitals also, and he does want constant affirmation of his masculinity. The problem is not that he is oversexed, but that he is overgendered.

He seems to be angry with marriage, and especially with the idea that he should restrict his sexual interests simply because he is married. He sees his marriage as belonging to his wife, and she uses it against him to prevent his appropriate freedom. He may, of course, express his anger and defiance of her in other ways as well. He may reassure himself of his masculinity by controlling things, like money, or refusing to do things, like calling home or taking care of the kids. He divides the labor, and assigns status to his jobs. He may well be violent, if necessary, to maintain his expected level of control. He may go around "commanding" things or "forbidding" things so his wife can let him be the boss. He may complain a lot about liberated women, and he likes to tell stories about how stupid and inept women can be. The less successful he is in his own life, the more dependent he is upon women, the more likely he is to put women down.

The hostile philanderer may be multimarried, and adulterous in all his marriages. He may have been raised in an ethnic group that encouraged, or at least accepted, his hobby, and he could have married a woman who was raised to expect that sort of arrangement in marriage. But he prefers to marry someone whose security would be most threatened by his behavior. He may blame each wife in turn, because each failed to satisfy him so totally that he would not want to screw around. If he screws around, it is her fault, and when he comes home from his philandering, he may berate her or even beat her up. The pattern may change for a while if he carelessly lets himself come under the control of a new woman who won't tolerate this nonsense, and who is willing to leave him if it continues. He may then give up the pursuit of new women, and be more or less faithful to this new mistress for months or years, until she relaxes and begins to like him or trust him enough to tolerate him. Or until she marries him.

SEXUAL HOBBYISTS

Philanderers like to think of themselves as oversexed, as people who are so masculine that they just like sex too much and too often. Most of them, of course, have a lot less sex than do the people who have a very sexy marriage and practice monogamy. A few, however, are accustomed to two or more orgasms a day, with a variety of partners in various genders and combinations, and the supplement of masturbation. One would think that a man who really wanted to pursue a lifelong hobby of sex would find a highly sexual female partner to marry. Some do, of course, and live happily and sexily ever after. Those who want even more sex come to marital arrangements that permit it with the least possible damage to the sexy marriage.

Philanderers don't seem to want sexy marriages. They don't marry women who share their sexual hobbies. If they are sexual hobbyists, they keep that secret from their wives. They may actively resist their wives' involvement. Back at the height of the sexual revolution of the sixties and seventies, many people tried sexually open marriage, with mixed success. It did not seem to solve the dilemma of the philanderer who loves both his gender and his sexuality. Few philanderers could tolerate having their wives screw around too. A man might go through the motions of urging his wife into swinging, but he is really pushing her to resist. Then he can maintain his mythology that men naturally have greater sexual needs than women, thus it is only right and fair for him to go out while she stays home. If the couple really did try swinging, he would probably be uncomfortable with it. He isn't seeking more sex, or greater harmony at home. He's seeking victories over women, and an open marriage is threatening in its equality. His jealousy might become intense, even reaching paranoid levels. He knows firsthand how much hostility goes into screwing around. He knows the feeling of gloating over the husband of the woman he seduces. He doesn't want another man or his wife or girlfriend to feel that way about him.

Despite his distrust of women, a philandering sexual hobbyist may be capable of forming a very friendly relationship with a female philanderer, a woman who has given up all romantic and idealistic expectations of men. He cannot marry such a woman, of course, since the relationship requires their mutual independence and total lack of romance. There are no illusions between these people, and a man may develop erotic friendships with one or more philandering women, women whose gender anger meshes with his own. One female philanderer, who had such a relationship with several men, told me cynically, "All married men sleep around, at least everyone I ever went to bed with did."

THE BORDERLINE PHILANDERER

There are men who have the attitudes of a philanderer, but are too civilized, too cautious, too wise, too busy, or just too comfortable to take on such an engulfing and alienating activity as philandering. Mostly these men have not been able to do what true philanderers do—they are not able to overcome the guilt. They may have tried screwing around and discovered that they worried about the effects of this activity on other people's lives. They felt out of order, so they don't do it much any more. They don't try to get close in their marriages either. When they aren't working, such men may hang around with the other guys and complain about women. The reaffirmation of gender differences and gender conflict seems to bring the guys together in a tighter fraternal bond.

Such a man, unable to drop his guard enough to establish a friendship with a wife, may go through a midlife crisis and start a desperate search for human contact and reassurance. The classic solution for such a man is to fall into a romantic affair, but that requires some capacity for singling out a specific woman, and giving her power over him. A career of philandering may not even begin until middle age and failure. When these men fail to achieve success in their competition for financial success, they turn to that other arena for proving masculinity—they can start competitive seductions of women. Their failure has left them so dishonored, according to their standards, that they can relax some of the other values that contribute to their sense of honor. Having already let their family down, they feel they should take their needs elsewhere, and not burden the family further.

A friend of mine from childhood had an extremely unappealing experience with middle-aged philandering. I'd felt very close to him and his wife, and watched helplessly as he sank into alcoholism, into philandering, and into bankruptcy. Nobody was surprised when she and the children left him. He was already living with another woman, a woman who wasn't very stable, and certainly wasn't as tolerant as his wife had been. This woman had set fire to his car when she found it parked in front of his ex-wife's apartment. She finally left him too, after the umpteenth time he got drunk and wandered off with another woman. Then he was just a loose pinball. He made a suicide attempt, carving up his wrists with a Trac II razor blade, and showing up drunk and despairing at his ex-wife's place. She called me and I went out. He was lying in a dark room, his wrists bandaged. When he saw me come in, he said, "Pitts, you old square. I bet I've had more women in the last year than you've had in a lifetime." Thereupon, he rose up a bit, vomited green stuff all over himself, and passed out. He was a man who wanted to be admired and envied—I understood that—but perhaps he didn't know how much I had once envied his wit and his energy.

THE IMPERSONAL PHILANDERER

There is an occasional philanderer who is neither hostile to nor fearful of women. He may be obsessively indifferent to women, and just use them regularly for exercise and relaxation when he is traveling. He has no particular objection to sex with his wife, if she happens to be there at the appointed time, but she wants to make a night of it, and he is a busy man and he knows a woman or a phone number he can call that will deliver some highly efficient sex and not tie him down for the whole evening. He has no personal interest in these women. Of course, he has no personal interest in his wife either. He barely notices which woman is with him in the bed. He is a busy man.

Such a busy philanderer protects himself from anything very personal, and the impersonality of his marriage extends far beyond the sexual patterns. He may in time discover that it is even more efficient and impersonal to stick to masturbation and leave women out altogether.

THE GAY PHILANDERER

If the criteria for philandering involve (1) an obsession with masculinity, (2) determination not to come under the control of the "opposite" sex, and (3) sexual competitiveness with other men, the ultimate philanderer would be homosexual. And surely enough, the gay subculture (pre-AIDS, at least) has been incredibly promiscuous. The gay life seems to center around phallic symbolism, polite avoidance of women, and frantic seductions of other men. There are celibate homosexuals who use the gay world to avoid what they see as the dangerous competition with other men. Those men may have little interest in sex, but are concerned about gender and a stereotype they don't think they fulfill.

There are a fair number of monogamous homosexuals who want to be married, but not to a woman, and occasionally manage to find with a man a very stable, equal relationship. With AIDS, homosexual monogamy is suddenly far more popular. Traditionally, liaisons between two males had to accommodate considerable infidelity, so they were not often stable and long lasting, and could be violent. The gay life has usually been intensely sexual. Those who pay the enormous price for being gay in our society are making quite a sacrifice for the sake of their sexual freedom, so they have tended to demand their rights to the promiscuity they have purchased. Homosexual infidelity has always been just as destructive to monogamous agreements as heterosexual infidelity. The gay community, unlike the straight community, has faced the AIDS epidemic, and is changing accordingly. In the gay marriages I treat here in the era of AIDS, a homosexual infidelity is increasingly seen as tantamount to an act of suicide/homicide.

Whether it occurs in pure or exclusive form, or alternates with heterosexuality, we don't know what "causes" homosexuality. It might be inappropriate even to think in terms of causation. Homosexuality used to be considered something any man or woman was perfectly capable of, and might well do if the circumstances were right. Some people might like doing it better than others. (Obviously, it would never have been considered a sin unless it had been seen as something ordinary people might be tempted to do.) But the concept that some people are "homosexuals" seems to be a fairly recent one, and I frankly don't believe there is anything different about those men who prefer to have sex with other men, except that they are not as comfortable having sex with women. We are all perfectly capable of having sex successfully with men, women, children, animals, machines, and certain kinds of plants. Which of these we prefer is a matter of taste.

A fair number of married men are actively bisexual, leading an underground gay sex life, generally a highly promiscuous one. Such a man may be so terrified of women that he must keep polite distance from his wife, and can only relax sexually with the other boys. Perhaps he feels his sexual performance is being tested and graded by women. Perhaps he fears coming under the control of a powerful woman. He may, on the other hand, be quite comfortable sexually with women, but may like variety, even more variety than a selection of other women would have to offer. There really is little difference, to my mind, between heterosexual philandering and homosexual philandering, even though almost everyone, gay and straight, seems to make a big issue of the difference—as if heterosexual impulses were voluntary while homosexual impulses were irresistible. Obviously that is nonsense; no one, straight or gay, is required to act on sexual impulses. Each of us chooses what impulses we will act upon, and that is no different whether the impulse is straight or gay.

This sort of bisexual philandering is increasingly unacceptable. While it protects the man from facing his fear of women and marriage, or his fear of coming out into a gay life, it exposes him and his family to AIDS, and assists in its spread. It seems hard to believe that these double lives can go on for decades without any suspicion from the wives, but these are stilted, formal, not very intimate marriages that keep the lid on many secrets.

FEMALE PHILANDERERS

Philandering is a predominantly male occupation. It is one of those activities for which women seem to lack natural talent. There are women who attempt careers of philandering, only to find that they mess it up by falling in love. The common mythology is probably generally true, that women just can't screw around as cavalierly and impersonally as men can. Most promiscuous women are not philanderers. They are unattached romantics, merely using their sexuality in the search for romance, magic moments, or someone to love. Certainly there are large numbers of adulterous women who have lost interest in and allegiance to their husbands, and are screwing their way around town in search of new partners, sometimes partners for sex, sometimes partners for life. As with men, the problem behind their promiscuity is not that they are oversexed. These women just haven't found a steady partner quite yet. They go through their daily rounds with hope rather than hostility. They don't degrade their partners; if anything, they glorify them. They like sex, and they like men, and every time they hope they have found Mr. Wonderful. They are naively optimistic romantics, seeking the magic wand.

A few women are capable of being philanderers, though. There is a small but growing number of female philanderers who go through a series of hostile seductions, using sex to exercise power over men. Such a woman ordinarily sees men as philanderers, and is determined to beat them at their own game. She may be quite comfortable with male philanderers, the more outrageously hostile the better, and may even have erotic friendships, sexually intense and emotionally hostile, with one or more male philanderers—a comradeship based on the fulfillment of each other's nightmares. In a sense, these are often very good relationships.

The female philanderer was probably sexually abused by men during her childhood, and was thus led to see herself as an object and to see sex as an act of exploitation, degradation, and aggression. She is furious with sex and with men, and she is going to make men pay. She could turn this anger into a career, and go into prostitution. The steady dose of anger in everything she does is rather wearing, and prostitutes in my practice have had a hard time separating the sheep from the goats. They seem to go automatically for the most abusive man, until they give up on men altogether.

An amateur female philanderer may hope it will be different next time, that a man will be loving despite the hostility with which she approaches sex and men and relationships. Or she may, more likely, enjoy the anger and the victory over men.

Female philanderers aren't usually married. In their determination to avoid coming under male control, they will make themselves as independent of marriage as possible. In this way, they differ from male philanderers, who seem best able to protect themselves from female control by staying married, at least in name. When female philanderers are married, they can be extraordinarily hostile and abusive to their husbands.

Each female philanderer I've seen had a father who was a philanderer. Sometimes the father had deserted or died, so she could idealize him, but often he adored her and saw her as different from other women, less inferior in his mind than other women. (Such a doting philanderer-father might almost declare his favorite daughter to be an honorary man.)

Each of these women then also had a husband or fiancé who humiliated her with his infidelities. She is furious, though she never seems clear about whether she is angrier with men or with the restricting and treacherous institution of marriage. The man she dislikes most, of course, is her husband, and she may deprive or hurt him sexually, while she sleeps with whomever it would hurt him most for her to sleep with. She likes to torture and humiliate men, seducing them in the most embarrassing manner she can. If possible, she will break up other men's marriages, and wreck their friendships and careers. Naturally she is depressed, and constantly angry with men and the world they control. She believes that all men are out to fuck her over, so she'll beat them to it.

Female philanderers are most often affairees, enjoying the opportunity to break up another woman's marriage and mess up a man's life. Just at the point of the divorce, a female philanderer may break off the affair, escaping as she humiliates all concerned.

One female philanderer kept a card catalog in which she logged all the men she had slept with. She ranked them according to size, technique, and endurance, and would show them their rank, always lowering their score if she found them a bit too cocky.

Philanderers, male or female, have a hobby that is not much affected by marriage. These people may give up their philandering at times when the marriage is threatened and needs attention, but they wouldn't keep that up for long. Marriage, especially as it gets comfortable, may be so threatening that they have to philander even more (philanderers do, however, like to hold on to bad marriages).

Some male philanderers might appreciate a wife who is dumb, passive, and incompetent, but a female philanderer is not pacified by male passivity and certainly could not tolerate a competent partner any more than a male philanderer could. There really isn't anybody female philanderers can live with comfortably. (They may try marriage to male philanderers, and the results may be unsettling until a marital arrangement is achieved. I know a few female philanderers who remain married, but don't live with their husbands. This may be their best solution.) Female philanderers are likely to get divorced a lot, because they just can't work out a satisfactory partnership. They are better off unmarried. Between marriages, they can be just as awful to the men who cross their paths, and they can do it even more openly.

A particularly beautiful female philanderer, temporarily between marriages, was invited to an office weekend of an accounting firm. A former lover, an associate new to the firm, invited her in order to impress the partners. She had never quite forgiven this man for betraying her with a sorority sister back in college, so she accepted his invitation and went to the mountain resort. As soon as she arrived, she began to overtly ignore her date, busying herself with his distinguished boss, who was there with his increasingly indignant wife. The boss and his wife had a rather tense encounter, and the wife returned to the city in a huff. The boss, finally free at enormous cost, announced his availability. But the young woman went straight for the least attractive of the partners, making a show of leaving with him. She returned, giggling, a few minutes later and for the rest of the weekend giggled pointedly whenever she saw him.

I was impressed with this young woman's efficiency. With one sex act, she had ruined her date's career and possibly his boss's marriage, and had turned another partner into a laughingstock. With delight, she pointed out to me that each of the three men had brought it upon himself. She had merely behaved the way male philanderers do, and she understood why they enjoyed it so. To her, as to most philanderers, sex is the most potent of weapons.

PHILANDERERS' WIVES

That most lovable of 1940s screwball film comedies, *The Philadelphia Story,* was from a play by Philip Barry. It concerns the carryings on of *High Society* and the comeuppance of a "cold goddess," played by Katharine Hepburn (and, in the later musical version, by Grace Kelly). The heroine's father, blackmailed and humiliated by his infidelity, attempts to ingratiate himself with his wife. He says, "What most wives fail to realize is that their husband's philandering has nothing whatever to do with them." He then goes on to blame his behavior on his insufficiently loving daughter.

If women married to philanderers make sufficient show of subservience and incompetence, their husbands may treat them very kindly. Male philanderers usually demand that the wives make a show of their sexual attractiveness, that these women stay thin, if thin is in style, and "feminine," by whatever standards are in vogue, and that they behave in whatever manner would make the man appear most "masculine." The philanderer's ideal wife might be a pretty little airhead, something like a Barbie doll. Philanderers want their wives to appear sexual to the other guys, but not to be sexual, either with other men or with them. They don't want sex at home to interfere with the real business of masculine conquest. So they like the notion that the wife doesn't like sex much. Philanderers are threatened by either competence or sexuality in wives. Philanderers may insult their wives regularly, in public even more than in private, as they try to make themselves look grand and their wives look insignificant.

Many women are attracted to philanderers, even when they should know better. These men can be charming, wonderfully comfortable and adept at sex, and can seem to be winners in the world. They can be successful, or on the way to success, and may exude masculine power. They may know how much weakness and vulnerability to display. Perhaps most important, they generally know how to make an impression, and the woman who seems to have hooked a philanderer can become the envy of all her friends. She has achieved a competitive victory.

If the philanderer is successful enough in life and amasses enough power, the wife may feel she has a pretty good deal. She may get only a fraction of his sexuality, but she gets all the legal rights and prestige that would come to a real wife in a real marriage. The price she pays in anxiety, loneliness, and humiliation may make the rewards look meager, though. If the philanderer is unsuccessful enough, which is even more likely, the wife may hope she will finally feel needed and appreciated. She won't, but she often keeps trying.

Obviously, philanderers, preoccupied as they are with their masculinity, are likely to marry women who are equally preoccupied with their femininity. As long as nothing changes that, the relationship may continue along its stilted and determinedly unequal course. If she recovers from her acceptance of subordination, the marriage will be threatened. If he becomes comfortable enough for a real partnership, that will also threaten the marriage. The major crisis occurs when the infidelities are somehow revealed (and these wives may go to a lot of trouble not to notice them), and the philanderer feels humiliated, not because of what he did, but because revelation of the secret becomes a sign of weakness. If the wife tries to make this husband feel guilty or punish him, he may have to rebel against her even more.

SURVIVING UNDER SIEGE

A philanderer's marriage is guerrilla warfare. His wife is the enemy to be escaped or subdued. He will bully her, charm her, disorient her, whatever it takes to keep her from understanding him and getting him under her control. The philanderer's mate may rely on punishment or guilt to try to turn him into a normal husband. Such an effort is, of course, doomed. His masculinity and thus, to him, his survival are dependent on escaping and defeating his wife. That part of the game is a lot more important than the other women.

Philanderers don't give up their chosen occupation in obedience to a woman scorned. Some give it up for a time when the marriage is threatened or when they have fallen in love temporarily with a new affairee. Changing marriages doesn't seem to help for very long. These men must not be controlled by women, whoever the woman.

I have said that I've only known one philanderer who gave it up completely on his own, and he did so only after becoming paralyzed and confined to a wheelchair. That's an exaggeration. Philandering comes in various degrees, and the borderline philanderers may have no difficulty giving it up after a crisis. The friendly ones, the impersonal ones, the hobbyists, and even some of the charmers may give it up if they can be convinced that it really is hurting themselves and other people. But the heroic ones, the more desperate charmers, and particularly the psychopaths and hostile ones are far too frightened to give it up without a fight.

I wish there were support groups for philanderers, as there are for alcoholics, drug addicts, gamblers, and even child molesters. But at the moment I don't know of such a program. Philanderers, and their families, must be treated one at a time—and they need treatment. I envision a self-help organization, perhaps Philanderers Anonymous, where these people could help one another. Philanderers may themselves be the best source of help. Many philanderers have benefited from group therapy and the opportunity for confrontation—by people of both sexes—about their lifelong misinformed view of the world. The message, especially if it comes from other men, can be heard, and with time and practice incorporated.

What should a philanderer do? Well, obviously, the philanderer might give monogamy a try, but this means much more than just stopping the extramarital sex. It means a different level of honesty and equality, a shifting level of marital sexuality, and, above all, a rethinking of everything these men think they know about gender. The changes required of the philanderers' wives would be equally extensive, drastic, and disorienting. Many men and many women in these situations are not willing to make such drastic changes, and if they did, there might be little basis left for the marriage. The divorce rate is very high.

In the past, many wives were taught to expect philandering and to tolerate it by being careful not to get too close to their husbands. This formal gender dance is no longer acceptable to most women or men. When there was no divorce, philandering destroyed the marital relationship but not the marriage itself, which was legally indissoluble. So some aspects of security were not threatened. Now, a philanderer can skip out or fall in love or dance away from his depersonalized marriage.

Despite the disadvantages and the risks, a great many women still choose to stay in such marriages, but they should remember the fate of poor Evelyn, Hickey's tragic wife in Eugene O'Neill's *The Iceman Cometh*. Hickey, the salesman who brings hope to the denizens of the skid row bar, tells the story of his marriage, how Evelyn loved him and believed in him despite all the lies and the broken promises and the other women. She would always forgive him and take him back, reassuring him that she knew he would change. And each time, he'd let her down again. There seemed no escape. He couldn't leave her—that would break her heart. So he killed her, after she finally forgave him once too often.

If a woman is determined to live with a philanderer, she must be careful to keep her distance. She must realize that she is the feared enemy, that the reason for his behavior is that he believes his life is dependent upon escaping her control. There is no way in which she can please him sufficiently, or impress him enough so that he declares her his equal. She must pursue her own life, giving him as much independence as he requires, while she takes as much freedom as she needs to develop her own self-esteem. Guilt-producing dependency will only bring out the worst in him, and will deprive her of a life that could be fulfilling.

It usually makes matters worse for the wife to threaten the philanderer, to put him on some sort of probation or under surveillance. These men are above all, bad little boys. But it can be helpful for the ever-betrayed wife to go ahead and kick him out. These men are not as stupid as they seem. When their usual weapons of charm, put-downs, and pitifulness fail to work, they can have a go at doing sensible things.

In the era of AIDS, people can't safely stay married to philanderers. Bisexual philanderers have already brought this deadly virus home. The sexual community of mankind is small—the sexually promiscuous are all eventually connected with one another. The merry-go-round of *La Ronde,* in which a bracelet passes from sex partner to sex partner until it is returned to its original owner, is instructive. The danger of AIDS for heterosexuals is growing. Living with a philanderer, who is scared of you anyway and can't treat you as an equal or even as an individual, is just not worth the danger. If you can't get the philanderer to change, then you probably should leave. Leaving may be the best hope of bringing about change, and that's a long shot.

I am not optimistic that long-standing, dedicated philanderers (the sort who started it in the first few years of marriage, or continued it through more than one marriage, or institutionalize it into a regular schedule, or brag about it and defend it as a hobby) will change easily, and certainly not without a serious crisis and continuing therapy. They don't think there is anything wrong with them, and they don't like being told that there is.

Philandering is addictive behavior, and, like all addictive behavior, is difficult to change without great honesty and the willingness to put yourself under someone else's control.

10 / Romantic Affairs: Temporary Insanity

"We're not here to be happy—we're here to ruin ourselves, to break our hearts, to love the wrong people, and to die."
NICHOLAS CAGE IN *MOONSTRUCK*, WRITTEN BY JOHN PATRICK SHANLEY

"Man is sometimes extraordinarily, passionately, in love with suffering."
DOSTOEVSKY, *NOTES FROM THE UNDERGROUND*

"**F**alling in love has to do with summoning up inchoate, rapturous feelings of engulfment in a safe and intimate world—one in which two are as one, perfect company, and in which perfect nurturance exists. It has to do with the visions of Eden, buried within, before human aloneness had been perceived," says Maggie Scarf in the recent book *Intimate Partners*. The thing about the in-love state is that it removes whoever is in it from the world, and from reality. From inside, falling in-love may feel like a regression to the womb or a union with the infinite, but from outside, falling in-love looks like temporary insanity.

Falling in-love has little to do with loving, and more to do with romance, which is a form of exotic and narcissistic suffering in which the specialness of a loving relationship gets distorted into an obsession with suffering and sacrifices to keep things intense enough to make the world and reality fade away. The in-love phenomenon tends to occur at points of transition in people's lives, and it can serve the purpose of distracting them from having to change and adapt to new circumstances or a new stage of development.

Unlike loving and being loved, which gives us the security to find comfort and joy in the world, falling in-love can be a dangerous episode of torture and adventure and emotional exercise. It is not a sickness that we diagnose, nor do we ordinarily lock people up or give them medicine for it. The in-love state is a sacred form of insanity, as sacred as cows are in India. We let people who are in-love wander around loose, messing up the landscape, tying up traffic, and doing any damn fool thing they want. They're not responsible, they're just in-love.

Romantics go even further: they fall in-love with love, find their security not from loving and being loved, but from the irrational, distracted high of falling in-love, making sacrifices to prove their love, and having sacrifices made for them. The specialness that people feel when they love one another becomes a willingness to give up everything for the romantic object, and a disregard for all other people and relationships. Falling in-love is even more crazily romantic if it is unrequited. Goethe, who understood romance perfectly, said, "If I love you, what business is that of yours?"

I don't get to stay home and watch the soap operas, but I understand that each character is in at least one love affair, as many as he or she can squeeze in between cups of coffee. In the glitzy evening soaps, like "Dallas" and "Dynasty," I understand these very rich families made up of old movie stars are always having affairs and murdering one another. I do read *People* magazine, which specializes in pictures of whole families in the bathtub together, and in stories about how minor celebrities have finally found true love with someone they met on their latest honeymoon.

Sometimes I go a half step further into romanticism and pick up the *National Enquirer* at the grocery store. Such tabloids try to provide hope for people who no longer expect life to make sense. Having given up on thought, planning, discipline, and knowledge, they prefer to believe in magic and luck. They believe in astrology, in faith healing, and in diets where you get to eat more and still lose ten pounds before the weekend. Tabloids exult in stories of true love, when a ninety-two-year-old woman falls in love with a fourteen-year-old Boy Scout and goes to live with him in a tree house. While slick magazines help women to cope with dry skin and rejection, and tell men how to get the money, the muscles, or the car that will funnel strange women toward their bed, readers of tabloids are given the hope that Elvis' ghost or visitors from outer space will give meaning to their humdrum lives. Many of us really do seem to believe that the best thing in life is the intense disorientation (the "picturesque unusualness") of being in-love.

The romantic, as opposed to the classic, tradition in literature concerned itself with passion rather than reason, with imagination and inspiration rather than logic. Romantics believe that the secret of happiness lies in freedom from reason and logic and responsibility and order, and that cutting loose will indeed set them free. Normal adolescents—especially in the first fifteen minutes after puberty—are innate romantics, trusting the basic nature of the human animal, the "noble savage" of the romantic Rousseau. The true romantic experience would come from defying all the forces of civilization and order in the pursuit of a love experience that seems most "natural," i.e., most socially inappropriate, disorderly, and unreasonable. If it seems wrong enough, then it must be right. Such is the nature of romance.

Romance seems safe only for adolescents to play around with, since they aren't ready for marriage and are just practicing. They may become immune to romance if they have a bad enough case of it in childhood and recover. Romance, like other adolescent illnesses, is far more dangerous for grown-ups, who may well confuse it with something real and important like marriage. People of all ages die for romance, usually from suicide. They do it regularly in the last acts of all the great operas, but they do it in real life too. Adolescents have so much life in them that they search for something or someone to give it all up for. Adolescents find dying for love quite romantic. Some people we think of as grown-ups do too.

The romance of the in-love state is a revival of adolescence. The pulsation of romance, like the rhythm of the music so appealing to adolescents, is an escape from the civilized world—the boring world of grown-ups who think and feel, who worry about the future and mourn the past and go through the full range of human emotions on a daily basis. Romantics and adolescents seem to believe that aging is a side effect of too much thought. But for a romance to work at totally erasing thought, it must short-circuit the brain.

The ideal shared romance would be the one that is most intense, the one that receives no support from anyone, that exposes the lovers to mortal danger, and that ends in the death of both, preferably at the very moment of consummation. Romeo and Juliet were perfect for each other: they came from warring families who went around killing one another on sight. The danger was absolute. The young couple devoted most of their energies to struggling against the forces that were keeping them apart. They managed to spend one night together, and when they were reunited, it was in death. The whole experience from first glance to death only took a few days. They never got a chance for boredom to set in. There can be no better romance than that.

The romantic tradition saw its greatest fulfillment in eighteenth-century Germany, with the writings of Goethe and Schiller, filled with melancholic longings for love and death. All this romantic suffering was set to music in the nineteenth century, and formed the plots of our most romantic operas. One of the most romantic opera librettos comes from Schiller's first play, *Die Räuber.* As Verdi's *I Masnadieri,* it tells of a banished nobleman who has been forced to become the leader of a band of robbers. His faithful fiancée maneuvers to get his status restored, and succeeds. But at the point of marrying her, his robber friends arrive and tell him that he has promised always to stay with them. Since his honor is at stake, he does the only thing a true romantic can do—he turns and kills the woman he loves, right there at the altar. Thus he protects her from the shame of his return to the robbers.

The ideal price for a memorable romance is death. In almost all of the great romantic operas, such as those of Verdi, the ill-fated lovers try to get together over the opposition of their parents and political forces. They come together and then they die for their love. The idea of the plot is to find the lovers who are most mismatched, who are absolutely ill-suited for each other, lovers whose mating could guarantee disaster. Accordingly, Don Carlo lusts after his stepmother, King Gustav lusts after his best friend's wife, the court jester's daughter lusts after the married duke. The prude's son chooses a prostitute, Joan of Arc is in love with the dauphin. The Ethiopian slave girl wants the princess's boyfriend, who has just been made commander of the Egyptian forces to invade Ethiopia, where her father is the king. The idea is that the love is unquestioningly doomed from the beginning, and everybody knows it—even the lovers. They fully expect to die from their love. And they do. (The only happily married couple in Verdi's operas are the Macbeths, and they are childless and overly ambitious.)

The summit of romanticism is Wagnerian. Tristan and Isolde betray her husband, his uncle King Marke. They then go on to die quite romantically, as illicit lovers must. Tristan dies from a wound he receives in carrying Isolde away with him. Isolde dies a "Liebestod"—a death purely for love—no superfluous natural explanation like a gun or a knife or poison or whatever. She just lies down beside Tristan's body and dies.

One of the standard rules of romance is that the love cannot be socially sanctioned. Romance, at all costs, must not be comfortable. It must not be functional. It must be in conflict with the world, so that the lovers have to choose between living in the fantasy world of being in love or in the real world of going around setting priorities and balancing realities. The romance must require sacrifice, and it can start with the sacrifice of all of one's other relationships and priorities. To do this, it must be illicit.

The most romantic of modern films was surely *Elvira Madigan*, in which the married aristocratic officer runs off with a circus performer. They hide in the woods, eating strawberries and cream and chasing butterflies to music of Mozart. They know they can't survive for long in hiding, and they know they can't stay together if they return to the world. They know from the beginning that they must soon give up either their love or their lives. Finally, they run out of time and resources, whereupon he pulls a gun out of the picnic basket and shoots them both.

For those who want all the pain of being in-love, and are diffident about death and dismemberment, there is an alternative. The couple can fail to consummate the affair, and thus suffer eternally, but in good health, from unrequited love. Dante did this with Beatrice. He saw her on the Ponte Vecchio one day, fell in love with her, and stayed in love with her forever, without ever speaking to her. We aren't even sure he nodded as they passed. Charlie Brown does the same with the "little redheaded girl."

Scarlett O'Hara, if we are to believe Margaret Mitchell, never quite got it together with Ashley Wilkes. Scarlett could have any man she wanted, so she threw herself at the one man who didn't want her. He kept telling her things like "How could I help loving you—you who have all the passion for life that I lack? But that kind of love isn't enough to make a successful marriage for two people who are as different as we are." Ashley was right, but Scarlett refused to take a practical view. Instead, she went through three marriages to men she didn't love so she could support Ashley and his family and stay close to him. She wasted quite a few years and lives and husbands, including Rhett Butler, as she pined away romantically for Ashley, who was too pure and noble to betray his wife Melanie or his honor. It wasn't until Melanie died and left Ashley to her that Scarlett realized that she really had very little use for him around the plantation. She suddenly preferred her husband, the dashing Rhett Butler, especially now that he no longer gave a damn. Poor Scarlett, toughest woman in sixteen counties, but she only wanted whomever she couldn't have.

It should certainly be apparent that romance does not lead smoothly into marriage and settling down and raising a family and living together happily ever after. In fact, marriage and romance may be antithetical. In speaking of love, poet John Ciardi said: "Love is the word used to label the sexual excitement of the young, the habituation of the middle-aged, and the mutual dependence of the old." Getting from the first definition to the second and third requires optimism, practicality, wisdom, patience, and all sorts of patterns of thought and emotion that are in direct opposition to romance.

ROMANCE AND MARRIAGE

In-love and romance have little to do with love, which is concerned with bringing pleasure, comfort, peace, and security to one another, rather than pain, excitement, and anxiety. Yet those intense, disorienting passions have served, in our society in recent decades, as the basis for marriage. Despite the dangers in letting something trivial and fleeting dictate something permanent and vital, there may be much value in letting romance be the starting point for marriage. Couples spend only a short segment of their lives in the throes of burning passion and suicidal romance, but as the romance settles into a real love, those memories of crazily intense passion are pleasant, and they serve the function of making the marriage seem very special. A marriage that began as a great love has a momentum and a magic that less inspired matches lack. Romance doesn't have to be revived to bring back that sense of specialness; the romance can merely be recalled.

The great romance can't last, and probably shouldn't, but it is a wonderful way to start. Spencer Tracy rather romantically describes how he feels about his wife, Katharine Hepburn, in *Guess Who's Coming to Dinner?* "Mrs. Prentiss says that, like her husband, I'm a burnt-out old shell of a man who cannot even remember what it's like to love a woman the way he loves my daughter. . . . I think you're wrong . . . I admit that I hadn't considered it—hadn't even thought about it—but I know exactly how he feels about her, and there is nothing—absolutely nothing—that your son feels for my daughter that I didn't feel for Christina. Old, yes. Burnt out, certainly. But I can tell you. The memories are still there—clear, intact, indestructible—and they'll be there if I live to be 110."

Couples couple, and they marry, and in time the poetry becomes prosaic. The hotter the romance, the cooler the ashes when the ardor wanes. If the couple were well suited to each other, if they had the basis for friendship and they have established a life together and they have gotten good at sex, they may then have the basis for a marriage, and they may live together happily ever after. When they need romance, they may sort through their "clear, intact, indestructible" memories of their romance, and they may be knowingly amused at the clumsiness of it, and at the loveliness of its innocence, and they may be glad they are beyond that now, but just as glad that they can still do it and still feel it. The true love comes after the romance is cool ash and memory, but it may never come unless the romance was there at the beginning.

People in love come in two varieties: those who are in-love with their partner, and those who are in-love with their love. Those who are in-love with their partner can form the union and then together join the world and make a life that brings comfort and joy to both. Most people who can do so come back down to earth and join the real adult world.

Those who are in-love with love can't do that. They, the true romantics, have become addicted to the high of romance. When they don't have it, they feel betrayed and angry. If the romance cools before marriage, they may panic, call off the wedding, and start looking for someone newer and more fantastically unusual, more clearly unsuitable, more outrageously inappropriate, and more deadly—someone who can fire up that sense of dangerously disorienting differentness, that feeling of romance.

But if the romance they must have cools after the marriage, as the world intrudes and they must think as well as feel, they can't seek out a new romance immediately. They must wreck the marriage first. Romantics are furious when the lights go on and everything is clearly real, and they attack. They may lash out angrily at the very real person who seemed, a moment ago in the dim light of romance, to be a god or goddess who had no connection to the real world at all. Romantics don't tolerate real people very well.

Philanderers can substitute any member of the gender in question, and feel no concern about the substitution. In fact, they are uncomfortable with any limitations on their rapid succession of substitutes. But romantics want only the loved one—there are no substitutes. (Juana la Loca, or Joanna the Mad, the Spanish queen, daughter of Ferdinand and Isabella, was crazily in-love with her husband, Philip the Fair. Philip died, and Joanna carried his embalmed body around with her for decades, explaining that she loved him so much she couldn't do without him. Romantics don't care whether their loved-one is alive or not; the loved-one is merely the object of the in-lover's affections and fantasies. The less real the better.)

Romantics are, by definition, not very realistic. They are not necessarily very nice either. They don't like anybody they aren't in-love with, and they don't really love the one they are in-love with. They've fallen in-love with being in-love, and they demand that their chosen loved-one play the reciprocal role in their fantasy. Romantics are not necessarily nicer people than philanderers. Philanderers at least like one gender, and have some use for the other. But romantics divide the world far more narrowly into those they are in-love with and those outsiders with whom they are not in-love, and are barely aware of anyone except their love.

As the romance cools, the in-lover lashes out at the loved-one, perhaps with jealousy, assuming that if reality is setting in, it could only be because the loved-one is losing steam, and to a romantic the only thing that could bring about a loss of intensity would be another love. If a whole lot of carrying on perks the loved-one's interest, then there is hope. The romance can continue, on an intermittent basis, anytime one partner has the energy to get homicidal or suicidal or psychotic or violent with the other partner. There are romantic marriages in which every week or every month the couple get into a wild fight, breaking furniture and chasing each other around in cars through the neighbors' flower beds or whatever. Or they may go after each other with knives or guns, or just with fists. They may kill each other in their efforts to keep their love alive. Much of the marital violence in the world is part of a power struggle in which the man thinks he is supposed to assert his dominance over the woman. But much more of the violence is an effort to become intensely involved in the marriage, and prove that the romance is still in effect.

KEEPING ROMANCE ALIVE

Romantics go around "falling in love with love," but they end up married to people, very human beings. Reality sets in, and romance cannot tolerate very much reality, as we've already seen. So romantics substitute fantasy to keep their love alive. Couples can go to bizarre extremes to keep their feelings of romance. They may dress up in costumes, carry on mock seductions in public, go off to strange places under assumed identities—all in an effort to prove their disdain for the real world and their utter absorption in the romance of the relationship. The complexity of the efforts to keep the romance alive can become a test of each partner's commitment to the relationship.

But the dangerous part comes when the test of romantic intent is the degree to which the loved-one can break ties to the real world, break off relationships with friends and even family (particularly children from a previous marriage). Loved-ones may be asked to prove their commitment to their romance by neglecting their job or their other responsibilities, and I have seen couples in which a jealous man demanded that his loved-one prove her love by quitting her job or dropping out of school so that she could become all the more dependent upon him.

The furthest extreme of sacrificing for one's love is the Indian practice of suttee, in which the widow throws herself (or is thrown) on the funeral pyre to prove that she loved her dead husband more than she loves her life. Romeo did essentially the same for Juliet. There are more subtle psychological forms of this in our society. People may make symbolic sacrifices to prove their love, as Burt Lancaster did in his courtship of the widow Anna Magnani in the Tennessee Williams play. He got a *Rose Tattoo* on his chest, just like the one her dead husband had had.

Some people go even further. A strange movie from 1927 called *The Unknown*, a film I've never seen, offers perhaps the ultimate example of this. I understand that in the film, Joan Crawford has been handled badly by men, and fears being touched. Lon Chaney is a knife thrower in a circus, and he loves this woman who cannot be touched. So he proves his love by cutting off his arms. I don't know what he does professionally after that, and I'm not sure whether Joan Crawford was pleased or not. But the point is made that people will go to great extremes to prove their love.

WHEN THE ROMANCE DIES

Consider the marriage that is based solely on romance, in which there is no friendship, no partnership, no companionship, no sharing of life and the world, no real love, but only the intense preoccupation with each other. Such a marriage ends up totally dead when the romance fades. Obviously, marriages in which the partners are quite different are most fragile. There are marriages in which the partners come from different cultures and traditions, perhaps even speaking different languages, and having no experiences in common. Such marriages are obviously extremely romantic—with fascinating differences to be explored and amazed at, and efforts at understanding that take up all of everybody's time. I think of war brides, or grooms, who fill the lonely hours in faraway climes, but who just don't fit in when you get them home. And when the romance goes, there is absolutely nothing left, and the desperation may be intense. Madame Butterfly, far from unique, committed suicide when she found that her American navy husband had left her for a more suitable American wife.

The end of the romance is a transitional point in every marriage, and it can be a major crisis that can destroy the marriage. Romantics just may not be able to live a normal life without all that excitement, unhappiness, and craziness. Some won't even try. They will seek out another romance right away. Such people may look like philanderers as they go through their search for someone to fall in love with. Their irresponsibility is just as innocent. But the difference is readily apparent in the degree of pain they feel as each potential loved one lets them down. They don't run away, they hang on. They don't want to escape any relationship, they want each to be magical. They are obsessed with the last relationship, not the next one. Each relationship totally absorbs them.

And the relationships may not be very sexy. It exists between the ears rather than between the sheets. The effect of this frantic search for romance, though, is to keep the marriage from accepting the end of the romance and settling into a friendly companionship. This will, before very long, wreck the marriage. Romantics are more dangerous than philanderers because they take it all so seriously. They can move in and out of marriage with amazing rapidity and total confidence that they are doing the thing that is right for them.

Mild romantics can drift along peacefully in a pleasant marriage, missing the romance and not knowing quite how to go about getting any. Their marriage is placid and workable, with no crazy excitement but all the comfortable love and unquestioned commitment of long-standing marriage. Such romantics may have no real complaints, but may have a vague sense of something missing. They may be reasonably happy, but vulnerable.

People who aren't really romantics can go through this too. There are sane people, who at not very sane points in their lives feel a need for the adolescent adventure of falling in-love. Some people go through this at a time when their bad habits are under attack, and they want a partner in crime, in effect, someone who shares the unhealthy habit their loved ones are trying to stop. Alcoholics and drug addicts can, under pressure, suddenly fall in-love with other users. Cigarette smokers have become so rare, they may begin to establish secret liaisons of this sort. There are people whose lives have been going so smoothly that they find them somewhat boring; they have a shortage of hardships and obstacles to overcome, and want some excitement before they are too old.

Romantic affairs can be used as a dangerous folk remedy for depression. Depressed patients have often said, "I'm depressed. If only I had someone to fall in love with." If brain chemistry does not reverse a depression with a manic episode, the depressed sufferer can go into a manic high by falling in-love. As with natural or drug-induced manic episodes, disaster is awaiting, back on earth, when all the air is out of the balloon and gravity prevails.

(The romantic is perhaps a bit more likely to be female than male, though the pattern is essentially the same for both. This pattern, unlike philandering, has little to do with gender or, for that matter, with sex. It is simply a search for a relationship that is illogical, dangerous, and inappropriate. And, of course, any affair is, almost by definition, illogical, dangerous, and inappropriate.)

THE ROMANTIC ACCIDENT

Affairs may start accidentally as romantics sexualize friendships or just find themselves in unusually sexually charged situations. Since they are romantics, they will do not what they think is right, but what *feels* right. Romantics, out to fall in love, throw themselves on the forces of passion, and may or may not land someplace safe and comfortable. Whoever they land on is bound to get hurt.

The impact of an accidental infidelity on a romantic is explosive. It unleashes all that frustrated romanticism. Romantics with their pants off go wild—not necessarily sexually, but emotionally. These people imprint whomever they sexualize, and they clamp on like snapping turtles, and you can't make them let go. Romantics will throw themselves desperately and suicidally at strangers, offering plans for the two of them to disappear and die together. The stranger may have trouble remembering the romantic's name. This sort of thing could even make a philanderer go straight, and will cure the accident-prone forever. This is the plot of the film *Fatal Attraction,* in which it was demonstrated that the romantic passion of a passing stranger is the most horrifying of nightmares.

THE ROMANTIC AND THE PHILANDERER

Romantics are easy prey for philanderers. (I asked my philandering fellow club member whether he knew anything about romance. He told me that of course he did, it works with some girls and it doesn't work with others.)

The classic way for people to get themselves killed is for a philanderer and a romantic to mate. The romantic will be determined that the loved-one will fulfill all the expectations of romance, and the philanderer will escape anything that looks permanent or controlling. Romantic women are for some reason especially attracted to the intense, dangerous charm of philandering men, and will then try to stop the philandering, even if they have to kill him, or themselves. Even more explosive is the pairing of a romantic husband and a philandering wife. The most dramatic presentation of that conflict is Bizet's opera *Carmen,* in which the homicidal soldier Don Jose is seduced into running away with the gypsy spitfire Carmen. After he has gone to prison and given up everything for her, she loses interest and takes up with the bull-fighter Escamillo. Jose stalks her down and kills her, while she sings that she'd rather die than give up her freedom and he sings that he'd rather kill her than give up his love for her. Such is the reasoning of philanderers and romantics.

THE ROMANTIC MARITAL AIDE

The romantic woman is at risk with the philandering man, but the romantic man's greatest threat is the damsel in distress, the woman who is unhappily married and suffering a lot in his direction. He, being a romantic, does not understand marriage, and may have no concept of the strength of the unhappy marriage. He may not have experienced an unhappy marriage, only a pleasantly placid one. He hasn't been needed desperately in a while. So he may sacrifice everything for a woman who is in need of someone to help her with her marriage, and is using him as a marital aide, with no intention of going off into the sunset with him. And as soon as she gets things worked out at home, she may not return his phone calls, even his suicidal ones. He may settle in, and take care of her in various ways, even at great risk to himself and his own marriage, while she goes through whatever maneuvers it takes to keep her own marriage at just the right level of chaos.

In the films noir of the forties, a slinky femme fatale like Barbara Stanwyck, Lana Turner, or Rita Hayworth keeps seducing our romantic hero into helping her get in or out of her marriage. The hero usually ends up dead or in prison, but wiser about the relationship between marriage and romance. A more recent example is *Body Heat,* in which Kathleen Turner seduces William Hurt into helping her with an unpleasant domestic situation. He falls for her, and kills her husband for her. She pins the murder on him and escapes with the money.

In an utterly different and less cynical genre, one of the most painful stories of romance and marriage is *Ethan Frome*, by Edith Wharton. Ethan is a dour, laconic New England farmer. He has suffered all his life, doing his duty toward his sickly parents and his barren land. He marries his cousin, Zeena, a morose woman who has helped him nurse his dying mother. Then Zeena falls sick. Mattie, a cheery servant girl, comes in to help and brighten the gloom. Ethan falls in love with her and comes to life. Zeena sees his transformation and sends Mattie away. Ethan is to take Mattie by sled to the train. He plans to run off with her, but realizes he can't desert or escape Zeena. He plots a joint suicide, which sounds lovely to the romantic Mattie. En route by sled, he tries to decide which course of action to take. He aims the sled at the suicide tree, but hesitates. They hit the tree. Mattie is left paralyzed. Ethan is scarred and crippled. Zeena must pull herself together to be caretaker of the two lovers forever. Twenty-four years after the accident, the atmosphere in which the three are living together is chilling.

ROMANTIC PAIRS

Another truly explosive combination is the coming together of two romantics: Tristan and Isolde, Lancelot and Guinevere, Romeo and Juliet, Héloïse and Abelard, Bonnie and Clyde. They mesh so perfectly, they just go wild. The landscape is strewn with bodies before they are through with each other. When two romantics fall in-love, all else disappears and fades into the mist, as in a perfume commercial. The rest of the world just ceases to exist, and anyone who objects is blown away. The couple are so overheated that when they finally come together, they go up in smoke.

Romantic-romantic pairings can be seen as manic folie à deux. These people are crazy, but they reassure each other of the intense sanity of their love. Before one of them cools off and backs away, they may have gotten divorced, thrown away all their money, alienated all their friends and relatives, and wrecked their health.

One common pattern of this type is the rich older man who suddenly breaks away from his lifelong caution and falls crazily in love with a glamorous girl young enough to be his daughter, or even granddaughter. He sees in her his lost youth and his forsaken naturalness. She, a child of deprivation, finds in the old man her idealized father. While some may think she is only a fortune hunter, she really does love the old man and is eager to devote her life to his care and happiness. But in order for this mismatched couple to get together, at least one has to get out of a current marriage, and they must go to war against the forces of reality. Only after all the barriers to happiness have been removed does it become apparent that they really don't fit together. But then it may be too late for both of them to go back to the lives they have wrecked for love. The usual duration of this process seems to be about six months, but it can be prolonged if there is sufficient opposition.

I could make a few generalizations about the nature of romance: it has little to do with love; it never works out for very long; the more illogical it is, the more intense it is likely to be; the more intense it is, the sooner it becomes a disappointment; no matter what happens, everybody gets hurt.

TRIPS TO HAPPINESS

A case in point involved Hap, a nice, hard-working, self-made man who had, with his wife Joy, built a successful business. He charmed all the customers, while the energetic, cheerful, and very ambitious Joy really ran the business. Their business had several locations, and they had made lots of money. They had raised their children successfully and had launched them in careers of their own. As they passed their fiftieth birthdays, they realized they could now travel more, as they'd always planned to do. Joy began to think of all the things she'd wanted to do. She felt free now to pursue romance and pleasure and even some frivolous toys. Hap just liked to keep working and had no interest in any of the things she suggested. She did talk him into buying a new sports car, but he worried a lot that it would get scratched, so he usually left it at home under a blanket. Joy thought of travel and brought him folders of cruises they could

take. They did go on a cruise once, but he got seasick. He had never
learned to play, and was far more comfortable working. Joy was
losing patience with him.. They actually were in some conflict for
the first time in decades.

Joy decided that she was ready to stop working, so she could visit
her grandchildren more and do some of the many things she
enjoyed. She had to hire several people to replace her, two people
to handle the money and the business, and a woman to receive
people at the front desk. Joy found a young woman who lacked
education and polish, and overdressed, but was cheerful and eager
to keep everybody happy. Joy thought Cherie might even please
her increasingly surly husband, who was feeling a bit lost now that
Joy wasn't going to be around full time.

Actually, Hap found that he liked Cherie very much. She reminded him of his favorite daughter, who, he'd always hoped,
would come to work with him, and who never did. But Cherie was
just fine. She did her job, and she began to go to lunch with him
and tell him about her problems. She told him about her marriage
to Spike, who ran around on her, beat her up, and made her support
him. But she loved him. Spike was out of prison at the moment,
and refusing to concern himself with the deep financial troubles
they were in. Hap offered Cherie money, but worried that Joy
wouldn't like that, so he did something he'd never done before—
he decided to keep a secret from Joy, even tell her a lie, and he
urged Cherie not to tell his wife about their financial transactions.

Over the next few weeks, Hap began to feel a bond between
Cherie and himself, and he would have told Joy about it under
ordinary circumstances, but he felt uncomfortable because he was
keeping a secret from Joy, and then he somehow just didn't want
to talk with her about it. He didn't quite see the young woman in
sexual terms, though he did notice that he began to think about
her when he was having sex with Joy. That was OK. He and Joy
had a great sex life and they both had fantasies about other people
and that was fine, but somehow this was different, perhaps because
he hadn't had fantasies about the same person so consistently
before.

He felt that he was being unfaithful to his wife, something he'd never done before, so he tried to clear his mind of the fantasies. The more he worried about them, the stronger they got. He decided Cherie would have to go. He called her in to tell her she'd have to go, and she started crying and he held her, and then somehow they were half naked and on the floor. Well, he couldn't keep her after that, but he couldn't let her go either. So he met her for dinner, and he could not for the life of him remember how he ended up in bed with her, but he did. It wasn't very successful sexually, not the way it was with Joy, where they understood each other so well. The sex with Cherie was quick. He was not the sort of man who did this sort of thing. He must be in-love.

Joy could not believe Hap when he asked for a divorce, and all the children agreed that their father must have lost his mind. Hap was adamant. He was going to give up his wife, his children, and his business and go off with Cherie. He had Joy pack his bags and get him a reservation at a nearby hotel that specialized in grownups who were running away from home.

He then called Cherie to tell her that he had moved out and was ready to start his new life with her, and save her from the degradation of her life with Spike. She rushed over and they had some more inefficient sex, and he gave her some more money. Cherie was furious that Hap had told Joy, because now she'd probably lose her job, and she had to support Spike. The time was wrong for her to leave Spike right now. She was worried about him, especially if he found out she'd lost her job. Hap had really messed things up by telling Joy. Cherie cried a lot about how hard Hap was making it for her and for poor Spike. So they would have to cool it for a while. Then she went home, and he sat there all alone in that strange room and thought about the glory of love.

Hap waited for Cherie's call. When she didn't call or come, when he couldn't reach her, he called Joy and threatened suicide. Joy didn't quite know what to do, so she humored him. He was desperately worried about Cherie. Somehow, the resolution of all of this was that Cherie kept her job, Hap went back home to Joy but not to Joy's bed, and Cherie stayed with Spike, but she continued to have intermittent sex with Hap. This arrangement went on for many months. Spike got arrested for drunk driving, with some parole violations, and was sent back to jail. Cherie was distraught, inconsolable. Hap brought her to me.

The situation was very simple. Joy loved Hap and would do anything to make him happy, even if it made her miserable. Hap loved Joy, and had always been happy with her, but now he was in-love with Cherie, who made him miserable. Cherie appreciated Hap, but she couldn't show it because she was in-love with Spike. Spike, whom I didn't see, was a philanderer: he didn't love anybody, which made his life a great deal easier, even in prison. Spike was the only happy member of this family.

Cherie was a classic romantic, as Spike understood and exploited. As long as he could make her miserable enough, she would remain in-love with him. Hap would seem to be the least romantic man alive: he had never done anything frivolous, selfish, or impractical. But when his wife was calling on him to cut loose, he couldn't do it. Instead, he fell crazily and painfully in love, as people so often do at points of crisis and transition. It really had very little to do with Cherie. It had to do with Hap's fear of changing his relationship with the world.

And what about Joy? Joy, not really a romantic herself, had always loved Hap in a mature, comfortable, sexy way. She had looked forward to a bit more romance at this stage of life, but it had scared Hap too much. She understood that Hap was a bit crazy right now, and decided to hang in there.

I saw them. I advised sending Joy back to work at the business, and finding a job elsewhere for Cherie. In time, Hap woke up and wondered what had hit him. He and Joy decided not to retire, and instead of living in luxury and traveling, they worked together and took dancing lessons on Thursday nights.

KEEPING SANE AMID THE ROMANCE

My family and I took a bobsled ride down an Olympic bobsled course. It was exhilarating, terribly exciting, utterly inexorable, and very uncomfortable, though we didn't notice how uncomfortable it was until it was over. While we were in the sled, racing eighty miles an hour out of control on the ice, being slammed from one icy wall to the other, we only felt the excitement. The whole thing lasts less than a minute. Romance is more dangerous. It too is totally compelling and almost completely impervious to outside influence. But romance can last for weeks or even months, and can interfere with one's real life.

I urge people who are in-love to slow down and enjoy it, and not to take it seriously. But they can't do that any more effectively than a bobsled could. The in-love are out of control, out of their minds, and out of reality. So it is the other people in the lives of the in-love who must keep their heads.

The betrayed partner has the difficult job. Cuckold spouses of people caught up in the throes of romance feel that their marriage is threatened, their dreams shattered, their security gone, but even more awful is the insult. Suddenly their partner in a love that was once this special too has declared them to no longer exist. There can be few greater insults than that. But in addition, their mate has come to life in another relationship, displaying a capacity for happiness and joy that has not been readily apparent up until now. The insult and rejection seem total.

It is very difficult to recognize that this craziness and disorientation should not be taken personally. The person who has been betrayed may not even realize that the infidel is likely to return home. It is difficult to survive such a degrading and depersonalizing situation, yet there are advantages to holding on. Nothing the betrayed spouse can do will affect the romance, but the romance is time limited, and will most likely fall apart. The aggrieved partner might want to be there when that happens.

I advise spouses who are waiting for their mate's romance to end: don't try to out-romance a romantic. Don't bother to arouse jealousy. Don't try to get your partner's attention, increase your partner's guilt, or threaten some sort of unpleasantness. Just express your point of view and then go off and do whatever holds you together during this time.

11 / Marital Arrangements

"Marriage resembles a pair of shears, so joined that they cannot be
separated; often moving in opposite directions, yet always punishing
anyone who comes between them."
SIDNEY SMITH, *LADY HOLLAND'S MEMOIR*

"Though marriage makes man and wife one flesh,
it leaves 'em still two fools."
WILLIAM CONGREVE, *THE DOUBLE DEALER*

In all the years I've been working with people whose marriages were
in some sort of trouble, I have run across very few marital problems
for which the ideal solution would be to go out and have an affair.
Having an affair does not solve a marriage problem. But having an
affair may stabilize the marriage by bypassing the problem and
making it unsolvable.

Nonetheless, people assume that when someone has an affair,
unless it is clearly an "accident," it must be because of a problem
in the marriage. There are a lot of people who are unhappily
married and who are having affairs, but the unhappy marriage is
not causing the affair. More likely it is the other way around.
Obviously, when people have affairs, that makes the marriage unhappy. Romantics get into intense affairs, and turn a comfortable
marriage into a prison from which they must escape so they can
sacrifice for love. When people find themselves too married and
decide they want to have affairs, they must first make their mar-

riage unhappy. Philanderers keep marriage in a state of hot or cold war so they can have their affairs.

It would seem ludicrous to assume that people first decide that they are unhappily married, and then go out secretly to have an affair. Yet there are a group of marriage situations in which the couple have a problem they don't want to solve, and they decide to stay married—at least for a time—while one or both have affairs on the side. These affairs are not necessarily particularly secret. In fact, they are part of a marital arrangement.

All marriages do not seem to have been made in heaven. Despite all the glorious expectations—or maybe even because of them—the marriage fails to fulfill the needs it was expected to fulfill. The marriage just doesn't work. Yet it isn't awful either. These people can live together, more or less, without too much danger of suicide or homicide. And unless they are hopeless romantics, they might consider themselves well favored by Dame Fortune. While that may be a hell of a lot saner than being hopelessly and desperately in-love, as they were when they got married, it's not as exciting.

There are reasons for staying together even when things are not blissful. It really isn't that bad an idea to stay together for the children's sake; that is, it isn't such a bad idea if neither partner is violent, or an alcoholic or druggie, or trying to punish the children for making the parents stay together in misery. It may make sense financially for people to stay together; it really may be possible for everyone to have a more comfortable life if the couple stay married. Divorce is often a luxury that people can't really afford. There are people who stay together because it suits their social life to do so, or it pleases their family, or it is an advantage professionally. And, of course, there are people who stay married because they fear being alone and they are convinced that no one else would have them.

Don't knock all these reasons. Only the very young, the very idealistic, and the romantic lovers of misery would criticize a marriage that is a comfortable, or almost comfortable, arrangement that protects people from the desperation out there among the singles who are looking for somebody wonderful enough to make the divorce, or the wait, seem worth the sacrifice.

I'm haunted by a recent survey that shows that only 10 percent of couples believe that they are *both* better off five years post-divorce. My experience has convinced me that when a marriage isn't a threat to life and limb, it is probably worth the effort to keep it afloat. That is not a popular point of view nowadays, when marriage is seen as disposable and replaceable, and I can certainly sympathize with those people who refuse to risk either degradation or AIDS by living any longer with a philanderer. In my practice, I see some people give up on a marriage that would seem to be nearly ideal, while other people sacrifice a lifetime to make a hopeless mismatch work. I guess people have to decide for themselves what they will accept and what they won't. There are certainly no agreed-upon standards about what makes for an acceptable marriage.

The state of marital unhappiness seems to be a matter of decision. People, using criteria of their own design, choose whether they will consider themselves to be in the category of the "happily married" or the category of the "unhappily married." The differences in circumstances may be minimal, but the differences produced by the choice itself are profound. Often one partner will decide to be happily married, while the other will choose to join the ranks of the unhappily married. Being unhappily married would seem to be a strange choice for a person to make. The unhappily married are required to go around being dissatisfied, refusing to enjoy their domestic life, finding little things to be displeased with, complaining and griping about one thing after another, and making sure that no one can set things right. While being happily married permits people to go cheerfully about their business, being unhappily married becomes a major investment of time and attention. It is a hard job, practically a full-time one.

Why in the world would people choose to be unhappily married when they have a choice? I've worried over this for twenty-seven years of treating the transitions and crises of marriage. I think many people are afraid that settling into a happy marriage would require them to give up all their other options, all other potential partners. The happily married drop their guard and settle in to comfortable intimacy. They stop fighting against the forces that pull people quite naturally into a complete fusion in which, like couples married too long, they even begin to look alike. The unhappily married make an enormous sacrifice in order to keep differentiating themselves as separate and distinct individuals rather than half of a couple.

People have a certain range of closeness or distance with which they are comfortable. This is the most important point in the understanding of both marriage and infidelity. There really is an incompatibility of sorts between those who want intense closeness and those who don't. Family therapist Salvador Minuchin speaks of relationships as being intensely close or "enmeshed," or being desperately distant or "disengaged." Those relationships in which one partner wants to be enmeshed while the other wants to be disengaged are bound to be conflictual, and the couple will have great difficulty deciding whose rules will be followed in conducting the conflict. It is not that enmeshment is good and disengagement is bad, or vice versa, but that both partners have to be in agreement or everybody will be uncomfortable. The most serious problems come when one or both partners are inflexible about closeness and distance, and have a narrow range of comfort with it.

There are a few couples who insist that their marriage works best if they live in separate cities or even separate countries. I'm working with a couple now in which the wife insists on living in Luxembourg, the only country in Europe to which her husband, because of some tax difficulties, cannot go. She visits him in various other countries several times a year. But if he starts getting too personal, asking about the man she lives with or something like that, she huffs off and returns to Luxembourg. I ask why he continues to be married to her, and he tells me he loves her, his religion teaches him that divorce is a sin, and he thinks it best for the children if their parents stay married. Anyway, he thinks his wife is a little crazy and needs the stability of marriage. When I ask her why she stays married, she says "money," but she then goes on to explain that this is the ideal of marriage in her culture—she provides certain services and the status of being married to her, and in return her husband supports her according to her specifications.

If both partners want distance, then the marriage can work beautifully for them—if they can get far enough apart. In John Irving's *World According to Garp*, the nurse Jennie Fields doesn't like men very much, but decides she does want a child, so she hops astride a dying patient whose brain damage keeps him totally oblivious to anything going on around him, and gives him an erection. She is promptly impregnated, but she hasn't bothered to look up the name of the man who impregnated her. He dies immediately after his ejaculation, so she names her son after his dying word, "garp."

Many a man would not want to be married to Jennie Fields, who wants such a small part of what he has to offer. But many a man, especially in wartime, marries someone he has just met, impregnates her, and then ships out, taking her picture and address. He wants for her to insure his immortality, but he really wants very little personally from her, and he offers even less. She, of course, may want little more. She may well have married him just to get her parents' permission to move out on her own. I occasionally see a young woman who doubts that she is attractive enough to get a man of her own in this country, so she will go abroad and marry someone who wants to emigrate. Once he gets here, he may or may not stick around.

We cannot assume that all couples want to be intimate partners, even if the very close marriage is in vogue in this country these days. In most of the world, couples don't aspire to such closeness to a spouse. Their closest relationships are with their children, with their parents and siblings, or with their same-sex buddies. In some parts of the world, the spouse is treated with great respect and dignity, while the greatest closeness is with a mistress or master who functions as lover and companion. If that's what everybody wants, it may be no problem at all.

The point is that marital closeness is not everyone's ideal, and is not the ideal in every society. There may be advantages to marital closeness, such as flexibility and compactness of the emotional unit.

There may be advantages to marital distance, such as a greater range of close relationships and greater independence of functional roles. Close couples may tend toward interchangeable functional and emotional roles. As they get closer, they learn from each other, develop each other's skills and talents and interests, and model themselves after each other. They may even begin to look alike. Distant couples, on the other hand, may tend toward greater gender differentiation. They may avoid negotiating things and sharing things, and instead divide the tasks and roles according to something impersonal, like which is male and which is female, and that way they don't have to deal with each other very much. Either approach can work, though the implications are enormous.

The real difficulty comes when one partner wants closeness and the other wants distance. They then are in constant conflict, with one trying to start fights that will require interaction and discussion and attention being paid, while the other uses conflict to justify leaving the house, going to another room and locking the door, or going into a silent snit—anything to reduce interaction. One pursues, the other runs away. The pursuer pursues harder, the runner runs farther, and round and round they go, each believing that their model of marriage is the "right" one.

Either the partner who wants distance or the partner who wants closeness can achieve it by getting involved with someone else. The marital arrangement requires a third or fourth person to stabilize a relationship that is alternately too intense for one partner and too flat for the other.

There are a variety of marital arrangements by which a less than ideal marriage is stabilized through the addition of a marital aide, someone who is willing to sacrifice or complicate his or her own domestic life for the sake of preventing this mismatched couple from having to get a divorce. Marital aides are willing to settle for the mistress or erotic friend role, or they can play rescuer when the marital battles get too intense and somebody runs away from home. The marital aide may be the prospective second husband or wife, just waiting while posing an ever-present threat to keep the current spouse in line. The affair with the marital aide may keep the distancer distant, or give the snuggler someone to snuggle with.

The marital aide solidifies the marital arrangement, protecting the marriage from getting any better or any worse. A triangle is amazingly stable; it won't wiggle and it won't bend, so if you want to change its shape, you have to break one of its sides.

TYPES OF ARRANGEMENTS

Here are some of the marital arrangements people can make when they decide they want to be unhappily married, yet stay in the marriage. Rather than solve the problems that they blame for their marital unhappiness, they decide to stabilize the marriage in its imperfect state, and they do this by bringing in an affairee, a marital aide who turns the arrangement into a triangle. There is no secrecy about the marital unhappiness, and usually not about the affair, though the identity of the affairee may be kept secret. These arrangements may not really be infidelities at all—they may involve little dishonesty or secrecy. However, adulterous marital arrangements do keep the partners from solving a marital defect in a more efficient manner. Types of arrangements include "the permanent separation," "the permanent triangle," "just shopping," "psychiatric nurses," "importing love," "importing sanity," "importing sex," "revenge affairs," "the power struggle," "guerrilla theater," "jealous lovers," "flirtations," "sex therapists," and "the swingers."

The Permanent Separation

Men who are "in the process of getting a divorce" keep getting involved with women who are in the market for a husband. The process of getting a divorce can take many years. For many people, the midpoint of the divorce process is their marital ideal. They may refer to themselves as separated. They are not married, in the sense that they have a commitment to someone else, but they are not divorced, in the sense that they are free to marry someone new. One partner may be trying to get a divorce, while the other may be trying to prevent the divorce; or, sometimes, this in-between arrangement suits everybody just fine. It may have financial advantages for somebody, or it may fulfill some religious qualms about divorce, or it may protect some family members from pain.

But, most often, the state of prolonged marital separation is a way of preventing remarriage. Now, who would want to keep someone from remarrying? Well, the outgoing spouse may be holding up the divorce out of disapproval of the incoming romantic entanglement. If the divorce can be postponed long enough, maybe the forces of sanity will bring the romantic back to earth. Or perhaps the betrayed spouse is too angry with the affairee to set the betrayer free until that particular affairee is out of the picture. This may work sometimes, but romances thrive on opposition, so keeping the lovers apart may simply postpone the disillusioning discovery that the romance was ill-advised.

More frequently, the state of permanent separation serves the purposes of a philanderer, who is thereby protected from being married or from getting married. He can give each new conquest hope that the divorce will finally come through during her time at bat, that she has a chance to win the grand prize of the newly single man. Desperate affairees, like small children, will believe almost anything, even that old one "The divorce is in the works."

People who want to be married get married and make it work. People who want to be divorced get divorced, and pay whatever the cost. People who want to be separated are protected from marriage in either direction. People who don't want to be married are likely to be philanderers. They have found their ideal state, and are not likely to change it.

This marital arrangement has more stability than might seem apparent. The marital aide, the affair partner who keeps hoping that the divorce is in the mail, is crucial but interchangeable. She can be readily replaced, and will be in due time.

The Permanent Triangle

There are people, mostly men, who don't want to be married, who don't want to be divorced, and who don't want to be separated either. They want to have control, without the risk of being controlled, and they want it all as stable as possible. These men are terrified of coming under the control of one wife. They know, perhaps from experience, that they won't achieve the desired level of distance by changing to a brighter and shinier new wife. They certainly don't want the disorder and confusion and obsessive effort involved in philandering. They have passed through their romantic phase and are too mature and wise for that now. The quest is for efficiency without sacrificing comfort, and above all without having to get too interdependent with one woman.

Bigamy or polygamy would suit them fine if it were legal. Those societies that permit plural marriage find that only a small number of men choose it for personal, as opposed to economic or political or status, reasons. And in our society only a small percentage of men want this particular balance between distance and control. Those who do sometimes take on a mistress. Mistresses, in our society, don't usually have legal status and job security. Sometimes the mistress is also married and, like the man, is participating in this arrangement part time. Or the genders are reversed, and a woman keeps a man. Of course, it is hard to find a good mistress or mister these days, with so many other career opportunities. So the turnover rate is fairly high. And sometimes mistresses attempt to elevate themselves into the wife position—which may be grounds for dismissal.

The point of the permanent triangle with the steady mistress or mister is that it stabilizes the marriage. It protects it from intimacy, and it provides a safe outlet for a semiphilanderer who might otherwise be prowling more loosely, or a semiromantic who might otherwise be falling in-love.

Frequently the spouse is well aware of the mistress or mister, though it is not usually discussed openly, as that would be too intimate. The permanent triangle ordinarily starts when a philanderer makes an effort at being a romantic and falls partially in-love, but can't quite let the self-destructiveness of romance overcome the self-protectiveness of gender war, so he settles into a friendly relationship with his affair partner, likes it, and makes it permanent. This may not seem too different from the erotic friendship arrangements of full-blown philanderers, but it is a lot closer and involves much more than just sex. A man's mistress may well be his best friend, as long as she doesn't threaten his marriage and the basic stability of his complicated life.

When a man starts screwing around on his mistress and tells his wife about it, things have become confusing indeed. But that happens. I have also seen cases in which men will change wives, but keep the same mistress through both marriages. These men are stability freaks, but they surely are afraid of intimacy.

Just Shopping

Many people have chosen to declare themselves "unhappily married" and to be seeking a more suitable mate. Such people are not really philanderers, but are certainly not romantics. They keep trying, but they can never quite fall in love. They are shoppers. They are looking for the mate who is just right for them. These shoppers sort through the available possibilities, try on some of the more likely candidates, and find some shortcoming with each in turn.

Even though shoppers never seem to find the perfect mate, they remain married to a highly imperfect one, and make no effort to improve that domestic situation, since it clearly is temporary and "someday my prince or princess will come."

The shopper's mate is in a helpless situation, unable to get the shopper to invest any attention to repairing or improving the marriage that has been rejected but not deserted. The shopper's mate may not even be able to divorce and end the marriage, as the shopper will then worry endlessly over divorce lawyers and details of settlement. The more freedom the shopper has to make a choice, the more extensive the areas in which he or she can express dissatisfaction.

A shopper may one day have to leave the marriage, and may at that time need a getaway driver, someone to take him or her away from all of this. The shopper, knowing that day could come, may keep one or more getaway drivers on emotional retainer for emergency use. Shoppers, and various other kinds of people who are unhappily married but reluctant to divorce, may be terrified at the thought of running out of mates. So the next possible mate is kept on hold, to be brought out in case of emergency.

Psychiatric Nurses

There are people who choose to stay married to quite damaged people, manic-depressives who undergo wild mood swings, schizo-phrenics who are frighteningly fragile, or depressives who are so shell-shocked by life that they seem to require constant padding and insulation. There are alcoholics and drug addicts and others who are delicate and unpredictable. They need caretakers, and may expect the caretaking as part of the marriage contract. A marriage centering on one partner's dysfunction requires the other partner's overfunctioning. People who have been prepared by family circum-stances to overfunction may become professional or amateur psy-chiatric nurses, and may actually seek out a marriage partner who is excessively needy. I frequently hear people say that they married because "he needed me so," "she couldn't take care of herself," "I couldn't break it off."

It is a hard job to take care of the incompetent. It may be an added challenge to keep the incompetent incompetent, by over-functioning so reliably that the incompetent never has to function at all. Any possible equality in the relationship is lost, in a way that need not occur in the marriages of the physically disabled, who may need extra help in some areas but gets to be a competent party to the arrangements. The marriage between the psychiatric nurse and the psychiatric patient may require extreme imbalance. The nurse has the more appealing job, and I have noticed through the years that it is the patient, not the nurse, who is most likely to leave the marriage.

Such marriages may be extremely stable, unless the patient-spouse is a manic-depressive who gets involved in great romances during high periods. The nurse-spouse has signed on for this job and will stick with it. It would seem impossible to find someone else to take over if the nurse resigned.

The nurse-spouse may need emotional support too, and there-fore may keep a friendly affair going. These affairs are chosen with great care, as befits the incredible conscientiousness of the care-taker. These are supportive affairs more often than erotic or roman-tic relationships. They are likely to be long-term, and they fre-quently involve an effort to get help for the damaged spouse. I notice the frequency with which clergy, therapists, or physicians are chosen as affairees in these situations.

The classic depiction of this arrangement is the Clifford Odets play and film *The Country Girl*, in which Grace Kelly alternately pampers, protects, and humiliates her alcoholic actor husband, Bing Crosby. She has an affair with William Holden, the director of her husband's comeback play, so Holden can hold both Crosby and Kelly together. Holden pampers and bullies Crosby into com-petence, so the actor can stand on his own and survive when the director runs off with the wife. Crosby is just as insufferably obnox-ious as a competent success as he was as an incompetent failure, but Kelly spurns Holden and stands by Crosby through thin and thick. At the end, Holden realizes that he's been used.

Importing Love

Some marriages could be called "efficient arrangements." They may produce and raise children, create a home and a life, and do it all with seeming ease. Such marriages may work well financially, socially, and even sexually. Efficient marriages may even develop expertise in problem solving. The various family members may schedule "quality time" with one another. There would seem to be no logical reason for complaint. But the marriage may have an emotional flatness. And so an affair is tempting.

In such impersonal marriages, role assignments and family rules are likely to be set up on the basis of gender. Husbands can devote their energies to the masculine business of working, and wives can stay at home and tend to the house and children. For greater efficiency, the couple may avoid discussing each other's life. Friends and relatives may think they "make a beautiful couple."

However, little that is emotional transpires between them. One or both partners may feel horribly lonely, and may sink into depres-sion and desperation for someone to be close to. The lonely one may appeal and cajole and threaten in an effort to get the other's attention, and may finally be told to get it elsewhere. The partner who is satisfied with the average twenty-eight minutes of closeness a week and does not want to be bothered with more than that may provide the opportunities for an affair, may implicitly encourage it, may even give the explicit message to go out and find intimacy elsewhere.

Most often, it is the wife who finds herself in this situation. She may choose an old boyfriend for her affairee, someone with whom there is a history of friendship and understanding. If such is not readily available, there are well-spoken romantic younger men who seem to specialize in paying court to lonely married women, but are not in a position to support them. It seems important that the courtly lover not be a serious threat to the comfortable, but flat, marriage.

These affairs can be wonderfully romantic, but they may not be very sexual. The affair is about inefficiency, about hanging out together and wasting time, so the talk-time to sex-time ratio should be as high as possible. The contact may be primarily via telephone and over lunch. The lonely wife does not really want to leave the marriage, but is flattered by the attention and even by proposals of marriage and other urgings to take her away from all this.

Importing Sanity

Truly stormy marriages are hard to maintain, what with everybody carrying on and running off in all directions as they keep everything very intense and very exciting and as unstable as need be to make sure no one relaxes for a moment. Some couples really like to fight and run away, and scare their partner into running after them, so they can feel that love takes priority over whatever was on the schedule. With all the ups and downs, ins and outs, offs and ons of such marriages, both partners need an emotional haven. People who lack sanity themselves may have to import it into their marriage.

Those in stormy marriages generally include alcoholics, manics, hysterics, and people with a great need for attention and very little self-control. They have to have an audience and a sparring partner, but they also have to have sane buddies and rescuers to whom they can turn when they burn out. Such stabilizers may be built in. The classically intense, crazy marriage may be a second marriage that began as an illogical and ill-matched romantic affair. The stable, boring first marriage partner may remain in the wings, ready to step in and provide sanity on cue.

I once worked with a couple I called the "Friday Night Fights." Every Friday night, the couple would go out for a drink or two after work, and before the night was over, they would have thrown each other out of second-story windows, or chased each other naked through the neighborhood, or rammed their cars into each other. Sometimes they would show up at the same emergency room, and start it up again. When the situation began to frighten even them, he would crash at his ex-wife's house. His wild present wife had a former boyfriend, now a bartender, at whose apartment she could collapse to sleep it off. The ex-wife and the bartender became important and much appreciated members of the Friday Night marriage. Unfortunately, the bartender decided to marry, and his new bride would not tolerate "that crazy, drunk floozie," so the stormy marriage fell apart for want of sanity to import.

Importing Sex

Some people just don't like sex. They don't like to say so, though, and they may insist that they like sex but their partner doesn't. It can get rather confusing.

The jokes men tell would suggest that their wives don't like sex. I run across a few women these days who are militantly opposed to sex, and I see some men who are determined not to have sex with their wives. Some of these sexless men prefer to masturbate, some of them are doing God knows what with God knows whom and just not telling me about it, but some really don't like sex. Some of them started very young, some had bad experiences, others just never got much of a sexual pattern going—I can't explain this problem. My best explanation is that these men are frightened at the thought of what they see as a sexual demand when they are not ready to display themselves at their most splendid. They wait until they are ready, which seems to happen quite rarely, but they refuse to be coaxed or ordered or scheduled or seduced into sex. They must have an erection before they enter the room.

Sex, after the age of thirty or thereabouts, is a habit rather than a drive for men. If men don't use it, they will indeed lose it. Those men who wait for their sexual desire to reawaken have just committed sexual suicide. Most of the wives of these men who have retired from sex seem to muddle along without it. Some import it.

In recent decades, women's popular culture has done a good job teaching women how to enjoy sex, but many still don't like it. Some haven't learned to have orgasms, others don't like to let themselves go sufficiently to have orgasms, still others find sex an intrusion into the fantasied chaste romance. There really are marriages that have been sexless for years, even decades.

Sexless spouses frequently tell their still-sexual partners to take their business elsewhere. Most of the partners find they don't like doing this, and become sexless themselves. A few, though, try to maintain outside sexual relationships that don't threaten the marriage emotionally. And, of course, just because someone tells you to go outside the home for sex doesn't mean he or she will like it when you do. Wild domestic violence and bitter divorces have centered on affairs the spouse suggested, encouraged, or even paid for. People who want a sexual marriage want something far more personal than the sort of sex philanderers want. This is not something that can be purchased. One ingredient in it is sex, but another is familiar old romance, and still another is just the personalness of having no barriers to intimacy with your partner. These people want a relationship, and if they can't have sex at home, they're likely to fall in love with whomever they're having sex with —including prostitutes. Several men who wanted sexual relationships with their wives found themselves falling into rather bizarre in-love states with expensive call girls.

Some philanderers justify their behavior by insisting that their wives don't want sex often enough or with quite the desired variety. Some complain that their wives do not respond exactly as they'd like. It isn't always clear that such a man wants his wife to respond as he says he does. Often he is merely justifying his dissatisfaction. When I work with such a couple, I suggest to the woman that she provide as much sex as her husband says he wants, and do so enthusiastically—thus calling his bluff. (If a couple want to achieve sexual compatibility, it seems sensible for them to have sex as often as the partner with the higher libido desires, but in the manner preferred by the one harder to arouse. If a couple are doing anything other than that, they are clearly trying to make sex incompatible for some reason.)

A philanderer may claim that his wife no longer fits his erotic fantasy; perhaps she weighs more than he might prefer. None of this has anything to do with sex, and if she achieved what he considered the perfect weight, he might then start in on changing her height. No woman could keep transforming herself into whatever a man might choose to fantasize. It works far better for him to overcome his belief that he can only have sex with someone who physically corresponds to his erotic fantasies. If he would restrict himself sexually to her for a while, after a steady stream of orgasms with her, she would become arousing to him. There is no sight that can be as arousing as the memory of sexual pleasure. This may seem unromantically Pavlovian, but it works when people try it. There are limits, of course.

Revenge Affairs

The revenge affair is a nasty thing. Sometimes, when an affair is discovered, the crisis cannot be resolved until punishment is exacted. The biblical injunction of "an eye for an eye, a tooth for a tooth" has its own compelling logic. So the enraged spouse may embark upon a revenge affair, torturing the offending partner with the gorier details. Even the most confirmed philanderer cannot compete in sheer meanness with a spouse driven toward a revenge affair.

The hapless affair partner who innocently steps into a revenge affair is likely to be caught in the cross fire of other people's marriages. Even if the unfaithful husband has given his wife permission to exact revenge, he isn't going to like it. The man she has chosen for her act of revenge is going to be the object of the husband's anger as well as that of the revenging wife. The revenge affair cannot possibly relieve her rage; there is no way to satisfy this kind of anger. Postcoitally, the affair partner has failed to resolve the situation, and thus becomes the new target.

The revenge affair, somewhat romanticized, was featured in the perceptive sixties comedy *Bob and Carol and Ted and Alice,* in which Bob has an affair and confesses to his understanding, forgiving wife, Carol. They are being oh so liberal about it all. She then decides to try an affair of her own, "not because you did it, but to see if I could do it." Bob is surprised by the strength of his jealousy and insecurity, wondering about the size of the affairee's car and whether the man in *his* bed with *his* wife was also wearing *his* pajamas. After that unsettling experience, Bob and Carol agree to not keep sexual secrets, but to have an open marriage. They then attempt an evening of swinging with their best friends, but that just makes everyone uncomfortable, and the film ends with the understanding that sexual freedom doesn't really work. The experiences and conclusions of Bob and Carol, and of Ted and Alice, struck me as right on target, but the atmosphere of emotional sweetness is not how it happens in the real world. In real life, these things hurt, and the anger is not easy to salve.

At times, the faithless partner will actively assist in the effort to exact the punishment, even going so far as to arrange a revenge affair for the betrayed spouse, often a threesome with a friend or with a professional. The arrangements can be a cooperative effort that brings the couple together, and the whole business can seem like a game—until it is over. At that point, the spouse has become faithless too and feels dirty, and can blame the original infidel for the humiliation of both the offense and the revenge. I've seen this happen a fair number of times, and the one originally betrayed usually ends up even angrier than at the beginning.

Revenge affairs don't work very well, and I don't recommend them. I did know one couple in which the husband had an accidental affair, and urged his wife to repay him by having one too. She did, but she told him she hadn't, and thus punished him through both the act and the secret, yet kept him feeling that he still owed her one.

The Power Struggle

Infidelity is the secret weapon of domestic warfare. Either spouse can threaten to have an affair, if necessary, to win a power struggle. The hope may be that the threat will be sufficiently alarming, and won't actually have to be acted upon. The inclusion of infidelity as one of the things people threaten does signify a commitment to fidelity. If it is clear that it would never be acted upon, such a threat becomes almost endearing. But if there is reason to doubt the partner making such a threat, it can be powerfully cruel. If the betrayer chooses to threaten infidelity, if that is what it takes to win a power struggle, what then is the other spouse to threaten— divorce, murder, castration? Even if an infidelity is never committed, the idea of it is intimidating.

Some people, generally philanderers, actually use affairs to win power struggles. Such philanderers don't like to keep their infidelities secret, but prefer to announce them and declare them the spouse's fault: "Look what you made me do." This shifting of responsibility turns a confession into an accusation, fueling the power struggle. Obviously it is practically impossible to make someone else be unfaithful, but marital battles of this sort are not logical; they have to do with hurting each other into submission by comparing each other's commitment to the marriage.

There are different ways of keeping score during a marital battle, and the scoring system can change constantly. Domestic power struggles usually begin with each partner giving his or her column points for the greater commitment to the marriage. ("I've listened to your mother's insane ramblings all these years." "I can't count how many times I've put you to bed when you were too drunk to climb the stairs.") Then a shift in the scoring system may occur, and one or both give themselves points for their ability to escape the marriage. ("I could live so comfortably if I didn't have to keep you and your fat ass in food." "Every man I've ever been to bed with could support me better than you do.") When a marital battle reaches that turning point in the scoring, it may seem more dangerous. It really isn't, because each player is just being reminded of the interdependency.

People do blame their partners for their own decisions to be unfaithful in secret. If people actually believe they are not responsible for their own behavior, they must be dillies to live with in other areas too. There is something truly outlandish in the statement "I am not responsible for my behavior. You are." One possible response is "I refuse to take responsibility for your behavior unless you do exactly as I say at all times." But marital power struggles aren't meant to make sense.

Frankly, as many times as I've heard this, I don't believe people really do have affairs as punishment. I think they just want to see whether that excuse will float. People on their way home from an affair feel guilt, and if they don't like feeling guilt, they may convert it to anger. They find some imperfection to blame the anger on, and then they walk in, loaded for bear, with a "Look what you made me do!" Any excuse may be worth a try in the plea for reassurance that you are still welcome at home.

Guerrilla Theater

Some couples go through elaborate rituals to keep their love alive. They may even put on shows in public, using a volunteer, nonprofessional supporting cast. The volunteers are not aware that this is a theatrical production, and the couple may not be either. The play involves courtship and seduction. It requires that the couple have a fight and split up, at least for a few minutes. One finds a new partner. The other then must break up the new partnership and seduce the partner back into the marriage. This sort of game was particularly popular in the screwball comedies of the thirties; Cary Grant seemed to be constantly struggling to get his ex-wife to come back to him. In *The Philadelphia Story*, it was Katharine Hepburn; in *The Awful Truth*, it was Irene Dunne.

Some more or less real people actually live this way. They can't really appreciate their spouse unless they have a rival. They obviously like competition with a rival more than they like being married. Such people are monogamous romantics. They don't want to go through all the disruption and turmoil of changing partners, but they enjoy winning the partner more than they enjoy having the partner, so they encourage the partner to have romantic affairs with which they can compete. Obviously, this is not the sort of thing one can be forced into. The partner who is willing to go through all these separations, romances, courtships, and reconciliations must be volunteering for the role. Occasionally, the partners may switch roles, but most often one is the courted and one is the courter.

The hardest role in this guerrilla theater belongs to the affair partner, who thinks this great romance is working toward marriage, and suddenly discovers that it is all play and that his or her role shifts in the last act from hero to villain to comic relief. Some of these scripts let the betrayer marry before returning to the ever-seductive spouse. While the couple may enjoy all of this, it does seem like a cruel trick to play on a trusting affair partner.

Jealous Lovers

Jealous lovers go through a simpler exercise in guerrilla theater, but they can wrap up the whole performance in an evening. One flirts; the other fights. They can go into bars or even museums if they're good at the game. There the flirt finds someone to flirt with. The fighter watches. If the flirt gets a response, the fighter jumps in and creates a scene. The responder to the flirt's flirtations is publicly humiliated. The fighter drags the flirt out of the joint. They go home and make love.

There is a slightly more sophisticated version of this game. Sometimes the fighter loses rather than wins the fight, and the flirt then rescues the fighter. And then they go home in each other's arms. There is surely a country song or two describing this game.

Flirtations

An even simpler variation is the solitaire version of the jealousy game. It is played secretly. The partner who needs reassurance of attractiveness goes out and flirts until someone responds. Once a stranger responds, the game has been won, and further play becomes optional. Of course, the one who needs reassurance may be in the mood now and may accept whatever has been offered. If anything actually happens, the flirtation has become personal, guilt-producing, and complicated. If the game is called before any clothing is removed, the winning flirt gets the desired reassurance, plus a powerful sense of self-control. And the story can be taken home for a response there too.

Sex Therapists

When sex isn't very good at home, philanderers rejoice and screw around more and romantics fall in love. But when the going gets tough, the tough go out for help. Some go to professionals, but sexual do-it-yourselfers find makeshift arrangements for sexual instructions. They take lessons from their friends, and then they race back home to rescue their marriage. Or they may stay with their instructor for advanced study.

There are a few couples who are so clumsy and amateurish sexually that someone has to show them what to do. I think of a virginal couple who could not consummate the marriage. She insisted that the boy's penis was much too big, and she threatened to faint at the sight of it. He was flattered, but unsatisfied. I had him measure it—it was five inches. Defying my suggestions, she took matters in her own hands. She advertised on the bulletin board at work for men with small penises. After auditioning a few, she chose one she liked, divorced her husband, and married the man with the smallest one. Years later, these two remain happy and tell me that sex is wonderful.

A man found himself to be impotent after his heart attack. His wife was mildly disappointed, but she avoided putting him in the embarrassing situation of having to attempt sex, assuming that he would fail in the effort. He finally discussed the situation with his cardiologist, who attributed the impotence to the man's medicine, and changed it. He still couldn't get an erection. He and his doctor thought perhaps fellatio would be easier for him, and he suggested that to his wife. She found the idea distasteful, and refused. But she did offer her permission for him to find someone else to perform this service. He checked with the women at work, and found one who agreed to assist in his sexual retraining. She gave him regular sessions of fellatio until his sexual courage returned, and he could take erections home to his wife. As the sex resumed in his marriage, his wife felt grateful to the woman at work, but preferred not to know her name.

A decade or two ago, I saw quite a few women who did not achieve orgasms in their marriages. They had affairs with men who had been recommended to them for such services, learned to have orgasms, and brought the information back home to their incredulous husbands, who had never considered the possibilities. I haven't seen this phenomenon in recent years, since more specific sexual information has been made publicly available.

The Swingers

There are sexual hobbyists in the world, people whose major interest is exploring the joys of sex in whatever variations can be imagined. Such people, if they pursue their curiosity to its limits, will become omnisexual, and will overcome any fear or anger toward the opposite sex. These sexual hobbyists may not ultimately be philanderers, though they may start out that way. Sexual hobbyists seem perverted to most people, since they enjoy voyeurism and exhibitionism, sex with creatures of all varieties, and may be willing to try out some pretty risky things. They may thus be like normal adolescents. An attraction to the kinky is neither unusual nor abnormal at certain transition points of life, but most people get their fill rather quickly.

There are people who retain a lifelong preoccupation with the outer sexual limits. Most, but not all, of the adult sexual hobbyists I have treated have been rule-breaking, risk-taking, antisocial people in other areas of life as well. They seem to get more pleasure from the defiance and the risk than they do from the genitals. Whatever is forbidden is sexy, and when they run out of things that are forbidden, they lose their interest in sex. For these people, sex is an expression of anger rather than an expression of love. Generally, they are not good at relationships.

True philanderers dabble in the sexual underground, and keep it secret. They would not tolerate mate swapping—the philandering game is gender and domination, not sexual freedom. True sexual hobbyists don't seem to tolerate this domestic secrecy. They want their wives, husbands, and sometimes their children involved in their hobby. Exposure to the world of orgies and swinging and sadomasochistic animal shows can blow the minds of certain mates, who will run screaming out of the marriage. Sexual hobbyists seem to do best when they marry people who share their interests, after giving up custody of their children to their more inhibited ex-mates.

In the sixties and seventies, I saw a fair number of couples who had attempted swinging, and those who came to me were usually repelled, if not by the sex, then by the other swingers. Some major crises were triggered by these experiences. Most couples were embarrassed and uncomfortable about it later, and often angry with whoever talked them into it. There were some exceptions: couples who enjoyed threesomes, foursomes, and larger groups. Some were glad they had had this experience, though few felt much desire to continue it. Nowadays, people get so much explicit sexual exposure and adolescent sexual experience, there is little sexual curiosity and adventurism left for them. I know there are adults out there who still do this sort of thing. I don't know them, and I can't imagine who would be doing it during the AIDS era, or who would stay married to those who do.

Lately, I have seen a few people who have abolished sex from their marriage because their partner is determined to be the last surviving homosexual or heterosexual swinger. Swinging and "free sex" seem dated and dangerous now. Maybe they always were.

MAKING ARRANGEMENTS

People go into marital arrangements voluntarily, as they try to avoid solving some problem that scares them too much. Sometimes people get into arrangements that they don't like, and don't know how to renegotiate the arrangement. The obvious solution in all these situations is just to discuss the arrangements.

Most people are uncomfortable with their affairs, and are reluctant to discuss them. They seem ashamed of them. I've seen a few people who were glad for an affair they had had. They credited the affair with helping them to leave a marriage that they were too passive, too angry, too helpless, or too polite to fix. Others credited an affair with helping them survive an awful marriage until they could make their getaway. But in general, infidelity, even if it works for one who is unfaithful, is a catastrophe for the marriage.

I've seen very few cases in which *both* partners believed that an affair and its crisis had been more helpful than harmful to a marriage. The likelihood of an affair helping a marriage is on the same order as the likelihood that the marriage could be improved by some other major crisis, such as the house burning down or the baby dying. A fine watch may be repaired by kicking it, but that seems risky. Any crisis stirs things up, and the outcome may be better or worse, but things will never again be the same.

The imperfectly married need therapy, formal or informal. A crisis may be necessary to get people into therapy, and few things trigger a crisis quite so dramatically as an affair. There are mules to whom people are married, and, as we all know, you must talk very gently to mules, after you've gotten their attention by hitting them over the head with the two-by-four. Still, it seems far more efficient to discuss the problem before taking heroic action that will push things to a crisis.

In my experience, the only affairs that work for the marriage are those marital arrangements that enable people to survive badly flawed marriages that no one wants to fix. And even when the purpose of the affair is to increase distance within the marriage, those affairs that work involve a minimum of secrecy and confusion. People who want distance in their marriage seem frightened of dealing openly and honestly with issues of infidelity. They fear such openness will bring about the marital closeness they are using the affair to avoid. Some people finally try negotiating closeness and distance, and discover that it can be done. Afterward, they may or may not feel a need to go on with the affair, but at least they aren't confusing or torturing anyone with it.

There is some comfort in knowing that even if your life and your marriage are crazy, they're honest. When your secrets aren't secret any more, you can feel at home at home.

12 / Infidelity and Divorce

"Love has got to stop somewhere short of suicide."
SINCLAIR LEWIS, *DODSWORTH*

"I swear, if you existed, I'd divorce you."
EDWARD ALBEE, *WHO'S AFRAID OF VIRGINIA WOOLF*

Once a marriage has jelled, has been together for a while or has produced a child, it is not easily dismissed. In established marriages, there is no such thing as divorce. What the law puts asunder continues at full tilt emotionally. If people hate each other enough, no divorce is strong enough to keep them apart. Divorce does not seem to come about because a marriage is bad, but because it has been broken.

As I see it, when a couple divorce, it is probable that someone is being unfaithful and won't stop it. In my practice, about half of the unfaithful couples divorce. However, divorce is unusual among established couples who are being faithful. In long-standing marriages, over 90 percent of the divorces involve infidelities. That may come as a bit of a surprise.

Divorce is not generally thought of in this way. We don't ordinarily point out that divorces and affairs are linked. *People* magazine shows pictures of couples in romantic affairs, crediting them with providing solace to each other as they dig out of the wreckage of crumbling marriages. There is rarely the connection that the affair *caused* the marriage to crumble. When people talk about their divorce—even to therapists and certainly to family and friends—they explain that they married "too young" or "too soon after the last divorce" or even "too late in life." They describe how great the differences were between them and their former husband or wife. The idea is that the marriage, even if it worked quite well for twenty years or produced twenty children, was not really what God or fate had intended. The marriage was somehow invalid from the beginning.

Those who are explaining their divorce may acknowledge that there were "difficulties communicating" or that they "grew apart." What they don't say is that they were having affairs and telling lies and keeping secrets, and staying as far apart and communicating as little or as confusingly as possible. In all fairness, they themselves may never have made that connection.

There are occasional marriages in which a woman finally escapes a violent or alcoholic husband after the children grow up or after the beleaguered wife attains some financial independence. Ordinarily it is like pulling teeth to get victimized women to leave their persecutors. Those who work at shelters for battered women often despair about changing these situations because the women stay so loyal to these awful men. Men (whose needs from marriage may be more functional) seem to be less loyal to awful women than women are to awful men. Still, some husbands tolerate great psychological and even physical abuse. Divorces occasionally happen in these situations, but even then those who want out frequently wait until there is a comfortable place to go and a traveling companion for the trip.

People don't often leave marriages without first being unfaithful. We usually assume, as was pointed out in chapter 2, that affairs happen because the marriage is so awful, and that does seem to happen about a fourth of the time. The rest of the time the marriage was serviceable prior to the affair, and became awful after the affair. One partner has the affair, ruins the marriage, and then flees the wreckage. And it is ordinarily the betrayer—not the betrayed—who makes the decision to divorce. That may come as a surprise too.

The process of divorce is different in each of the four kinds of infidelity. Those few divorces that are entered after accidental affairs are panic attacks, so clearly crazy that someone usually stops them before the divorce actually takes place. People who have settled into marital arrangements in destructive or dreary marriages may have great difficulty detaching. These people have made arrangements that prevent divorce, often at a dreadful cost. If they do try to get out, they are so skittish and ambivalent that they rarely leave the marriage—they merely seduce a marital aide into helping them keep the marriage both awful and intact. Romantic affairs lead inexorably, almost hypnotically, toward divorce, without regard for consequences, and in a powerful hurry. They too are likely to get stuck about halfway between the two relationships, but there is nothing comfortable about that position.

Finally, the spouses of philanderers may file for divorce, in a desperate effort to get attention. These spouses don't really want divorces and hope they will not happen. However, the philanderer may initiate a divorce, usually to get more control, and then not want the divorce. The philanderer may even stop philandering during the divorce battle, since divorce is a more dangerous and therefore more interesting game than philandering. Philanderers can be dangerous during a divorce, even when they are instigating it.

The process of affair-induced divorce can get pretty wild, but the basic pattern is fairly predictable:

1. *The betrayal.* First, someone breaks the marriage bond by having an affair. The affair is kept secret. Lies are told. Life becomes disorienting. The marriage grows increasingly confusing. Sanity can only be maintained by creating distance. The situation develops into a state of crisis.

2. *The battle.* Rather than acknowledging an infidelity, the couple choose to fight about it. The partner who has been unfaithful insists upon denying what is obvious, while the spouse insists that the obvious be explicitly confessed. They both go underground

and keep secrets, one using confusional tactics while the other plays detective. If the affair continues to be secret, they try to confuse each other. If the affair comes into the open, they battle over who is to blame. The cat and mouse games can get dangerous. The couple must be fighting in order to detach, since getting the secrets out into the open might lead to resolution and intimacy.

3. *Blamelessness.* Each blames the other for the situation, and since there are no rules of logic in such matters, neither has to make sense. These people are not trying to salvage the marriage. They are trying to prove that its failure is not their fault. Each seems to believe it is important to be the good guy and prove that the mate is the bad guy. They take this quest for absolution to whatever judge and jury they can find, which includes all the relatives and friends. When that isn't sufficient, they find a judge and jury to assure them that their marriage is not their fault. The struggle for blamelessness can become so intense that they may not even notice that they are, incidentally, getting a divorce. If the marriage is bad enough, the divorce may go fairly well. If the marriage has seemed satisfactory prior to the affair, the divorce can look quite crazy. At this stage, the effort to discredit the other partner makes each partner look so unappealing that both appear to be monstrously defensive and attacking. Each goes around town publicizing the other's most embarrassing secrets and most repulsive habits, which is extremely unattractive to the captive audience. It is particularly burdensome for the children. Soon, everyone believes these two really should get a divorce.

4. *Emotional incongruence.* One infuriating feature of divorces in which there is an affair going on is the incongruence between the divorcing pair. The betrayer may already have found a new partner, or may simply be someone who has had practice at finding new partners, and does not feel the loss of the marriage. Meanwhile, the betrayed spouse is shattered, terrified of the future, and therefore collapsing on friends and relatives. The happiness of the escaping one, of course, is the unkindest cut of all. And the one who has been unfaithful can be excrutiatingly insensitive, detaching totally during this period.

5. *Waking up.* The deserted partner makes contact with the

world outside the marriage and discovers that life goes on, perhaps even better than before. As the betrayed spouse recovers, the infidel's great affair or great freedom or great power play or great panic attack comes to an end. These two events often coincide. As the rejected spouse is feeling increasing strength and survival skills, getting everyone's support and seeing the advantages to being free, the infidel begins to feel the disadvantages of the divorce, and reality sets in. As the enormity of the emotional, physical, and financial sacrifice becomes clearer, the strain on the affair grows. Philanderers no longer have a spouse to escape from, and little pleasure in having sex legitimately. If the affair continues, the divorce puts a heavy burden on the affair partner, now being called upon to make all those sacrifices seem worthwhile. The partner who has been unfaithful can get caught halfway between two relationships.

6. *Human sacrifice.* The affair partner is usually sacrificed somewhere in this process. The couple, so used to fighting in their own way, are experts at a game the affair partner is just learning. So the couple, even as they divorce and battle, may delight in ganging up on the affair partner, who seems baffled at everyone's anger. Affair partners may not understand the power of marriage to consume anyone who falls into the internal machinery.

7. *The return of the infidel.* Almost always, the betrayer makes a pass at returning to the betrayed. Some of these efforts are suspect, such as suggested arrangements that include the affair partner. The betrayed spouse is generally given a chance to decide whether or not to go through with the divorce.

8. *The Mourning.* If the divorce is halted partway through, the couple celebrate. If the divorce goes through, each is granted a period of mourning. And both have lost a great deal, even the romantic who fell in love. A romantic affair, once out into the open, devastates children and looks ridiculous to grown-ups. It usually falls apart during the divorce process, as reality sets in. If there was no romantic affair, the betrayer can make an even better case for being the victim of this domestic disaster.

Whoever brought about the divorce now gets the desired divorce, gets to be surrounded by disaster, and gets to seek everyone's support for the resultant state of mourning. Infidels, in seeking everyone's emotional indulgence during the divorce process, only occasionally cry about how their spouse didn't want them to have affairs. Instead, they talk about how hard they tried to satisfy someone who wanted them to change in some way. The distortions can be astounding; people might not recognize their own marriage from their partner's description of it during the divorce.

Even after all of this, divorce does not finish a marriage. Until the marriage is understood, and its problems mastered in retrospect, the survivors really can't go on to new marriages. Those who have been betrayed and deserted have soul searching to do, and they may have the time and the solitude to do it. Those who ran away may not stop and comb through the wreckage of their lives, and may not learn what they need to learn before they try marriage again.

Divorce has got to be painful if it is to do its work of finishing one marriage and preparing people to try again—perhaps with someone fresh, perhaps with someone familiar.

ACCIDENTAL DIVORCE

In the wake of an accidental infidelity, the unfaithful partner is tortured, and may reveal far too little to orient the betrayed spouse. The sudden desire for a divorce comes as a surprise, especially since the marriage seemed reasonably satisfactory until right now. The affair itself rarely continues, though it may do so in an embarrassed guilty alliance.

It is not usual for a divorce to take place under these circumstances. I have heard of it happening as an item of past history, when an infidel panicked and ran all the way through a divorce without revealing what was going on. A few young men have described an early divorce in a short marriage, where they felt sexually deprived but too protective of their inhibited bride to push the matter at home. Instead, they fell into accidental affairs, and realized they liked the sex but not the dishonesty. After deciding against the life of a philanderer, they chose to divorce and live as bachelors instead. These young men then sowed some wild oats, found a relationship more sexually compatible, and married again more maturely.

People have gone through separations after an accidental affair, but those I've seen have reconciled. I know of a few cases that involved inhibited, anxious, and controlling people who were caught up in fundamentalist religions. When they learned of a spouse's infidelity, they immediately considered divorce. However, the same religion that was so absolute required them to "forgive" the miscreant and stay in the marriage, and they then punished the poor sinner through eternity.

In accidental divorce, the unfaithful partner has made an error, and wants to keep it secret even though it is causing psychological trauma or systemic confusion. The impulse is to run. This leaves the mate confused and baffled, perhaps with self-blame for some imagined defect. If the mate does try to accept blame, there is no one to notice that something crazy has happened.

If the couple could achieve a few moments of emotional congruence, the problem would be solved and the divorce prevented. If the betrayer feels sufficiently guilty, and the betrayed feels sufficiently insulted, divorce can happen before the frightened and disoriented couple realize what they are doing. Any therapist—or even any sane bystander—could prevent the disaster. And fortunately that usually happens in time.

An Accidental Near-Divorce

Eve had an anxiety attack. She called my office, referred by a relative I had seen, and told me she was dying. She was hyperventilating and in panic. Her husband, a dentist accustomed to such reactions, rushed in (the maid had called him) while we were talking. I sent her out for a walk with him, and a second phone call was far calmer. She was scheduled for an appointment the next day. She insisted it be an individual appointment. The next morning she called to cancel it, saying she had decided to divorce her husband and move to California later in the day. My wife (who is also my co-therapist and office manager) talked her into coming in anyway, by pointing out that she was obviously upset about some secret, probably an affair, and we were accustomed to dealing with such things.

She came in alone and confirmed our suspicions. Eve was thirty, had been married ten years, and had three small children. Her well-to-do parents had not considered college important for her. She went for a year, and then got married. She was still a virgin when she married. Her husband, Egbert, was five years older. Egbert was a large, quiet, handsome man, who worked long hours as a dentist; his feet hurt at night. He was nice to her and gave her whatever she wanted. She had three children, a Mercedes, a big house, a maid, and a tennis court.

Eve hoped she could get Egbert to exercise and was taking tennis lessons so she could play with him. The tennis instructor, a college student, gave her a book to read. She'd never read a book before, nor had Egbert. She tried to get Egbert to read it too, but he preferred the *Wall Street Journal.* She talked about the book with the tennis instructor. More books followed. Finally he brought her *Fear of Flying.* By then, they were talking about things she'd never talked about with anyone. One hot day the tennis instructor asked if he could take a shower, and she just stood there as he walked out of the shower naked; they fell into bed for a few frantic seconds. They both felt foolish. She hurried him out and had an anxiety attack.

She tried to act calm when Egbert came home, and he didn't notice anything untoward. She called the young tennis instructor and asked him what she should do. He acted helpless and begged her not to tell her husband. She fired him, rehired him, and fired him again. He left his phone off the hook. She went to his apartment to take him back his books, then feared Egbert would notice, and went back to get them. That night she seduced Egbert and it was, as usual, good. She felt some relief, but she didn't sleep all night. She was hyperventilating the next day and called me.

She told me the story and calmed down. She had already told Egbert she was going to divorce him, but wouldn't tell him why. I told her to tell Egbert the whole story and bring him in a few days later. She came in alone. She hadn't told him, she hadn't slept, she wanted sleeping pills, and she'd planned an escape to California. I told her I wouldn't see her without him.

She brought Egbert in. She had now told him she wasn't going to leave. He was baffled by her plan to leave him, since he thought the marriage wonderful. She'd never complained before. Now she wanted to talk about things and have him read things. He preferred to solve problems rather than talk about them. He wanted to know what to do. As he saw it, Eve had gone crazy. The dalliance was not mentioned, and he left more confused than before and rather hostile about the pointless confusion.

That night she told him everything. She felt great relief. He was angry for a few minutes, then felt panic with the fear that unless he changed to be more like the tennis instructor, he might lose her. She was so comfortable, she suggested rehiring the tennis instructor. He actually cried for the first time in his adult life.

By the next appointment, Egbert felt more secure that Eve would stay and playfully threatened to have affairs of his own. Mostly he was awkwardly, frantically responsive and attentive, offering to take her dancing, offering to read the books she'd read. She loved it, but he was sweating.

They spent six months in a couple's group, while she tried to teach him to communicate about the things she had learned. He gradually became a little more playful, but not too much, as she basically liked him as he was. They quit coming to the group when a new couple came in and he could not face the embarrassment of reviewing the affair again. He saw the problem as solved.

A year later Eve called to report that Egbert was working less and enjoying it more. She was happy, he was happy. She was glad the whole thing had happened. She could get his attention very easily now.

There was no question that Eve's reaction to her dalliance was too intense to permit it to go unexplained. The result of the confession was positive. Some day Egbert may have such a dalliance himself, and he will tell Eve about it, and they will handle it OK. A marriage that has survived such revelations is not always better for it, but it certainly can be.

PHILANDERING INTO DIVORCE

Philanderers aren't really fit for marriage, of course, but that doesn't stop romantic partners from trying to housebreak them. Philanderers have even been known to fall in love, at least long enough to go through a divorce, especially if everyone is lined up in opposition to the divorce, and anticipate remarriage. When the circumstances are sufficiently inappropriate, a philanderer can actually get a divorce, or at least push the spouse into going ahead.

The spouses of philanderers can be exceptions to the general rule that the partner who has the affairs is the one who gets the divorce. A philanderer can finally go too far for even the most masochistic mate. Or perhaps the spouse has just become more self-confident or independent. Perhaps she's finally given up on getting him into therapy, and has gotten herself into therapy so she can save her own life. Perhaps the philanderer won't stop the current affair (which the philanderer can't do, of course, without committing an act of obedience to a wife). The philanderer may be protecting himself by spreading himself around. It isn't unusual for these men to be divorcing a wife, planning to marry an affair partner, and sneaking away from the mistress to make love to the wife. This can become extraordinarily crazy as the philanderer goes (in all directions) through a divorce.

Frequently the philanderer figures out a way to stop the divorce without giving up the affair. Sometimes he has to give up that particular affairee and find another. Philanderers have been known to marry their affair partners, but it is not the usual pattern.

When a female philanderer is married to a male philanderer, it can be even more complicated. When a female philanderer is married to someone monogamous, the male spouse suffers and clings and tries to use the threat of divorce to get the philanderer under control, which doesn't work any better for a female than for a male philanderer.

Philanderers must win and don't care if they play fair, so the divorces can be cruel and nasty. A philanderer will deny all wrongdoing and attempt to prove in court that the monogamous (or sometimes incidentally unfaithful) spouse is the true philanderer.

The philanderer may be so expert at lying that he can seduce a jury too.

The philanderer's spouse must be prepared for some unpleasantness in the process of escaping the marriage. The philanderer doesn't want her as a true partner, but may well want her as a housekeeper or as an opponent. He does not see her as an equal, but as a possession. In a divorce settlement, he assumes he owns everything—all the property and possessions, and her. He may believe he owns the children, though he generally thinks it is her responsibility to take care of them. The divorce may provoke monstrous behavior in men who seemed civilized apart from their inability to practice monogamy.

To a philanderer, marriage is a betrayal of *his* rights to independence and dominance. These experts at seduction can seduce everyone into seeing them as the aggrieved party. The philanderer may try to convince the spouse that he has learned his lesson, and the first few times he tries this, he may succeed in seducing her back. The spouse may beg and plead for another chance to please him totally. I've known a few philanderers who went straight if no one would tolerate their behavior any longer, but as long as there is any other alternative, the odds are against it. Generally, by the time such marriages come to divorce, everyone is ready.

Philanderers don't believe in divorce any more than they believe in marriage. They tend to drop by to seduce their ex-wives. The wife, who wants to believe some miracle has happened, may fall for this pleasantry and postpone a sorely needed divorce. As the divorce proceeds, philanderers get together with other philanderers and complain about the high cost of women, and their threats to the cult of masculinity. They manage to emerge from divorces with regret about the treachery of women, but no guilt and thus no insight.

A Philanderer's Divorce

Stan was a winner. He was handsome, charming, and successful. He'd learned to play and win every game there was. He even played a game with marriage.

Stan and Blanche had been married less than six months when he spent the night with a woman he met on an airplane. While he certainly had no interest in a woman who would sleep around like that, Stan realized that he would not have slept around unless he had married the wrong woman. This was exactly the same thing that had happened to his father, uncles, and brother, and they'd handled it by getting divorced. He didn't want to leave Blanche— she was fun, beautiful, loving, and sexy; it was a shame that she wasn't the one he could be true to.

After that he kept screwing around—not all the time, of course. Sometimes, he'd be so busy he would go months, even a year, without "a piece of strange." He really felt happy with Blanche, but he reminded himself that they had "irreconcilable differences," primarily in that she believed in fidelity and he didn't. He didn't keep records, and had lost count of how many women he had had, but he felt sure he'd done better than his father and brothers, and he didn't even have to get divorced to win the contest.

Stan and Blanche had long since stopped fighting about his infidelities. He explained that that was the way things were done in his family. Blanche went to the priest, who agreed that this was the way men were, and she should accept it.

Stan couldn't understand why Blanche left him. This business with his partner's wife was no different from any of the others, except for the temporary breakup of the business, and, of course, everybody knowing about the woman's suicide attempt. By then, all Blanche hoped for was that Stan wouldn't embarrass the children. And now he'd done that. Everybody knew. The children joined in demanding that their mother divorce their father. One of the children even threatened suicide. The child psychiatrist got Blanche into a woman's group after Stan refused to see the family therapist. The group and the children were putting pressure on Blanche to leave him. She cried a lot. She loved him.

She told Stan she couldn't take the humiliation of his affairs. Once again he explained the nature of men. The children were worried about AIDS. Blanche told him of their concerns. He was insulted and furious and said he only had sex with women. Blanche gave up and drank more so she could be cheerful for him when he came home.

Stan's business was divided after the crisis with the partner's wife. He moved from Colorado to South Carolina, where they had a home and business interests, and he expected Blanche to follow him. She didn't. He commanded her to move. She refused. He reasoned. She refused. He finally begged and cried, and she still refused—unless he would see me. He agreed. They both came and told me the story. Blanche had filed for divorce. Stan had agreed to all her terms. He begged her to come back. Blanche said she would do whatever I said.

Blanche said she loved him and missed him (and it showed). He said he'd be faithful, though he thought that was a strange thing to ask a man to do. She reminded him that he'd said he'd be faithful the seven or eight other times too. They giggled as they confessed they'd been meeting secretly for sex, sneaking around on the children, the women's group, and the divorce laywers.

They had flown in from Charleston and Denver to ask me what they should do. What would you have had me tell them?

ROMANTIC DIVORCES

Romantics enter the divorce in a romantic haze. Nothing matters except the romance. The marriage, and perhaps the children, no longer exist. Like King Edward VIII, they will give up everything for the man or woman they love. The romantic may even delight in making sacrifices for the sake of the love.

The betrayer may boast about the great romance, or may show a little caution in keeping it under wraps during a quick divorce. The spouse may try to counter this sudden determination to end a life together. But all the mate's pleading and anger and threats are simply unpleasant racket. The betrayer may even move out abruptly to a secret place. So the confounded spouse carries on a battle all alone.

People in love are merely fulfilling some cosmic destiny. The forces pulling the romantic couple together are greater than any-one's will. The lovers are ecstatic. Everyone else is baffled and devastated. If the divorce can just be slowed down, reality may catch up with the fantasy. The betrayed, deserted, and almost erased spouse may have little patience or support for hanging in there. But my own experience indicates that more in-love roman-tics end up back in the marriage than married to the affair partner a few years later. If the infidel can be induced into being honest with the marriage partner and telling lies to the affair partner, everything begins to make sense, and the guilty alliance begins to come unglued. And suddenly the affair partner is the one left out. At this point, the deserted spouse may have suffered quite enough. Most of these deserted husbands and wives do get to choose whether or not to return to the old marriage.

Some of the most miserable people are those whose spouse just "fell in love" and walked out. They keep going through a mourning process in their effort to find out what they did wrong. And it may be hard for them to believe that they didn't really bring this about. The romantic couple in a new marriage seem gloriously absorbed by their love and happiness. If the new marriage fails—as it often does—that may bring some comfort to the one who was deserted, even if the one who was betrayed chooses not to return to the potentially treacherous marriage.

A Romantic Divorce

Nick was a great big bear of a man, 360 huggable pounds. He was a florist, and went through his day at work exhausting himself in his attention to detail and duty and the feelings of everyone else. He tried to bring beauty into everyone's life. Then he'd go home and collapse.

Sex was difficult for Nick. He could handle the mechanics of it, but he couldn't believe that any woman would want him. He had been in better shape as a sailor twenty-odd years ago when he'd found Nellie in that little Irish village. Nellie had been a tiny, dependent, inexperienced virgin who had given up hope of ever marrying. She was living at home with her invalid father. Her only obvious talent was cooking.

Nick got fatter and fatter, and his self-loathing became intense. He couldn't imagine that Nellie would want him if she knew any better. He couldn't bear the sight of himself in sexual embrace, so he lived on fantasies of some other man making love to Nellie. His preoccupation with sexual fantasies grew, and he devised costumes for Nellie and playlets for them to enact. Nellie didn't enjoy this. She liked Nick's size—that enormous man made her feel secure. The fantasies and games meant to her that he had no self-confidence, and that scared her. She wanted to cuddle next to his big warm body, and he wanted to live out fantasies in which his body did not take part. They remained faithful and had sex, but it never was quite what Nick had in mind.

They rocked along like this for years and had five children. When the children grew up and left home, Nellie returned to school, got her degree, and did what she had always wanted to do —taught school.

One day Lola walked into their lives. Lola was only twenty-five, but had just left her third husband. Lola had had a rough life, with poor, inept parents and a reputation that made it impossible for her to go back to the islands where she grew up. She traveled light, and touched down in Atlanta. She knew she could make it anywhere on looks alone. Her first job interview had led her to Nick, and when she sashayed into his office, she gave a look that set 360 pounds of flesh aquiver. It was all over for Nick.

Lola got whatever job she wanted and was rarely out of Nick's sight, day or night. Nellie didn't know what had hit her, and Nick didn't care. Lola wore all the costumes and played all the games Nick had been dreaming about for a lifetime. He would lie on the bed and watch over the mound of his belly as she performed for him. He paid for her divorce, her apartment, and her wardrobe.

Nellie met Lola and decided Nick was insane. All his family agreed. She tried to stall the divorce, but Nick was determined and it was just too humiliating, so she gave him the divorce he wanted. He and Lola were married the next day.

I saw Nick and Lola two months later. Lola had put Nick on a diet, and she refused to wear the costumes anymore, insisting they were degrading. She was saying all the things Nellie had been saying. He couldn't understand the change in her. And she was expensive, refusing all the "sexy" clothes he'd bought her and preferring very expensive tailored things.

Nick began to call Nellie, finding excuses to get together to discuss the kids or the settlement. Lola became jealous and began to have temper tantrums over Nick's friendship with Nellie. How could he be friends with his ex-wife? He was treating Lola like a mistress or a whore, just there for sex, she complained. So she cut him off sexually. Within the month, Nick and Lola were fighting, the police were called, and Lola filed for divorce. She'd found her fifth husband by then anyway.

Sadly, Nellie wouldn't take Nick back. She was sorry she hadn't found a new man, and she wanted to be friends with Nick, but she could never return to the marriage. Overall, she'd never felt better in her life.

DIVORCING ARRANGEMENTS

There is great stability to those marital arrangements that require a sexual supporting cast to keep the loving/hating pair at just the right distance from each other. But sometimes the complex stabilizing structure fails, and the couple are left with no choice except to get really married or get divorced. The divorce seems less real and therefore less dangerous.

The possible range of adulterous marital arrangements is enormous—from those thoughtful oh-so-civilized couples who insist on giving the other a sexual weekend off each year to those sadistic battlers who keep a matched pair of sex slaves chained up in the basement. These couples are going through their idiosyncratic patterns in order to prevent divorce. As hard as it is for them to get together and address conflict, it is even harder for them to detach.

What holds the couple together is their helplessness, their inability either to solve problems or escape. Each feels a victim of the other. If the battle escalates to the more dangerous level of divorce, each is playing "Look what you made me do!" Couples like these can get a divorce almost accidentally, while each is trying to prove that the divorce was not his or her fault.

The primary emotional energy, for each partner, is still directed into the marriage. Infidelities are really peripheral, and merely serve a stabilizing function. The couple continue to fight, or make love, or bicker about the rules, or pursue and reject, or follow whatever pattern turns them on. Even after they divorce and remarry, they may follow the familiar pattern. One painful aspect of these relationships is their intransigence. No matter how much reality intrudes, the couple can't seem to change the pattern. I think of astronauts strapped into their little capsule looking out its little window, and having no control over the orbit the capsule follows or the speed at which it goes.

The affair partner in these arrangements becomes a servant to the marriage. I hear of sophisticated ménages à trois, in which everyone treats everyone with great respect, but I have yet to see one hold together for any length of time. Two always seem to take sides against a third, and it seems to be the affair partner who gets the most abuse. People who devote their lives to hating and fearing the person they stay married to are not likely to have much concern for someone outside their inflexible arrangement.

The divorce process has a life of its own independent of the marital relationship. The divorce may occur at any point in the couple's customary rounds, and while the divorce has a legal reality, it may produce no change in the patterns of the system. These marriages don't seem ever to end or ever to begin.

A Divorce Arrangement

Harry and Edna had a torrid affair, quickly leaving the boring people to whom they had been married. Then the wars began. How could his wife, her husband, all their children, care so little for their happiness? How could they stand in the way of a love so strong? The battles over the divorces, over the custody, and over all the problems with the children filled the next few years and kept Harry and Edna so embattled, so miserably unhappy, they often said they could not have made it through without each other.

They couldn't actually marry for a few years, and by the time the wedding itself took place, things had begun to cool a bit. They did have some fights over who would and would not come to the wedding.

It was just before their first wedding anniversary that all hell broke loose. Edna traveled a good deal because of her job, and was out of town. Harry, as always, called her, but she wasn't in her room. He worried, then panicked and finally drove all night to find her at that motel in Mississippi. She was not in her room. She insisted she was in that man's room because she had drunk too much and passed out. Harry didn't believe that. He hit the man, who proceeded to break one of Harry's teeth. Edna nursed him through this experience.

Harry then took up with Ruthie, a cheerful, low-key, young single woman at work. His affair with Ruthie was extremely open. Everyone, except maybe Ruthie, knew the affair was an effort to punish Edna. Edna was furious and divorced him. He refused to leave. When Edna forced him out, he made a show of moving in with Ruthie, but he still managed to spend most nights with Edna. If Edna went out with other men, he'd hide in the bushes and jump the guy as he brought Edna home.

Harry would arrange to spend the night with Ruthie, then drive the ten miles to Edna's house to pick up his favorite pajamas. He'd wake Edna up and either fight with her or make love to her, or both, and then return to Ruthie, who didn't like to fight and only wanted to make love.

Once Harry took Ruthie to their houseboat, knowing that Edna was there with one of her sons. A fistfight ensued in which Ruthie pushed Edna into the cold water and the boy tried to shoot Harry —but the gun wasn't loaded. It was after that that Edna and Ruthie came to me for help. Ruthie decided to back off, and Edna decided to give up alcohol. Harry was furious, feeling both his women were betraying him.

Harry, however, would not stop drinking. Edna would not re-marry him unless he did. Now he lives with Edna. He sees Ruthie from time to time, though Ruthie assures Edna there is no sex between them. Edna and Ruthie have made a pact of honesty, and each trusts the other. Edna says she doesn't care what Harry does with Ruthie. As long as they're not married, there is very little to fight about.

13 / From Romance to Remarriage

"Marriage—from the beginning of the world, such as are in the institution wish to get out, and such as are out wish to get in."
RALPH WALDO EMERSON, *THE SKEPTIC*

"What the hell, if you get divorced the chances are you'll end up with somebody else's castoff. What's so great about that?"
ANONYMOUS, QUOTED IN E. E. LEMASTER, *BLUE COLLAR ARISTOCRATS*

All logic would dictate that second marriages should be more successful than first. The choices are being made by people who are sadder but wiser, more mature, more experienced, and more cautious. They know themselves better. They should be able to make better choices. They should be better able to handle disappointment and frustration. They should have sowed their wild oats, and come to see life as less distractingly mysterious. They should be readier to settle down.

It may be that second marriages in general do have advantages over first marriages. Those who have been widowed, those who have been divorced for years, often seem to have success with second marriages. It may be that the disasters are only inevitable when people use romance to jump from marriage to marriage without a rest stop in between. There is something inherently doomed in those marriages that began as marriage-wrecking affairs. It is possible for them to work, but it is unlikely they will do so.

In my practice, while over half the people who get into romantic affairs end up divorced, only a fourth marry the affairee. Even then, three-fourths of those romantic marriages end up in divorce. There is a greater likelihood that the divorcing partner will be back with the original spouse in five years than that the romantic affair will be a stable marriage at that time. Why is the success rate so low?

THE DEFECTS OF ROMANTIC SECOND MARRIAGES

1. *The intervention of reality.* Divorce in these marriages tends to take place very early in the marriage. During the affair, the infidel and perhaps the affairee are in a state of intensely stimulating unreality. The second marriage itself seems to be a switch that throws the lights on and illuminates the mess that has accumulated. It is as if the romance had seemed real, while the divorce didn't. Only after the remarriage did the divorce become real enough for the lovers to see that it was all a horrible mistake. The affairs that become marriages typically were so intense they were never questioned at all. During the divorce, reality never set in sufficiently to let the romance be evaluated and questioned. The romance was so romantic no one ever got around to asking if it was sane.

A classic example of the truly romantic affair is the movie *Splash*, in which Tom Hanks falls in love with a cute fish, played by Darryl Hannah, and goes off to live underwater with her. She agrees to use her gills to protect him from having to breathe, but I thought that was a less than practical arrangement. When something seems too good to be true, it probably is.

2. *Guilt.* People who have wrecked a family have inflicted much pain, and they have a lot they could feel guilty about. As reality sets in, they see many things they were overlooking. They may have felt no guilt during the affair and divorce, and the guilt they feel after the romantic marriage may come as a surprise to both of them. It is generally assumed that people who don't permit themselves to be happy must be feeling guilty about something, and are unhappy as a way of punishing themselves for their misdeeds. One aspect

of guilt is the reluctance to enjoy one's ill-gotten gains. Another aspect of guilt is the urge to return to the scene of the crime and in some way make amends. As a romantic newlywed resists the joys of the new marriage, and worries instead over the sensitivities of the ex-mate who was deserted so blithely, the new mate can feel disoriented and betrayed.

One romantic man, who had capped his whirlwind romance with a divorce and a remarriage the next day, began to feel guilty at the wedding, and spent the reception on the phone with his ex-wife, who was mourning the divorce. He then suggested to his new bride that they take his ex-wife on their honeymoon, since she was unhappy and had no plans for the weekend, and they owed it to her since it was their fault that she would be at home alone. This led to a fight that ended with the marriage being annulled. (He did go off on the honeymoon with his ex-wife, but he did not enjoy it and they didn't get back together.)

3. *Disparity of sacrifice.* Divorces are expensive luxuries. Whatever the financial cost, the emotional cost is far greater. Anyone, after losing that much, will be drained, exhausted, and depressed. It is particularly difficult when the exhausted survivor of a debilitating divorce marries the triumphant winner of the struggle. If the romantic partner is marrying for the first time, and especially if the courtship has been treacherous and insecure, the new mate will be ecstatic. I look at pictures of big game hunters with their prey, and notice the difference in mood between the successful hunter and the unsuccessful trophy.

All divorces are not equally debilitating or equally costly, of course. A new couple may feel a disparity in what had to be sacrificed to bring them together. The partner who has never been divorced may have difficulty understanding the complexity of emotions toward the previous family. I regularly read letters to "Dear Abby" or Ann Landers in which a new mate complains that the divorced and remarried partner betrays the new marriage by appearing with the ex-spouse in the child's wedding pictures, or by sending Christmas cards to former in-laws. One such letter even referred to the children of a previous marriage as "ex-children." At the point of remarriage, there is little likelihood that the two new mates will be equally attuned to the sacrifices that have been required. A new accounting system starts with the new marriage, and the columns are unequal from the beginning.

As second marriages fall apart, it is common for people to give an accurate accounting of what had been sacrificed for the marriage. One wealthy and powerful politician had not been an exemplar in his personal life, but had maintained an unsullied public reputation. He had gotten into an affair with the wife of an associate. To avoid a scandal, he arranged to ruin the career of his associate, actually hounding the man into suicide, so he could marry the man's widow. She subsequently blackmailed him with this dishonorable information. She even used it to coerce him into passing over his sons from a previous marriage, and declaring her son to be his official heir.

4. *Expectations.* Then there's the feeling that anything that cost this much emotionally had damn well better be worth it. The greater the sacrifices, the greater the expectations from the new marriage. Now that the promised land has been reached, it should flow with milk and honey. But instead, the new couple are just two tired warriors with no fight left in them. Whatever these people were expecting, the best they are likely to find now is the ordinariness of real life, the dubious peace between glorious battles. Nothing could be good enough to make up for what this has cost. I watch films about the effort to get to the North Pole, with the sacrifice of men and dogs and fingers and toes. And when they get there, there isn't anything but snow and ice, like all the snow and ice along the way. The reward is in the going, not in the getting there. The more people enjoy the battles involved in wrecking and escaping marriages, the less they are likely to enjoy the business-as-usual of the new marriage that was the destination of it all.

People risk everything on the hope that they can achieve joy by changing everything in their lives except themselves. They would like to press a button and have the old life go away and the new life appear. The human animal has an unfortunate tendency to identify the source of any unhappiness as coming from outside itself. The fault, as Cassius informed Brutus, is not in our stars, but in ourselves. Our unhappiness is not in our marriages, but within us. Changing everything about our lives leaves everything important still the same, because we are the important factor in our lives, and we are the one thing left unchanged.

Eric Berne, author of *Games People Play*, told the story of the follow-up visit the fairy godmother paid to the newly married Cinderella and Prince Charming. After all their adventures, they had gotten together and it had been pleasant for a while, but the prince was now off playing with the feet of all the girls in the kingdom, while Cinderella had fired the servants and was cleaning out the toilet bowls. Berne's point, as I understand it, is that romance is so mysteriously and magically automatic, it doesn't produce awareness of anything inside the person. It changes people's lives without changing them.

5. *General distrust of marriage.* Of course, anybody who has been unhappily married is likely to develop a strong distrust of the institution of marriage. People whose marriages fell apart during affairs are likely to end up distrusting marriages rather than distrusting affairs. People who distrust marriage have a very hard time being in one. As the drown-proofing instructor said, the danger comes from the effort to protect yourself from being engulfed. You really can immerse yourself totally in it, relax, and breathe comfortably. But those who are recovering from a wrecked marriage may withhold and protect all manner of things from the new marriage.

People usually protect money from the new marriage, especially if they have children from old marriages. Some make prenuptial agreements that remind everyone that this could be a temporary relationship. Separate money is far more common in second marriages. There may be careful rules about access to the children, authority over them, etc., and three different sets of children may be treated in three quite different ways. Some people enter new marriages with a determination to avoid being hurt sexually. They may withhold either sexuality or sexual fidelity. Most of all they withhold themselves, and lose some of the honesty and openness that may have been present at one time in the earlier marriage. Some second marriages, even after a fiery history, are surprisingly stilted and formal arrangements. One would think that the history of an adulterous couple would bring them close enough, but that does not routinely happen. People in love may be in love with the love, not necessarily with each other, and I'm not sure they are noticing each other very much as they go through their adventure together.

One man who had been divorced twice seemed totally committed to his latest fiancée. He hovered lovingly as she went through her divorce and gave up everything in order to marry him. She emerged with nothing, except him. On the day of the wedding, he suddenly presented her with a prenuptial agreement that, in effect, reduced her to the status of indentured servant rather than partner in the new marriage. He explained that he had been burned by marriage before, and he had to protect himself, but he couldn't tell her his terms until he was assured that they would marry.

6. *Distrust of affairee.* Groucho Marx is credited with saying he would never join a club that would have him as a member. People may feel the same distrust of anyone who would sink into a secret affair with them. It might seem appropriate for someone to go out with them, or even to marry them, but not quite appropriate for someone to have an affair with them. Affairs are considered dishonorable acts, and people who feel guilty for having affairs believe that they are dishonorable and their partner must be dishonorable too. The level of disapproval and paranoia may be directly related to the level of guilt about the affair. But it does lead to the suspicion that if the affair partner "will do it with me, he or she will do it with someone else."

The level of distrust in second marriages is understandably quite high. People may find ways to explain and justify wrecking a marriage, but the guilty participants can't explain it away so easily to themselves; they know just who was doing what to whom. The very things that worked so well in the affair—the romantic abandon, the sexual adventurism, the expertise at deceit, the delight in breaking the rules—work badly in marriage. As a patient once said, "Of course I'm in love with her. I screwed up my marriage and messed up my kids for her, but I'm afraid to *marry* her. Even when I get my divorce, how can I marry her? How can a guy marry a woman who screws around with married men?"

7. *Divided loyalties.* During the affair and the divorce, the ro-

mantic couple isolate themselves. It is not only the betrayed spouses who are erased from awareness, but also the children, the families, the friends, anyone who attempts to pull the romantic couple from the quicksand of their affair. But after the remarriage, there may be a longing to reestablish connections with families and friends, and this may be more difficult than expected. Each close relationship—and some that were amazingly casual—may have to be renegotiated in view of the hurt caused to others. The two partners may differ strongly in the degree to which they can forgive the disapproval or rejection expressed during the affair.

Reestablishing the network will stabilize the marriage but dilute the romance (when they clung together against all opposition). Each time an old relationship that has opposed the romance is reopened, it requires some detachment from the tightness of the romance. And each new relationship that supports the new marriage helps make that fragile new marriage less vulnerable. Actually, everything that works toward stabilizing the new marriage dilutes the romance that has kept the couple isolated from everyone else.

The movie *Twice in a Lifetime* has a bittersweet ending, as it focuses on postdivorce family loyalties. Gene Hackman has left Ellen Burstyn and his children for Ann-Margret. He awkwardly returns for his daughter's wedding. Everyone is uncomfortable. His former wife, proud that she looks so good for him, tolerates his presence better than she thought she would. One of his children bristles at his presence; another glows warmly at his return. Everyone is relieved when the father doesn't go to the reception. He has a lot of regret, but there is no turning back for him. He's not sure how to connect the disjointed sections of his life. So he takes a bouquet from the wedding flowers back to his new woman. We aren't shown how Ann-Margret reacts to that rather complicated gift.

8. *The nature of infidels.* People who get themselves into affairs have some specific characteristics that must influence the course of their subsequent marriages. Each kind of infidel is different. Most of those who end up marrying an affair partner are romantics who drift hypnotically through this romantic high without taking much responsibility. Romantic remarriage seldom works, not only be-

cause of the unrealistic nature of romance, but also because of the reality-avoiding nature of romantics.

A few of the infidels who marry affairees are not romantics at all. Accidental infidels who would go through with divorce and remarry under these circumstances must be a guilt-ridden lot, and chances are they are entering this new marriage as an act of penance. After enough self-punishment, there may be no need for the marriage to continue.

For those who may have emerged from a faulty marital arrangement, the new marriage may be an attempt to stabilize the old marriage by turning it into a ménage à trois. Or the new marriage may have been a ploy in the lifelong battle of a previous marriage. Once this skirmish is over, the new marriage may no longer be needed. In any case, the new marriage is likely to be of secondary importance to the old marriage in the infidel's life.

Even philanderers can fall in love briefly, and in those states in which divorce takes only a few weeks, they may actually marry an affair partner. However, the new mate becomes the enemy—and the new cuckold—very quickly.

9. *The nature of affairees.* Affairees want whatever they want from a relationship, just as everyone else does, but what makes them unusual is that they seek their goals among the married rather than among the single. They choose partners who are not in a position to marry them, and who are engaging in the relationship at great risk. People like this are clearly angry with marriage, and perhaps with the opposite sex. They believe marriage doesn't work, and they demonstrate that by breaking up another marriage as they find a partner for themselves. They substitute a belief in romance for a belief in marriage, and it is frightening to watch people put their trust in the temporary rather than the permanent. If circumstances conspire to bring such people into a marriage, they are not likely to have the sympathies for marriage that would make them good defenders of the institution.

Some affairees do believe in marriage and in relationships, want to make them work, and are willing to take whatever pragmatic steps are necessary. Such affairees may be romantic social climbers who try to displace someone else and go into a ready-made marriage. Women who do this are seen as calculating, but they may make sure they do a good job once they reach the level they are seeking. At least they believe in marriage enough to be practical about selecting a partner.

The nurturing marital aide who sacrifices her own chances for marriage in order to hold someone else's bad marriage together may also be a strong believer in relationships and responsibility. She might be a loving if somewhat self-sacrificing spouse for a self-centered man.

Single male affairees are an interesting phenomenon. They are often emotional beggars, trying to get some goodies without the risk of commitments or responsibility. Since most women who are having affairs fancy themselves as somewhat in love with their affair partner, they treat these men well. Male affairees are experts in recruiting damsels in distress, emotional cripples, as well as women who are being deserted. They are not likely to be shopping for wives. In my practice, few single men were trying to persuade married women to leave their marriages and marry them instead. Nonetheless, accidents happen, and romantic couples can miscalculate. So far, I haven't seen these new marriages succeed for long.

All in all, I would say to an affairee: unless you are seeking the bittersweet tragedy of romance, it is wise to wonder why a married someone would wreck a life for you.

10. *Romance.* People who believe in the chemistry of romance don't bother to learn much about the physics of relationships. When the romance begins to fade, romantics know little about how to solve those problems that they have relied on romance to transcend. It is painful to watch a romantic relationship dissolve. It happens so suddenly, and so totally. These people have already demonstrated that they would rather get divorced than learn physics, so it is far easier for them to follow the same pattern. At the first sign of problems, the couple declare it a mistake and split.

James Thurber drew a cartoon showing a battling couple. One is saying to the other, "Well, who made the magic go out of our marriage, you or me?"

11. *Scapegoating of cuckolds.* During the affair and divorce, the romantic couple conspired to convince each other that the defec-

tive marriage was the fault of the cuckold. To acknowledge otherwise, now that remarriage has taken place, seems a betrayal of the rescue fantasies that fed the romance.

To me, the most crucial step in moving from one marriage to another is the understanding of the past, and particularly of the past marriage. Most people put their energy into justifying their behavior, and protecting themselves from having to feel responsible. That doesn't help. The past marriage must be reviewed with full understanding that it was your marriage, and you were a partner to making it good and you were a partner to making it bad. Whoever broke the marriage, by stepping outside it and telling lies, must take a hefty portion of blame for its final failure.

The legal process, and particularly the divorce process, encourages people to defend their own actions by blaming one another. Infidels often manage to go through the entire divorce seeing themselves as the innocent victim of an imperfect spouse. Sometimes they can convince judges, juries, friends, and families to see things that way. And thus they pay all that money and suffer pain for an experience from which they learn nothing that will prepare them for the next marriage.

Romantics, no less than most people who are keeping their guilt under wraps, don't like to be criticized. One recently remarried romantic went through his first marital squabble with his bride. He went back to his first wife, saying, "If I've got to listen to any criticism, I'd rather hear it from my own wife in my own bed."

12. *Unshared history.* Even if the new marriage survives all of these obstacles, there is one further characteristic of all second marriages: the absence of the shared history that brings familiarity to relationships that began earlier in life. If a romantic marriage has wrecked a previous marriage or two, the history of the relationship is painful to both partners, and possibly somewhat embarrassing to others. The new partners keep thinking about it and justifying it, but it is hard to talk about lightly, in the familiar, safe manner of people who can tell their old war stories without guilt. However intense their commitment, people who share a guilty past aren't totally proud of their new marriage.

We have a family friend who persisted throughout her second

marriage in introducing her husband as "John Doe, my second husband." We suspected that that marriage was doomed, and we were right.

PRINCIPLES FOR SECOND MARRIAGES

Richard Stuart and Barbara Jacobson have written a guide called *Second Marriage*. Much of their advice centers around getting a good understanding of the failure of the first marriage. More of their advice concerns the communicating and negotiating that is crucial for conflict resolution in any marriage. There are special problems in second marriages, especially the management of money and children that belong to one partner rather than to the couple.

Stuart and Jacobson are clear about the criteria for choosing a second mate. Their principles of second-mate selection are the following. (1) "If there is anything we very much want in a partner, we should find someone who already has it. We can't trust the power of our love to create what is not there initially." (2) "We shouldn't marry anyone we don't love, but we should never make the mistake of marrying for love alone." (3) "While we may be stimulated by people who are different from us, those most like us tend to be better choices as mates." (4) "Marry for yourself, not for anyone else."

I would add a fifth principle to those of Stuart and Jacobson: "Don't marry someone with whom you were having an affair during your last marriage." I realize that I am stating something categorically to which there are some obvious exceptions. Through the years, I've seen people work and sacrifice and suffer in an effort to salvage a marital situation that was ultimately hopeless. It is a painful and tragic process, and I joined enthusiastically in the effort to keep these doomed marriages from self-destructing. Nonetheless, I have encountered a few relationships that began as affairs, survived divorces, and then worked as marriages. These are unusual, but not unheard of. There do seem to be circumstances under which affairs are less clearly doomed.

Those that worked had most or all of the following characteristics:

1. The original marriages broken by the affair were truly awful marriages. The infidels had been tied to people who were violent, alcoholics, drug addicts, philanderers. These marriages were not left frivolously. And the commitments and loyalties and responsibilities were taken so seriously that the infidel could not seem to break loose all alone. He or she needed an accomplice in escaping the engulfment of the original marriage.

2. The infidels had not had previous affairs, or at least not often. An act of infidelity was a special and uncomfortable activity. They gave considerable thought before sexualizing the extramarital relationship. They had a history of sexual exclusivity and an enormous respect for marital fidelity.

3. These couples were friends or co-workers and had known each other intimately before things got sexual. The relationship had previously been conducted quite above ground and naturally, without any sense of guilt or infidelity. It did not start as an underground relationship.

4. These people were not romantics, and this was not love at first sight. The attraction was not a violent physical convulsion. It developed slowly as an emotional intimacy. The couple were not believers in magical relationships, and did not see themselves as being at the mercy of gods, goddesses, cosmic forces, magnetic attractions, or chemical reactions. They saw themselves as making decisions about their lives.

5. The new partners felt guilt and blame for the marital breakup. While these people may have had true justification for leaving their marriages, they were willing to take more than their share of the blame for the marital failures, and did not scapegoat the cuckold.

6. These people delayed and had doubts about the remarriage. They went through sacrifices and considerable misery over their divorces, and they paused and pondered between their marriages. They made sure that reality set in before they chose their next move.

7. The new partners delayed long enough before marriage and campaigned hard enough to win the support of their families, and

especially their children. They knew they needed the bolstering of the family, and they gave that a high enough priority to insure that they would receive it.

All experts urge divorced people to wait a while, live independently, examine themselves closely, and recover from the divorce before remarrying. Between marriages, people should get experience in guilt, blame, self-loathing, loneliness, desperation, independence, and enough reality to appreciate whoever is willing to give a little love. And they shouldn't marry anybody who hasn't gone through the same. *Slow down!*

Cole Porter said it in "Just One of Those Things":

> If we'd thought a bit
> Of the end of it
> When we started painting the town,
> We'd have been aware
> That our love affair
> Was too hot not to cool down.

14 / What Will the Children Think?

"Why is happiness such a precious thing? What have we done with our lives so that everywhere we turn, no matter how hard we try not to, we cause other people sorrow?"
WILLIAM STYRON, *LIE DOWN IN DARKNESS*

"Children begin by loving their parents; as they grow older they judge them; sometimes they forgive them."
OSCAR WILDE, *THE PICTURE OF DORIAN GRAY*

People who have affairs may think they are betraying only their mate (some may not realize that they are betraying anyone at all). Actually, of course, people having affairs are betraying the whole family. The betrayal of the children may be the cruelest blow of all, often blindly cruel because the unfaithful parent has no idea that this act could damage the children. Yet the impact of parental affairs on the lives of the children is very much the stuff of tragedy. Some of our most enduring dramas center on children whose lives are profoundly affected by their parents' affairs. We have only to think of *Hamlet* or *Electra* as powerful demonstrations of the universal child's suffering when parents betray the family, and therefore the child.

Children growing up in truly awful families have had so many encounters with the alcoholism, violence, instability, or treachery of one parent or both that they may have embarked upon their own depressions. In such families, children may finally wish that one or both parents would leave, and they feel more comfortable when it finally happens. But infidelity and divorce don't happen only in awful marriages. They can happen in marriages that provide considerable security.

Children rely upon the stability of the marriage and family. If secrets keep family members from being close to one another, the family undergoes disorientation. Children who experience secrecy and lies cannot trust what they are told; they become insecure and dependent. When the framework of the family finally collapses, there may be no honest relationships to fall back on. The children feel cast adrift.

Young children are egocentric, and tend to see themselves as the source of all parental misery and strangeness. They may even feel guilty and assume they are to blame. Even when the secret is out in the open, the situation can be disturbing. Children don't have the power to change their parents' behavior, but they do have the power to make life very difficult for themselves and/or their parents. They may lash out with horrifying fury at a parent who betrays the security of the family.

Worst of all is when a child shares the secret of infidelity with the unfaithful parent. Arthur Miller's play *Death of a Salesman* centers around such a secret. The play dramatizes the tragedy of a family in which the son becomes so disillusioned that he rejects his family and all the values his father has seemed to represent.

In *Death of a Salesman,* Willy Loman is the cheerful loser who tries to make it on a smile and a shoeshine, and puts great store in being well liked. But when the customers stop smiling back, he turns to suicide. Willy's downhill slide, as he struggles to achieve the American dream for himself and his loyal wife Linda, is shown in counterpoint to the failures of his sons, the worthless Happy and the tragic Biff. Biff, Willy's pride and joy, is a sports hero who has won a scholarship to college and enjoys every opportunity Willy can arrange for him.

A turning point occurs when Biff has a crisis with an examination and wants to find his father to ask advice. He goes to his father's hotel room in Boston and finds Willy with a strange woman. The woman flirts with the boy, and Willy doesn't see how horrified Biff is. Biff runs away. He feels betrayed, as if everything his father has stood for and believed in is no longer credible. From that moment on, Biff rejects the idea of success. Without explanation, he leaves home, carrying his father's secret with him. He is too furious with Willy to confront him, and he can't talk with his mother, who keeps asking for explanations. Willy never gives up on Biff, though, and his ultimate suicide is an effort to provide Biff with his life insurance benefits, to make up to his son for that infidelity in Boston.

Surely the worst position for a child is that of confidant to a secretly adulterous parent. This is the situation from which Biff Loman runs, and it has most of the characteristics of an incestuous relationship, in that the child is fused with one parent by a guilty sexual secret that could blow away the family. The secret makes it practically impossible for the child to get close to the parent who has been betrayed. Such a situation is a disaster for a child—of any age, even grown. Boundaries are blurred, alliances are too exclusive, and the parent-child relationship becomes too preoccupied with sex. A child who carries such a secret can blackmail the unfaithful parent, which is, of course, an extremely destructive way for a child to learn about power. The child may try to protect the parents' marriage, or try to wreck it, or may just use the secret for personal advantage.

The sons of philanderers are at risk to be caught up in their father's philandering. Philanderers are show-offs, and they feel alliances based on gender rather than on generation, so it seems quite appropriate for them to form secret alliances with their sons to hide things from the wife and mother. The son can be sucked into an undercover all-boys setup so the old man can prove he is not under the thumb of the boy's mother. The son, at any age, can find the father's pride in such an endeavor disorienting and profoundly disturbing. The son must deal with divided loyalties, feelings of protectiveness toward the mother (and a secret that creates a barrier of pity), and alliance (though it may be profoundly ambivalent) with the father. Sons of philanderers who grow up to become philanderers themselves often recall their fathers' revelations as the beginning of their underground sex life. But if they discover the father's philandering from some other source—local gossip or an outright scandal, for instance—they may feel no alliance with the father, and only protectiveness of the mother and outrage at the betrayal of the family.

THE CHILD IN THE CENTER OF THE STORM

Children can develop virtually any physical or emotional symptom while the parents fight out or wait out the threat to the family. If one parent is in a romantic affair and has forgotten about being married and having children, the children have the choice of either going crazy or forgetting that parent. The children may be further confused to realize they have been living above an underground life. Ordinarily, when children don't understand things, they are encouraged to trust their parents. Suddenly that trust has been misplaced.

Small children tend to develop symptoms of insecurity, regressing to the behavior of younger children. They may exhibit anxiety symptoms, with clinging, bed-wetting, thumb-sucking, fire-setting, temper tantrums, night terrors—in fact, anything that seems an appropriate response to the fear that their family is about to be wiped out.

Older children may also regress. But they generally try to manipulate the parents into stopping their behavior, or at least stopping the divorce. Shoplifting, running away from home, and setting fire to the house are frequent ways of acting out. These behaviors may have a certain metaphoric appropriateness.

Suicide attempts among children and adolescents are a frequent response to a parental adultery. Children may hurt themselves in attempts to shake the parent out of the affair, and if the parent doesn't give up the affair for them, children feel unloved and betrayed. The child is asking, "Who is more important? Your child or your affair?" The child may be shocked, and truly suicidal, upon learning the answer to that question.

Children may decide that one or both parents are out of control and need to be punished. Most children punish parents by hurting themselves, but some may play tricks on the unfaithful parent and the affair partner. Children can be mean when they are betrayed to this degree. (I know of two children who put finger-breaking mousetraps in the pockets of the mink coat their father had given his girlfriend. They wanted everyone to know how they felt about the affair.) Some children have even attempted to murder the unfortunate affair partner who broke up the parents' marriage.

If symptoms or tricks don't catch the needed attention, the child may try to detach from the untrustworthy parents. When adolescents give up on the parents, they may go underground, where drugs and antisocial behavior prevail. Some become prematurely sexually active, even destructively so, and develop their own sexual secrets. They may withdraw further and further from the parents, and finally avoid them totally.

INFIDELITY AND ADOLESCENCE

The traumas of infidelity and divorce are overwhelming for children of any age, even children who are fifty years old and grandparents. But perhaps they are hardest on adolescents, who are sexually supercharged, and alternately delighted and terrified by sex. A parent's inability to maintain sexual control can be frightening, stimulating, and permissive. They have enough trouble doing what's sensible with their sexuality under the best of circumstances. Under the circumstances of parental infidelity, they can be counted on to make a grand mess of it, either by overdoing sex or by underdoing it. Classically, they either become promiscuous and get themselves or someone else pregnant, or they render themselves sexually undesirable by gaining or losing weight, neglecting their hygiene, and dressing unappealingly.

There does seem to be a relationship between the child's adolescence and the parent's infidelities. Families with adolescents worry about their children's sexuality a lot, and can get rather obsessed with inhibiting it, investigating it, controlling it, or enhancing it. Adolescents may practice some of their flirting techniques in what should be the sexually safe atmosphere of the family. That atmosphere may become too sexually charged, and not very safe. The sexuality of the adolescents can stimulate the grown-ups, which might be fun for parents with a sexually comfortable marriage. But having to think about their children's sexuality can be too much for parents who are trying to inhibit or hide their own. Philanderers may manage to keep their hands off their daughters, but may not maintain such control with their daughters' friends or their sons' girlfriends or their daughters-in-law.

Fathers of adolescent sons don't divorce their families as often as fathers of adolescent daughters do. Maybe fathers do need friends to play with at that age, and without sons, the philandering fathers choose girlfriends. Philandering fathers may not know quite how to deal with daughters, especially adolescent daughters. This can be an awkward time in the relationship between philandering father and adolescent daughter, as the father has to either rethink his gender notions, or reclassify his beloved daughter as a member of the enemy sex. Raising daughters should be one of the best corrective experiences for philandering men, but some of them manage to escape involvement in child raising, become preoccupied with their daughters' gender, and find it too arousing for comfort.

Sexual tensions between parents and children are less likely to be a problem than the tensions between stepparents and stepchildren, who don't share enough of a common history for the generational boundaries to be clear, and thus may feel less of an incest taboo.

The parents may also be envious of their children's sexuality, and may compete by having sexual adventures of their own. During a child's adolescence or a parent's infidelity, the sexual atmosphere may be as supercharged as a TV soap opera.

CHILDREN OF DIVORCE

Recent movies, *Shoot the Moon*, *Twice in a Lifetime*, and Woody Allen's *Interiors*, have shown us the quandary of children caught in a romantic divorce. It is easy enough, at the beginning, for the children to cluster around the deserted spouse, but that alliance is fragile as both parent and children take turns trying to get the unfaithful parent back. The parent who is left can feel at odds with the children if they continue to see the parent who broke the family apart. But then, as the children give up on the departing parent, the abandoned parent may make an effort to reconcile. It's a vicious circle. The children who are trying loyally to reject the family betrayer can find themselves betrayed.

In *Shoot the Moon,* famous writer Albert Finney leaves domestically disorganized Diane Keaton and their four daughters for another woman. Dana Hill, the oldest daughter and the one most identified with her father, refuses to speak to him or to accept his gifts, even the symbolically loaded gift of a typewriter. She gives up on writing, and tries to run the household instead. She punishes her father with her silence and her depression. Then when she finds that her mother is still sleeping with her father, she turns against her mother too. The daughter is sacrificing to hold the remnants of family together and punish the father who betrayed them, and now her mother betrays her by going over to the enemy.

Several research studies have tried to understand and measure the impact of divorce on children. All show that it is a disaster. The most optimistic studies suggest that half the children of divorce are back to normal five years after the divorce. Every possible symptom has been blamed on divorce, probably accurately. It is not unique for the deserted spouse to recover completely while the children are still shell-shocked.

In *Twice in a Lifetime,* Gene Hackman leaves Ellen Burstyn and their grown children for widowed barmaid Ann-Margret. Oldest daughter Amy Madigan drags her mother into the bar to confront her father and his girlfriend. They end up screaming and hitting and making quite a scene, but Burstyn as always bows to her husband, whatever he does, and Madigan ends up frustrated as she realizes that she is angrier over the betrayal than her mother is.

Divorce may well be preferable to living in a situation in which someone is likely to be killed. Divorce, whatever its disadvantages, beats the hell out of homicide, suicide, domestic violence, or trying to keep an alcoholic at home. Divorce wrecks lives, but it can also save lives. It is a drastic procedure and a last resort. Yet during a romantic affair, it seems natural and harmless for the couple in-love to float off together, and the children who might object to it seem selfish and unworthy of the sacrifice.

In *Interiors,* the three grown daughters really side with their father, E. G. Marshall, in his effort to divorce their cold, perfectionist mother, Geraldine Page. They shelter their mother, but know she can be cruelly dependent and demanding, and she bullies them all with the threat of suicide. They sympathize cautiously with their father, knowing how deprived he has been. But when exuberantly life-loving Maureen Stapleton emerges as the mistress, the sisters feel their sympathy with their father has been betrayed. Stapleton is the antithesis of their snobby WASP allegiances, yet their father has been brought to life by her. This vulgar, plump, forthright woman in a red dress seems a betrayal of everything they have valued. She's like a big friendly dog, jumping up on the furniture, breaking things. The sisters are horrified, but attracted to this symbol of life. They lose all sense of who they are and what their life is about. They fight among themselves, and wreck their own marriages. They try, unsuccessfully, to prevent their mother's suicide, even if it costs them their own lives. Like their father, they are ultimately rescued by Maureen Stapleton. Stapleton is the hero and the good guy of the drama, but even her virtues are disruptive, and ultimately destructive.

When the parents go off duty, somebody has got to take over. While the parents run wild with lust, grief, self-pity, or self-righteousness, a child routinely becomes guardian of the family—usually far too big a job. Some children avoid this destructive position by developing symptoms to distract everybody from the dangerous crisis of infidelity; others manage to call for outside help. There are those who pretend not to know what is going wrong. And those who survive by deciding that their parents are too absurd to take seriously. Perhaps most commonly, children do whichever of the above seems to work, and then also lose their faith in marriage. They may decide that there is nothing wrong with their specific parents, but that infidelities are normal and marriage is impossible. They may go even further and decide to give up on the entire opposite sex.

ADULT CHILDREN OF ADULTERERS

Parental affairs can be the training ground for their children's adult lives. Crises of infidelity disfigure the pretty domestic fantasies about falling in love and living happily ever after. For children, these are indelible lessons about what they can expect when they grow up—from men, from women, and from marriage.

Children do survive divorce, but they pay a heavy price for their parents' infidelities. Perhaps the most common effect of parental infidelity is the children's subsequent infidelities. For the next generation, I think it would be a good idea if we had self-help groups for Adult Children of Adulterers. The impact and the problems of people who grew up amid secrets and deceits and constant threats to the marital stability are not greatly different from those faced by children growing up with alcoholic parents. Children are not likely to grow up normally surrounded by dishonesty, disorientation, gender obsessions, or the temporary insanity and fugue states of high romance. But if infidelity and divorce are considered normal, normal children can grow up expecting it and preparing for it.

People who have lived through these things may well need a chance to learn how to love and to trust again, before they can do a better job with marriage than their parents did. The long-term outcome of the family drama for the next generation will depend upon whether each child chooses the infidel, the cuckold, or the affairee as a role model.

Adult children of adulterers may have identified with the betrayer of the family. Children understandably identify with infidels, who manage not to let responsibilities get in the way of play. As children see it, adulterers are out having fun, getting the excitement the folks back home are missing. Children's anger at the parent who betrays them and destroys the family may not prevent them from growing up to take that role themselves. It looks like a position of strength. Children of infidelity, especially the sons of philanderers, are very much at risk to become philanderers themselves. A boy growing up amid infidelities, either his mother's or his father's, is likely to identify with the philanderer, marry and then screw around, in an effort to win at marriage and protect himself from it at the same time.

There are exceptions, though. Some adult children of adulterers —often the ones who were left holding the bag—have been horrified by their parents' behavior, and while they may love and honor the unfaithful parents, they don't emulate them. They choose and value fidelity, and make it part of their identity. These highly responsible people suffered directly in childhood from the parental infidelity, and built a value system around avoiding such activity themselves. These children dealt with the parental infidelity openly at the time, and identified infidelity as an error or a character flaw rather than as a normal activity or an appropriate solution to a marital problem. In general, both parents were in agreement that the infidelity was wrong, but they did it, and usually let this child be the mature one who held the family together.

Adult children of adulterers often grow up to be cuckolds, identifying with the helplessness of the betrayed parent. Children in adulterous families may adore and protect and rely on the parent who remained faithful to the marriage and to the family, but may still wonder if the betrayed partner might not have somehow caused it to happen. People who deliberately marry people who are likely to be unfaithful to them might believe they can do a better job of holding a difficult situation together than their parent did. Even for people who really like a challenge, that would seem like a poor choice. Many make this choice because the family infidelities have been seen as normal and universal, so these children are taught to believe that they have no other choice.

When families overcome their children's objections to infidelity by treating it as a normal event, they may be teaching their children to expect it. Children, given such a choice, may prefer to do it than to have it done to them. The daughter of a philandering father may grow up to distrust men and refuse to repeat her mother's fate. She may take a stab at being a philanderer herself.

Adult children of adulterers, led to expect infidelities in their marriages, may decide they'd rather spend their lives as affairees. They may then choose not to marry, and to raid other people's marriages instead. For instance, a girl growing up with the infidelities of either parent is likely to distrust marriage, and to battle against it by raiding the marriages of others. She's quite likely to avoid marrying and remain in the mobile and independent position of affair partner.

I once treated a family in which every member had been damaged by the infidelities over several generations. The one who came to me first was Amy, a woman of forty, the mother of three children and the wife of a protestant minister who was a chronic philanderer. She had tried everything she knew to stop his behavior: she had cried, threatened suicide, thrown temper tantrums, and threatened to leave him. (She said she couldn't really leave him, since he would lose his job if they divorced.) He refused to come to my office, insisting that his behavior was between himself and his Lord.

When I asked Amy about her own family, she described her late mother's alcoholism and unhappy marriage. Her mother had been miserable with her philandering husband, and even more miserable after he had left her. She had had a little antique store she loved, and her husband had belittled that as he made a fortune in water beds. Amy's mother had recently died, and she herself had been depressed, concerned that her life would repeat the unhappiness of her mother's life. Any thought it was strange that this would happen to her, since she had tried for a better marriage, even though she knew that "men are the way they are."

Amy was the oldest of five children, the one who nursed their mother through all the depressions and crying jags when the father went off with other women. Amy had tried to discuss the father's behavior with him once, but he was terribly angry and it made her mother cry, and it frightened her. Her thirty-nine-year-old brother, Ben, ran the family furniture business now that his father had retired. Ben was just like his father, always bragging about his succession of strange women. Ben had tried to molest Amy when they were in their teens, and he still joked about it. When the father was out of town, he left his oldest son in charge, the "man of the house," and the children had to do whatever Ben said.

Charlie, the next brother, was a psychotherapist in another city. He had been married three times, and had been unfaithful to all three, though he prided himself on how well his ex-wives got along with one another. Charlie moved back and forth between the three households, in part to see his three sets of children, and in part because his own prolonged psychoanalysis cost so much he couldn't afford a permanent place of his own. His wives indulged him and didn't expect much of him.

The other daughter, Diana, was thirty-three and had not married. She was independent and stylish, and had a good job selling office furniture. She frequently dated married men, reasoning that they were safe. One man divorced so he could marry her, but as always she backed out at the last minute.

Ellsworth, the thirty-year-old baby of the family, had taken over his mother's antique shop. He had just announced that he was homosexual. His mother had known for many years, but had not wanted to upset his father by bringing it out into the open. Now that his mother was dead, Ellsworth wanted to hurt his father with the truth. He especially enjoyed telling his father that he'd had sex with some of the old man's favorite football players.

I suggested to Amy that there seemed to be something wrong in this family. We arranged a session with Amy and most of her siblings. Ben refused to come, but Charlie, Diana, and Ellsworth showed up. All of them knew about their father's affairs, but it was understood that mentioning them would bring punishment. Half the time their mother was suicidal over his infidelities, and half the time she called them normal or none of the children's business. They didn't know their father well. They didn't trust marriage much, and none of them could think of a marriage that seemed to work.

The father, though he balked on coming in with his children, agreed to come in alone. He'd always tried to be a "real man" for his children, so he was confused by Ellsworth's revelation of homosexuality. He was pleased that Ben and Charlie had turned out fine, but felt that Ellsworth had been too close to his mother. He seemed surprised that anyone recalled his "little flings"; they weren't significant to him, since he assumed everybody had affairs. He offered to apologize to his children, and wondered why no one had expressed their feelings before. He did admit that his wife had carried on about his infidelity, but, as he put it, "you know how women are."

After that, the siblings put pressure on one another, and most of them entered therapy. Amy got her father and other siblings to join her in confronting her husband, and even he finally entered therapy and is struggling to change his ways. He'll have to; he knows Amy is strong enough now to leave him if he doesn't. Charlie gave up his analyst of many years—a philanderer himself —and is in therapy with someone who believes in marriage. He's thinking of choosing one of his wives to live with full time. Diana is dating a single man, and Ellsworth has stopped trying to shock everybody. Ben refused therapy, saying he didn't believe in talking to other people about private things. I understand, though, that his father bullied him into giving up philandering for several months, though Ben didn't tell his wife he was doing it. He didn't like fidelity, and went back to his previous pattern, though he didn't tell his wife about that either.

The old man seems to have gotten the most from his belated experience with therapy. He offered to pay for the therapy for his children, and came in himself for a while. He made tearful confessions to each of his children, and humbled himself just enough for them to start liking him and to start correcting the misinformation of their childhood, so perhaps they can have a better chance at marriage. The old man keeps telling his children that he'd never wanted to hurt them. He had just tried to be the kind of father his father had been.

WHAT THE CHILDREN SHOULD KNOW

The children are going to have to grow up facing whatever choices and situations the parents struggle through. The parents' job is to help the children understand that these things should not happen, but do happen, and can be survived. Despite their disapproval and distrust, the children should emerge with sympathy for their parents. Most important, the children should get through this without losing respect for the institution of marriage or for either men or women. It is far better for children to decide that their parents are foolish than for them to believe that the world is treacherous.

The children should know all the open secrets; they should be told whatever *both* parents know that is relevant to the stability and future of their family. There are many experts who disagree with me, but I believe that children should be told about threats to their parents' marriage, even told about their parents' affairs and the crises that result. Obviously how children are told what they are told, and in what detail, is in part dependent upon the age of the child. There's no point in turning it into any ceremonial big deal, but the situation should be explained calmly by both parents as soon as is feasible. The children have heard the parents carrying on at each other about these things already, and the disclosure is not so much a revelation as a clarification. The family history and the explanation for the life of the family should be open knowledge. There is a danger that isolated pieces of information will be whispered around, out of context, and be treated as if they are more important than they are. I see no point in keeping these things secret from children of any age. Alert children know everything anyway—they just don't know it's safe to know it and understand it and talk about it.

The best interests of the child should be a factor any parent considers in making decisions, especially decisions about marriage. But that is not be the only factor, and the child needs to know the other factors parents use in making such crucial decisions. Parents, whether together or apart, must explain each other to the children, and it is quite appropriate to belabor the circumstances, the tensions and alliances that help the children understand their parents' marriage and/or divorce. Children need to understand their parents and their parents' marriage both for their careers as children and for their later careers as adults. When grown-ups don't do what the children would think best for them, they need to know what the grown-ups are considering more important.

Some couples do stay together "for the children's sake." People who stay married to violent, incestuous, or substance-abusing people aren't doing the children any favors, unless the alternative is homeless drifting, and maybe not even then. But most people who talk about "not staying together for the children's sake" are trying to decide between a marriage partner and an affair partner, and would like to justify leaving any concerns with family and children out of the decision. Actually, it may be a wise investment for people to stay together in a less than exciting marriage for the children's sake, especially if they make the marriage work comfortably during those years. But it sabotages any benefit from the sacrifice (if it really is a sacrifice) for the parent to thrash around in misery and then tell the child that it is the child's "fault" that the parents are not in a continuous state of ecstatic wonder. A child may be naive enough to believe this is true. It is an enormous burden on children for frightened or selfish parents to stay married but suffer loud and long, and blame their unhappiness on their children. Are they hoping the children will take over as parents and make the adults go ahead and get a divorce? Children, at any age, are inappropriate marriage counselors for their parents.

Children deserve better than to be declared responsible for their parents' marriage, however it goes. Open explanations, which carefully avoid conspiring with the child or blaming the child for the marriage or the divorce, can relieve the burden rather than increasing it. Usually, one parent ends up having to do all the explaining, and that parent is characteristically, but not necessarily, the mother. Children thus tend to see the world and the marriage through the mother's eyes, while they see the mother through their own eyes, the eyes of a child. If the marriage ends, they may then get to know their father for the first time, and have a whole new perspective on everything they thought they understood so well. The confusion and the shifting loyalties will be traumatic, but enlightening.

It would be a shame if children did not process the history of their parents' marriage, whatever the sequence of events, from both perspectives. They must emerge with the understanding that their parents are both sympathetic people, who made whatever mistakes they made and suffered. And it must be acceptable for them to forgive their parents—once they are sure they understand the parents, and are sure their parents understand themselves. It is, of course, impossible to ever forgive people who consider themselves blameless.

15 / When Monogamy Works

"Love is no use unless it's wise, and kind, and undramatic. Something
steady and sweet, to smooth out your nerves when you're tired.
Something tremendously cosy; and unflurried by scenes and jealousies.
That's what I want, what I've always wanted really. Oh my dear,
I do hope it's not going to be dull for you."
NOËL COWARD, *PRIVATE LIVES*

"Fidelity gave a unity to lives that would otherwise splinter into
thousands of split-second impressions."
MILAN KUNDERA, *THE UNBEARABLE LIGHTNESS OF BEING*

Despite everything I've said up to now, monogamy works. It isn't rare —it's practiced by most of the people most of the time, and always has been. It isn't difficult—anyone can do it, even without special talents. It isn't dangerous—only the smallest sacrifices are involved, and none of these exposes you to danger. Monogamy isn't even dull —living without lies and secrets opens you up to being known and understood, and that isn't dull unless you yourself are dull.

I know there are cautious souls who are so in love with their masculine or feminine ideal, their dreams of romance, or their personal independence that they cannot commit themselves to the honesty, the equality, the interdependency of a monogamous partnership. And there are those intrepid souls who insist on living dangerously. This is all right, so long as they don't commit the cruel folly of marrying someone who *does* believe in monogamy. If no one tries to get too close to these people for too long, they can even be sources of pleasure for a time.

And many nonmonogamists make contributions to humanity

275

outside the domestic arena. Domestic restlessness may divert one to more public areas of fulfillment, to relationships with populations rather than individuals. Domestic misery may even spur creativity and ambition, and it does get people out of the house. (Where would we be today if Christopher Columbus had been so comfortable maritally that he didn't want to leave home?) Running away from home propels people toward adventures of self-discovery and exercises in resourcefulness. Monogamy is not the only way to live, and while it is surely the most pleasant and efficient arrangement, the alternatives have advantages too.

Still, most people—in polls on the subject as well as in my office —insist that monogamy is their ideal for themselves, and particularly for their mates. Over and over I have had to advise people in the matter. Here, then, is the best advice I have to offer to those who want to practice monogamy, or even those who haven't done so and are now wishing they had.

1. Don't marry people who don't like you. Some men and women gravitate toward the potential marriage partner who confers the most status, or elicits the most envy, or horrifies the most relatives. Those in search of mates may not ask themselves what *they* think of the object of their marital ambitions. Those suffering from a mating urge may speak of chemistry and electric shocks when they touch or kiss that person. I don't mean to denigrate love in choosing a mate, but the most important element is whether the two of you like each other. Friendship is an infinitely more stabilizing basis for marriage than romance. People can be passionately, desperately in love, and consumed at the same time with distrust, jealousy, rage, and even intense hatred for the loved one. That sort of violent love, though it seems to be a sexual attractant, is too temporary and angry to lead to good sex, much less to a good life. The best basis for good sex seems to be friendliness, as Dr. Ruth Westheimer keeps reminding people.

Obviously, it would be foolish to marry someone who doesn't like your ethnic group, your family, your friends, your religion, your heritage, customs, and style, even if that prospective spouse is fascinated by the differences between you, and sees you as greatly different from all those factors that make you you. Someone who wants to take you away from all of this will discover that you carry all of "this" with you. The belief that opposites attract explains magnets but misunderstands the nature of marriage.

Don't marry a man who doesn't like women, or a woman who doesn't like men. Someone who doesn't like your gender but who sees you as different from the other members of your gender will discover that you have indeed absorbed many of the hated characteristics of your sex. Both the woman who distrusts men and the man who fears women are crippled, perhaps by a father who deserted the family or a mother who was too clinging. Set up by these situations to become philanderers, they need to work that out before they marry. The best indicator of whether your prospective spouse can be your friend is whether that person has close, nonsexual friends of your sex.

You should consider also the degree of friendship your prospective mate has with his or her parents. Has this person worked out the generational conflicts well enough for a healthy marital relationship? People who are still at war with their parents may not be ready for peace in their marriage. The best indicator of how someone is going to be in a family is how that person has been in a family before.

Marry sane people who like you, who have nonsexual friends of your gender, and who are friends with their own parents.

2. Forget everything you ever thought you knew about the *opposite* sex. People, as we know, come in two genders, and this tells you far less about them than you might think. You need to see past the popular ideas of what a man or a woman is like, or should be like, before you can make a personal relationship with someone. We like to produce instant intimacy by pretending that we know more about people than we do: she is female, he is a Pisces, she grew up in Kansas, or he is Jewish, and on this basis we make certain assumptions. We might be right, we might be wrong, but even if we are right, our impersonal assessment interferes with getting to know the individual personally.

It would seem difficult to go through a courtship and a marriage and never see past someone's gender. Yet I see it happen regularly. It is insulting to your woman to assume that she should want to dress up in skimpy costumes that look like they came from the ads in the back of *Playboy*, even if Hugh Hefner tells you that "women" are turned on by these things. There are women who learn about "men" from reading *The Total Woman*, and they assume they are pleasing stereotypical Man by dressing or behaving as stereotypical Woman. The couple never get close enough to reveal themselves, and they may begin to feel increasingly ashamed for their failure to be perfectly Man or Woman.

There are authoritarian husbands who insist upon acting as the boss, and smart but self-effacing wives who pretend to be incompetent. They have learned this gender dance, and they go through it to reinforce their notions about how the sexes should be aligned and to distract themselves from recognizing the real situation. The impersonality of the gender dance is a setup for equally impersonal gender dances of philandering, or for escape into romances that seem personal but are really projections of our own fantasies.

Everything you need to know about the experience of your partner's gender or sex can and must be learned from your partner.

3. Be clear about the agreement between you and your spouse about what is and what is not an infidelity. Most couples agree to be faithful sexually, but some decide that certain activities under certain conditions will be acceptable. Couples may even agree to things that are impossible (not to feel sexual attractions to other people) or unworkable (to act freely, but always to keep it secret).

Couples probably should negotiate the appropriateness of such activities as getting together for lunch with a former mate, or former lover, making secret phone calls to a former lover, flirting with friends, flirting with strangers, going out for the evening with co-workers of the opposite sex, going on separate vacations, dancing repeatedly with someone at a party, leaving the party with someone, sexually fondling other people. Men and women who are trying to remain faithful would do well to set clear boundaries for themselves, avoiding those people and those situations where temptation to commit an infidelity is strong, and distancing people who breach those boundaries. If the temptation is strong enough to become a problem, you need help from your spouse, not from the person who is out to seduce you.

People tend to believe they themselves are trustworthy and under control, but their partner might lose control. So they are likely to grant themselves more latitude than they're willing to grant a partner. A man who feels quite comfortable staying out half the night drinking at a bar may be severely threatened if his wife does the same. A woman may get together for lunch with her former boyfriend, and then have a fit if her husband phones his former girlfriend.

I haven't noticed that people have much difficulty deciding in principle what is an infidelity and what is not (and almost everyone wants sexual exclusivity and interpersonal freedom, the pleasure of being turned on by outside people and the comfort of knowing that it won't be acted upon or reacted to). The difficulty comes with the exceptions. It isn't good enough for people to set their limits according to what *they* are comfortable with. They really must limit themselves to what their partner is comfortable with. And it is reasonable of them to expect the same of their partner. Unless they want to start a conflict and renegotiate the marital agreement, each must be bound by the other's comfort and tolerance.

Fidelity is something you do for the sake of *your* marriage, not because your mate requires it. When fidelity seems an act of obedience, a set of restrictions you "blame" on your partner to protect your partner's marriage, you're disoriented. You've forgotten that this is your marriage too. You keep *your* marriage working by keeping both your partner and yourself comfortable.

Be sure you know what is an infidelity and what is not. If in doubt, ask your partner.

4. Fidelity is a decision. Fidelity may not seem to come about naturally, and perhaps sometimes it doesn't. We are not always inclined to be faithful, which is fine if we know that fidelity is not supposed to be an inclination. The head decides what the genitals are going to do, rather than the other way around. It would be just as dangerous to let your genitals drive your marriage as to let them

drive your car. A decision must be made about who is boss here. You make a decision to be faithful and then you practice it, making a series of decisions along the way about which of your sexual impulses you are going to enjoy in fantasy and which you are going to put into full-scale production. Fidelity is not difficult, unless you have made the decision that you will grant yourself exceptions when either the attraction to another person or the anger at your spouse is particularly intense.

Infidelity can start as an accident or a punishment and become an addiction. Addictions are powerful. Some of the principles in the handling of other addictive behavior may apply to infidelity, and particularly philandering. My most personal experience with addictive behavior has been an addiction to nicotine. I used to smoke cigarettes, and I spent years intermittently acting as if I were trying to stop, with imperfect success. I finally realized that I was not really quitting. I was permitting myself to suffer from my deprivation, as if to stop smoking left me on the verge of psychosis, homicide, or suicide. I told myself I was stopping smoking for the sake of Betsy and the kids, as if I didn't care whether I lived or died. Then I would grant myself certain exceptions: if I had a particularly bad day, I would let myself have a cigarette. I found myself depressed, at war with my family, and having a series of really bad days, on which I had no choice but to protect myself from insanity by having a cigarette. Once I decided that I wouldn't smoke again, no matter how I felt, I've had no trouble doing without cigarettes. And I don't have very many bad days either.

Once you decide that you are going to practice fidelity, whether you want to at that moment or not, you may find it easy, comfortable, and rewarding to do so.

5. Honesty is the central factor in intimacy. Even the smallest lie can be hopelessly disorienting. As I've said to so many patients, and earlier here, if I gave you detailed instructions on how to get from Atlanta to New York City and threw in just one left turn that was a lie, you'd end up in Oklahoma.

People like to convince themselves that they are doing their loved ones a favor by hiding the unpleasant truth. Spouses usually know when they are being lied to; they just don't know what the truth is, and if it is bad enough to lie about, they expect the worst. The "I Love Lucy" show had the same plot each week. Lucy and her friend Ethel Mertz would attempt to hide something from their husbands and produce all manner of confusion, which would result in far more unpleasantness than the secret could ever have produced. Finally, the two wives would disclose their secret, which was never as awful as the husbands were imagining, and all would be relieved and forgiven.

Couples need not tell each other every detail of their activity and every thought that goes through their heads, but they do have to tell each other the bad news. There are things that are too insignificant to talk about. Fine, don't talk about them. The things people must be sure to talk about are those things that are unsettling, guilt-producing, or controversial.

There is no truth that is as destructive as any lie.

6. Sharing a secret with someone else, and keeping the secret from your partner, is particularly dangerous. A secret produces a bond between those who share the secret, and it puts distance between you and those from whom the secret is being kept. Monogamous people make sure their nonmarital alliances aren't threatening to their marriage. This means they can't be secret. If a friend wants you to keep a secret from your marriage partner, that person is asking you to betray your marriage for the sake of the friendship.

Friends of the opposite sex have to be especially careful of each other's marriages. Rarely, a friend might want you to keep something secret, but the circumstances would have to be extraordinary. Other people may divide their loyalties in a way that's different from mine, but no female friend would call me about some issue in her life, whether it be her concern about her love life, or help in getting her daughter out of jail, or just advice about growing roses, and insist that I keep it secret from Betsy. A friend would recognize the implications of such secrecy.

Same-sex friends do sometimes try to draw you into their secret lives, expecting you to keep their infidelities secret from your spouse and theirs. Such a secret can spoil a friendship between two couples, and put everyone in an impossible situation. But your loyalties must be to your marriage, and you have to concern yourself with how your friend got so confused about loyalties and alliances. Obviously, the relationships can never be comfortable again until both your spouse and your friend's spouse know the secret. Some friendships can become couples friendships and some can't, and it often depends upon the depth of the secret alliance between the same-sex friends.

Friends respect your marriage and don't expect you to keep secrets from your partner.

7. If you're doing something you feel you should lie about, your guilt is telling you to stop doing it. It works better to stop doing things before you think you should lie about them.

It really isn't that difficult to avoid doing those things that would make you feel shame and guilt. But once you've done something that makes you uncomfortable, it's hard work to keep up the deception. Confusing the people who are closest to you, so they won't understand what you are doing that is making you feel shame and guilt and act weird, is a tricky and time-consuming process, and one that is inevitably distancing.

It's more comfortable to control your activities rather than to try and control other people's awareness of them.

8. The revelation of an infidelity is most shocking and horrifying in those marriages that had seemed "perfect." The betrayal seems all the greater. Perfection, however, is inhuman. Moslem rug weavers make sure they weave imperfections into the rugs, since any human effort at perfection is insulting to Allah. People who must maintain an aura of perfection have to protect themselves from being seen, known, and understood. In their urge to be a hero, they lose their capacity for intimacy and openness, and maybe for marriage. (Someone said no man is a hero to his tailor or to his wife's psychiatrist.)

Undoubtedly, many affairs come about because the partners feel they aren't sufficiently perfect. People may feel paltry in contrast to the images they are trying to project, even at home. They think they should be godly or saintly, and fear rejection if they are discovered to be only human. So they may seek intimacy elsewhere, may take their shabby humanity to a humbler bed.

If you have somehow convinced your naive mate that you are perfect, it may be disconcerting for him or her to face the truth. It might be even more disconcerting for you to accept the fact that your mate already knows you're not perfect, and can tolerate you anyway. Your mate might conceivably be shocked and hurt at the revelation of your imperfection, but will recover, and will begin to feel closer to you once the shock wears off. Once it is clear that you are only human and that is OK, then the marriage can begin.

Reveal your human imperfections at home, so you can be understood and loved. You probably weren't going to be worshiped for your perfection anyway, so there's no loss.

9. The purpose of marital conflict should be to understand the issues and the emotions, rather than determine who is the winner. The winner of a marital conflict, if we must think in such terms, might be the one who understands the other's point of view first. Either both win or both lose.

People who try to be right, who want to establish that whatever they did was not their fault, can go into a frenzy when they are criticized. Blamelessness is all-important, and they are afraid they will be punished if it's determined that they are responsible for their own behavior. You are asking for explanations in order to understand better, and they act as if you are trying to hurt them. They feel like small children, and you become the parent. (Of course, if you act like an angry parent, your partner may respond by acting like a guilty child. When that happens, the conversation is too frightening to continue.)

People who need to prove they are right are not trying to be understood. They feel inadequate, and may have been overdisciplined in childhood. They see the marriage as a threat to something more important: their aura of blamelessness. They are fragile, and have to be treated gently. You can't live with somebody who does this very often.

You can't be right and married at the same time.

10. Know that affairs can happen, can threaten your life, and must be taken seriously. There is no infidelity that is too insignificant to talk about, none that is not the family's business, or none that is best forgotten. At the same time, it is important to stay clear about who is responsible for what. No one can *make* someone have an affair. An affair is never someone else's fault. What's more, affairs should not be taken personally. If your spouse makes the decision and then has an affair, don't assume you caused it. Don't let anybody talk you into believing that you made it happen.

Of course, this can be extraordinarily difficult. An affair is such a personal betrayal, *the* most personal betrayal, and the most personal insult. At least that is how it feels to the betrayed. But it does not feel that way to the betrayer. Most of the time, the unfaithful one is not "doing it" to the partner, but is doing it for quite different and more individual reasons. If you have been betrayed, your partner, the unfaithful spouse, should be approached as someone who has a problem, rather than as someone who doesn't "love you" anymore.

Even if a mate wants to give it all up and go die for someone new, that romance should not be taken personally. Philandering might be treated as an immaturity, like a defect in toilet training. Accidental infidelity might be equated with a temporary lapse in control, like a minor seizure. Marital arrangements are things you know about anyway, and go along with for reasons you understand very well.

Infidelity is your partner's nuttiness. Don't take it personally.

HOW TO DEAL WITH CRISES OF INFIDELITY

If you are the one who is being unfaithful, my best advice is to stop it, reveal everything, and throw yourself on the mercy of your family.

If you are worth salvaging in other ways, your family will almost certainly choose to keep you. It will require that you do several things differently, and even that you rethink aspects of life you may never have questioned. You may be kept on a short leash for a while. Nonetheless, you can recover from this. Your marriage can even be better as a result of the total experience (though the possible benefits drop and the dangers increase with each subsequent episode). Your main job is to keep telling the truth, however it hurts, and let your family and particularly your spouse react.

If you are the affairee, your continued presence is making things more difficult for everyone, especially you. The best thing for you to do is to go home.

You and I know you are a lovely person, but under the circumstances your affair partner is likely to have more pressing work to do than to hold you and your disrupted life together right now. You are, unfortunately and perhaps unfairly, going to get the blame for everything, and little or no support from anyone. I know these things aren't fair, but they are predictable.

You may wonder how a nice person like you got into such an awful situation. You may be startled by the sudden shifts in allegiances, when the person who had eyes only for you is suddenly being sucked away from you back into a family that seemed to hardly exist just a little while ago. Or your great romance is sometimes on and sometimes off, and you don't know which it will be from moment to moment, but it is clearly more of a problem than a solution.

You are ashamed and embarrassed and humiliated, and you want to explain to someone that you are not the sort of person you seem to be, but there is no one around to accept apologies or offer pardon. And you really don't have a life to go back to. This is all a disaster for you, and you need to examine yourself and understand how you got yourself into such a destructive situation. But there is no one here in this family that can help you through it. *Go home and save your life.*

If you know of a friend's or relative's affair, you have too much power, and you are in danger of becoming part of the problem.

How you deal with this information will depend upon what the information is, how you obtained it, and what your relationships are with the people involved. You have very difficult choices to make.

You may be aware that you have the power to hurt someone or to destroy a marriage, and that is more power than you want to have. You must remind yourself that it is the unfaithful partner here who is hurting a marriage, and the cuckold spouse can't repair the damage and save the marriage if the secret is maintained. You may say, "But if someone is hurt, I could be blamed." But if you don't reveal the secret, you could be blamed for that.

If you don't care about these people, you know just what to do —gossip about it, tell everyone else, but don't face them with it. If you aren't close enough to the couple to be deeply concerned about your allegiances to them, then their affairs really are none of your business.

But what does a friend or relative do? The secret information may be painful to you, and you might prefer to forget that you know it. However, it is very important to the people involved. If you are close to only one of them, you really should let that person, whether infidel, cuckold, or affairee, know what you know and how you know it. It may be painful or embarrassing, but either way it could be lifesaving.

In the more difficult and complex situation of having an important relationship with both, or even all of the people involved—if they are relatives or close friends—you can tell what you know to both partners. Tell the betrayer first and give him or her a chance to explain it to the spouse. Whatever your relationship with these people, even if the person betrayed is your daughter and the betrayer your bitterest enemy, take your information to the betrayer first. Let that person know that the information is out. If you know it, others do too. The betrayer can salvage the situation by revealing it personally. Of course, if he or she doesn't tell the spouse, and you care about the spouse, then you should tell.

An example of this is a mother who came to me after having discovered that her son-in-law and her younger daughter were having an affair, and her older daughter (the wife) didn't know about it. The mother's impulse was to tell the young, college-age daughter what she knew, and put her on restriction unless she ended the affair. But the mother realized that the alliances were entirely too complex to tolerate leaving things semisecret.

I suggested that she tell the younger daughter and the son-in-law, and give him a choice and a deadline for telling his wife. He did break off the affair and tell his wife, and the couple were grateful to the mother, though the younger daughter felt that once again her mother had been on the older daughter's side. She reasoned that her sister's husband might have chosen to divorce her sister and marry her if the mother had not forced the situation out into the open at that point. She thought that the secrecy was on her side, and the openness favored her sister. The younger daughter left home, and never did heal the long-standing rift between herself and her sister.

The mother pondered how she could have handled the problem in a way that might have brought the two sisters together, but she realized that the younger sister was declaring war when she got into the affair in the first place, and would not have been satisfied with anything short of total annihilation of the older sister. Perhaps it was time for the younger daughter to find a life, and even a husband, of her own.

If you reveal the secret only to the person who has been betrayed, you are displaying your distrust and disdain for the betrayer, which may be appropriate but not very helpful for your friend, who might value the marriage greatly. On the other hand, if you reveal the secret only to the betrayer, you are entering a conspiracy, which may be appropriate only if you feel no relationship or allegiance to the betrayed spouse.

If you don't reveal the information, you may not offend anyone, but you don't help anyone either. Both partners may already be well aware of the situation, but not know that anyone else knows. They may be stuck, and might appreciate your information or your help. If you are concerned about these people, and about your relationship with them, your best course of action is to tell both marital partners that you know and are sorry, and then *don't take sides*. Don't conspire with either of the partners.

Briefly, you may be the enemy. They will probably thank you in the long run.

If you are the one who is being betrayed, it is horribly unfair, but your marriage is in your hands.

This may be the most important job you will ever have to do. Don't mess it up by carrying on, indulging in your hour on the stage. Your initial response will, quite naturally, include anger, and you must certainly make sure that your spouse knows that you are angry. But you have many other emotions underneath the anger. Above all you are hurt and you are frightened. You will also be obsessed, and want to know various things; some of the things you'll want to know will surprise you. You will certainly find something to feel guilty about, and you may even be embarrassed. You'll feel stupid for not having figured it out earlier. Like the drowning man, your whole marriage will pass before your eyes, in vivid emotional colors.

Try not to let your anger or your guilt paralyze you; you have more important work to do. You must convey your hurt, which is a far more hospitable emotion than anger, so that your spouse knows you are calling for closeness, not distance, as the reparative action. Once that is clear, and the atmosphere is sufficiently unthreatening, show your curiosity and let your partner explain and reveal, while you shut up and listen.

As you explore this with your adulterous mate, who is probably terrified, try to remember that you are the sane partner of this marriage. Under these circumstances, you may never have felt less sane, but you are still the one who can save the marriage. Saving the marriage may require sacrifices, perhaps being a lot more tolerant of your betrayer than he or she deserves. (I'm sorry, but there are no rewards for being right, even for being faithful when your mate wasn't.) Your straying spouse might want to make it up to you somehow, but there is no payment that will erase the debt. You can exact punishment by being unpleasant, and you have earned the right to that, but it isn't likely to help much. So forget punishment, especially anger and rejection, or counteraffairs, both of which prevent reconciliation. If your wayward spouse is feeling rather shoddy, overcome with shame and guilt, that humiliation may be sufficient punishment. The nicer you are, the more guilt your partner might feel.

Don't take blame for someone else's actions. Nonetheless, assume that things will have to be different in the future, and consider with your mate how things should be different. You may have to get a new romance going in the marriage, find interests together, become attentive and involved with each other, be with each other, and try to recapture whatever it was that once made this relationship special enough and personal enough for the two of you to sign on for life, and then panic when it appeared about to end. Some of that specialness is still there somewhere. You might have to make sacrifices, give up some of your more irritating habits or develop skills you had previously avoided. You may end up being the one who makes the most changes, benefits most from the crisis. Your partner, even after what has been done to you, is still a partner to this marriage, and has a voice in how it will be.

If your spouse had a sexual accident that caused guilt and discomfort, great. That demonstrates that the commitment to fidelity remains. If your spouse fell in love, your marriage may seem to be over, but it may well not be. The romantic affair probably won't work, and the romantic infidel may bounce back into the marriage in due time. It is hard to live with someone who is in love with someone else, but if you see how crazy it is, you may be able to wait it out, and thus prevent a divorce and a disastrous remarriage. A few weeks, even six months of trying to stick it out may be a worthwhile investment, but a longer period of trying to tolerate a romantic affair becomes a marital arrangement that you might not be willing to live with permanently.

Philanderers are more difficult. These men (and sometimes women) need serious, prolonged gender retraining, and you may have to create crisis after crisis to keep a philanderer involved. You may be tempted to just live with him in a marital arrangement, and keep your distance. Some marital arrangements are not better than divorce, so you must carefully consider how much indignity and craziness you will have to tolerate in order to maintain the semblance of marriage.

If you do find yourself in a marital arrangement that seems to be protecting you from divorce, take a close look at it. It may be that the divorce would be preferable after all. But it might well be that the marriage could work nicely without the arrangement, and would benefit from either therapy or a crisis that might shake things up and rearrange the marriage. If some secret came out, or some pesky issue were resolved, the marriage might even work as a real marriage.

Montaigne said, "It is far better to commit adultery than to tell a lie." The lie, or the secret, is the real betrayal of the trust and intimacy of the marriage. Honesty and openness, even about the frightening and guilt-producing issue of sex, create the intimacy of marriage, and enable people to grow increasingly comfortable and special to one another. If people would only trust one another enough to reveal the secrets and tell the truth, then maybe they could do what everybody wants to do, and most people are afraid to try—they could live together happily ever after.

A CATERED AFFAIR

I'd like to end with a case on which Betsy and I worked together. It illustrates some of the things I'm saying about how monogamy works.

Mona was not the sort of person who would do this kind of thing. She couldn't believe that she had gotten into an affair. She was a happily married woman, and she'd already made the only sexual mistake she thought she'd ever make. As soon as she started college, just as her father was leaving home to marry an awful woman, she had gotten pregnant. She married Jimmy, the only boy she'd ever dated and certainly the only man she'd ever slept with, dropped out of college, and stayed home to have children instead. She had two sons and then a daughter. She loved Jimmy and both her sons, but boys were different. Mostly she loved her daughter Hope. When Hope was born, Mona was well into her twenties with two little boys, but she didn't feel like a grown-up at all. Even now, at forty-two, Mona often thought the eighteen-year-old Hope seemed to be older than she. As the boys grew up and did whatever boys do, Mona and Hope grew closer and closer. Hope was so sexually free that she made Mona feel deprived because Jimmy had made her miss the whole sexual revolution. And now Hope was leaving her, to go off to college and to sexual adventures and to all those wonderful things she herself had missed.

Jimmy was a good husband, a whole lot better than Mona's father had been (though the old man had certainly done better when he came back home after that brief second marriage). Mona's mother reminded her how grateful she should be that Jimmy had married her at all. He had moved up in the stockbrokerage, and he made a good living. He'd been a good father, especially to the boys. But since they had left home, he seemed to work all the time, and played golf when he wasn't working. Sex had gotten a lot better through the years, and they went on great trips to his professional conventions, and sometimes with his partners and their wives. He kept promising that one of these days, he'd arrange a trip for just the two of them.

Meanwhile, as Hope grew up, Mona had started a catering service with another woman she'd met at exercise class. Hope was very much involved in it, and had really become Mona's partner after the woman from the exercise class moved away. The catering business had made Mona feel wonderful about herself, though Jimmy ridiculed it, and complained that she never cooked for him anymore. Mona didn't tell him he was too fat anyway. There was no point in getting into that discussion. They'd long ago stopped fighting. Jimmy always had to prove he was right, just like his father. It didn't matter. The catering business thrived, more than Jimmy realized. Mona didn't tell him how much money she was making. That was a little secret between her and Hope. Jimmy had no idea how much Hope's clothes cost. It was just as well. Mona and Hope worked together, the business thrived, they both felt great. But now Hope would be leaving. How could Mona live without Hope?

After Hope left, Mona didn't know whether she felt old or young, but she was forty-two years old and still a child. She felt lonely, and began to take cooking courses. Somehow—it just happened—she found herself in bed with Luciano, a talented young pasta chef who had recently arrived in this country with startling ideas for sun-dried tomatoes. Lucky's English was not so good, but he had time to spend with Mona. She spent every day with him, and finally, after six months, she told Jimmy she wanted a divorce. If she had ever told Lucky that she was thinking of leaving her marriage, it had been lost in translation. He, in turn, had never mentioned his wife back in Genoa, and suddenly the situation between him and Mona was very different and very uncomfortable.

Jimmy was just as uncomfortable. In fact, Jimmy fell apart, and stumbled into our office. He knew he hadn't paid much attention to Mona in the last decade or two, but he loved her and didn't want to lose her. He felt terribly guilty about what he had been doing all those years, not just the neglect and the put-downs, but also a few affairs of his own that he had never told her about. When Mona announced she was thinking of divorce, she hadn't actually told him she was having an affair, but he'd known about Lucky for months, and he just hoped it would go away. Jimmy realized that if he confronted Mona, he might have to tell her about his affairs, and she would leave him if she knew.

Betsy and I pointed out the discrepancies in his thinking: why would he want her back after her serious romance, while she would leave him over his past dalliances? He feared he would lose control, display passion and emotion, even cry, and run her off. We reminded him that Lucky was Latin, and his emotionalism might be part of his appeal. We urged Jimmy to confront Mona, tell her everything he knew about her affair, and about his, and then beg her to return to him for a whole new marriage. He thought he could do that.

He did it, and called to tell us it had gone fairly well. Mona would be in with him to see us the next day. Both of them were depressed. Mona thought it was probably best for her to stay with Jimmy, especially since Lucky had disappeared after finding out that Jimmy knew, but she was bland about it. She couldn't get comfortable with Jimmy, and she felt guilty. She didn't know what to do, so she telephoned Hope at college, Mona's expert on sexual freedom. To Mona's surprise, Hope screamed at her, saying, "How could you do that to my daddy? How could you tell him things that would hurt him so much?" and hung up.

Jimmy started being wonderful to Mona. He hadn't tried this for a long time, and he enjoyed it. The nicer he was, the more uncomfortable Mona felt. She wasn't used to having Jimmy around so much. In a session with Betsy, she suddenly realized that she was angry over having to feel grateful, and beneath that was her sense that she was the blemished one, blemished both by the pregnancy in college and by the affair. She realized that she believed what her mother had taught her about men and women and sex and freedom, and who was responsible for what. So she was still keeping secrets from Jimmy: the biggest secret was that she still thought of Lucky, and of some sexual things that Lucky did that she wished Jimmy would do. She told Jimmy, and it amazed her that he was angry at her not for thinking about Lucky but for not telling him what she thought he could do to make her happy.

There were more crises as they stabilized and began to return to normal. But they didn't want to go back to what they had had. Mona still thought of Lucky sometimes, and Jimmy still got nervous when he thought she might be holding something back. Mona felt awful anytime Jimmy was angry with her, and she thought of her mother's warning that she would have to be eternally grateful to Jimmy for marrying her under those circumstances.

Betsy (more the romantic than I) had the thought that Mona and Jimmy had missed a step in coming into their marriage. They hadn't married in the ideal way. They needed the courtship they had never had. It wasn't the "chemistry" of sexual attraction that they needed—part of the problem was that they had had that, but the relationship had never gone further. They certainly didn't need the gender dance, with frills and flowers and all those Valentine trappings. They'd had that back in high school, when Mona was Queen of the May, and Jimmy was King. Of course, like any married couple, they needed the comfort of knowing that the relationship was solid no matter what each of them was feeling at the moment. And, through this crisis, they were gaining that knowledge. But something was missing.

Although they were becoming intensely aware of each other, they didn't know how to manage their awareness of themselves or of each other. They didn't know how to come together. Now we urged them to rearrange their priorities and simply experience each other, as people do when they are courting. They needed to hang out together, inefficiently exchanging reactions to the world around them and getting to know each other so well that they were inseparably special to each other. They needed to think about each other when they weren't together, and to know the other was thinking of him or her. They needed to run through the full range of human emotions with each other every day, until they became automatically, unthreateningly aware of each other.

We suggested that the two of them take off a few weeks to spend together and say all the things to each other that they hadn't said through the years. They went to the mountains, walked every day, had sex every night, and played some golf (he'd forgotten how good she was). Mostly they talked. It was interesting how little they talked about their children or their businesses. Jimmy finally even showed her some of his anger about the affair, but even more anger about her passively disliking him for all those years. Mona talked about blaming him for that first pregnancy, and about her anger for feeling obligated to him all those years. These issues somehow seemed more important to them than her affair, and certainly more important than his long past affairs. Both of them admitted how lost they were when they married, so young and so unready, and how they fell back on the models of their parents without ever questioning what they were doing.

When they returned, they were almost like married people. Mona said it was a new marriage. To her, it seemed as if they had started with passion, and were tied together by that, and then by guilt, and then by responsibility and what everyone expected of them, but this was the first time they were together because they understood each other, and felt understood by the other. What they had together was more special, more personal, and more intimate than anything they had had before.

This was not the old marriage revived, but a whole new open and honest marriage. They didn't think there would be any private lies from now on.

Bibliography

Abe, Kobo. *Woman in the Dunes*. New York: Random House, 1972.

Beauvoir, Simone de. *The Second Sex*. New York: Knopf, 1971.

Beavers, W. R. *Successful Marriage*. New York: Norton, 1985.

Berne, Eric. *Games People Play*. New York: Grove, 1964.

Coward, Noël. *Private Lives*. New York: New American Library, 1983.

Fowles, John. *The Collector*. New York: Dell, 1975.

Framo, James L. "Rationale and Techniques of Intensive Family Therapy." In I. Boszormenyi-Nagy and James L. Framo, eds., *Intensive Family Therapy*. Hagerstown, Md.: Hoeber Medical Division, Harper & Row, 1965.

Freud, Sigmund. "Certain Neurotic Mechanisms in Jealousy, Paranoia, and Homosexuality" (1922). In *Collected Papers of Sigmund Freud*, vol. 2, Ernest Jones, ed. New York: Basic Books, 1959.

Friday, Nancy. *Jealousy*. New York: Morrow, 1985.

Gilligan, Carol. *In a Different Voice*. Cambridge, Mass.: Harvard University Press, 1982.

Hamilton, Edith. *Mythology*. Boston: Little, Brown, 1940.

Irving, John. *The World According to Garp.* New York: Dutton, 1978.

Jung, Carl Gustav. *Contributions to Analytical Psychology.* 1928

Klein, Melanie. *Envy and Gratitude, and Other Works, 1946–1963.* New York: Delacorte, 1977.

Kubie, Lawrence. "Psychoanalysis and Marriage: Practical and Theoretical Issues." In V. Eisenstein, ed., *Neurotic Interaction in Marriage.* New York: Basic Books, 1956.

Kundera, Milan. *The Unbearable Lightness of Being.* New York: Harper and Row, 1984.

Lerner, Gerda. *The Creation of Patriarchy.* New York: Oxford University Press, 1986.

Mackey, Sandra. *The Saudis.* Boston: Houghton Mifflin, 1987.

Miller, Arthur. *Death of a Salesman.* New York: Penguin, 1976.

Minuchin, Salvador. *Families and Family Therapy.* Cambridge, Mass.: Harvard University Press, 1974.

Morgan, Marabel. *The Total Woman.* New York: Pocket Books, 1983.

O'Neill, G. and N. *Open Marriage: A New Lifestyle for Couples.* New York: M. Evans, 1984.

Pittman, F. S. *Turning Points: Treatment of Families in Transition and Crisis.* New York: Norton, 1987.

Russell, Bertrand. *Marriage and Morals.* New York: Liveright, 1970.

Scarf, Maggie. *Intimate Partners.* New York: Random House, 1987.

Stuart, Richard B. *Helping Couples Change.* New York: Guilford, 1980.

Stuart, Richard B. and Barbara Jacobson. *Second Marriage.* New York: Norton, 1985.

Styron, William. *Lie Down in Darkness.* New York: Random House, 1951.

Tiger, Lionel. *Men in Groups.* New York: Random House, 1969.

Updike, John. *The Witches of Eastwick.* New York: Knopf, 1984.

Wharton, Edith. *Ethan Frome.* New York: Scribner's, 1911.

Index